THE LIVING
UTTERANCES OF GOD

The New Testament
Exegesis of the Old

ANTHONY TYRRELL HANSON

D1420021

Darton, Longman and Todd
London

225.7

First published in 1983 by
Darton, Longman and Todd Ltd
89 Lillie Road, London SW6 1UD

© 1983 Anthony Tyrrell Hanson

ISBN 0 232 51553 0

21015762

British Library Cataloguing in Publication Data

Hanson, Anthony Tyrrell
  The living utterances of God.
  1. Bible. N.T.—Commentaries
  I. Title
  225.7   BS2341.2

  ISBN 0–232–51553–0

Phototypeset by Input Typesetting Ltd, London SW19 8DR
Printed in Great Britain by The Anchor Press Ltd
and bound by Wm Brendon & Son Ltd
both of Tiptree, Essex

CONTENTS

To
Professor Otto Betz
of
The University of Tübingen
this work is respectfully dedicated

A learned scholar
An acute theologian
A valued friend

FOREWORD

I wish to acknowledge my wife's never-failing assistance in typing the first copy of this book for the publishers, in reading the proofs, and in compiling the index. All these necessary activities were carried out under a certain amount of pressure, because of the exigencies of modern publishing. Only a wife – and an exceptionally tolerant one at that – would have put up with all the consequent minor worries.

I would also like to record my appreciation of the treatment I have received at the hands of Messrs. Darton, Longman and Todd. I have never encountered more courteous publishers.

Anthony Hanson
Thirsk
Feast of the Ascension 1983

ABBREVIATIONS

Evv   English versions
JSNT   *Journal for the Study of the New Testament*
JTS   *Journal of Theological Studies*
LXX   The Septuagint
MT   Masoretic text of the Hebrew Scriptures
NT   *Novum Testamentum*
NTS   *New Testament Studies*
RSV   Revised Standard Version of the English Bible
VT   *Vetus Testamentum*
ZTK   *Zeitschrift für Theologie und Kirche*

ACKNOWLEDGEMENT

The majority of Scripture quotations in this publication are from the Revised Standard Version of the Bible, copyrighted 1971 and 1952 by the Division of Christian Education of the National Council of Churches of Christ in the USA.

INTRODUCTION

The intention of this work is to set out the way in which the authors of the New Testament interpreted the Old Testament. I use the Christian terminology 'New Testament' and 'Old Testament' because this is the point from which I begin. But for the greater part of this book I shall rigorously avoid such language, because it misrepresents the way in which the authors of what we call the New Testament viewed what we call the Old Testament. For them of course there was no New Testament. They were its authors, but they did not (for the most part) regard their own writings as inspired scripture, and none of them would have dreamed of applying the term 'New Testament' to what they wrote. This is a term which seems to have originated in the second century after Christ, and is one which would probably not have appealed to them in any case. Nor did they regard what we call the Old Testament as being either a testament or old. For them it was simply 'the scriptures', and they no more regarded the scriptures as old or out of date than we regard the New Testament as old or out of date. So, until we reach the last three chapters of this work, I shall do as they did, and write 'the scriptures' or 'scripture', meaning the books of the Hebrew bible as recognized by the Jews.

The subject of the New Testament interpretation of scripture has been growing in importance for students of the New Testament ever since the beginning of the twentieth century. For this one can suggest three main reasons:

1   Exploration of the cultural background of the New Testament, greatly inspired by the 'history of religions' school of the first quarter of the century, has proceeded apace. Nobody who has any knowledge of the subject can deny that late Judaism formed the greater part of this background. The 'history of religions' school tended, it is true, to stress rather the Hellenistic or near-Eastern element in this background, and this certainly cannot be ignored. But it can be said with some confidence that the Jewish element in the culture of the New Testament has been assuming greater prominence during the second half of this century. Admittedly, we have also come to see that the Judaism

of the first century AD was a Judaism that had already been heavily
Hellenized. It could only survive the immense cultural assault of
Hellenism during the third and second centuries BC by borrowing
extensively from the weapons of its adversary. But survive it did
to become the matrix of Christianity. Now the centre of that
Judaism was the Torah, the law of Moses as set out in the Pentateuch, reinforced (it was believed) by the prophets, and
commented on in the writings. Since, therefore, scripture was so
central to the Judaism out of which Christianity emerged, we
cannot understand the New Testament unless we try to understand
the way in which Jews interpreted their scriptures. The New Testament writers inherited the various exegetic traditions current in
Judaism. However much they modified them in the interests of
Christianity, this is where they began. We cannot hope to understand the thought of the New Testament writers unless we take
account of their interpretation of scripture. And that means examining contemporary Jewish methods of handling scripture.

Moreover, during this century, and particularly during the last
forty years, a series of startling discoveries has thrown a flood of
new light on this topic. Very early in the century came the discoveries by Samuel Schechter in the *geniza* (muniment room) of the
Old Synagogue in Cairo. He found what proved ultimately to be
two manuscripts of a work of the Qumran community, and also
some fragments of the *Targum of Palestine,* a targum which scholars knew had existed, but which up to then was known only
through a series of marginal notes on an extant targum. It was
believed, rightly as was later established, to contain a good deal
of exegetic material which predated the Jewish-Christian controversy. Then from 1947 onwards came the discoveries of the
Qumran documents. When the dust occasioned by the absurd
claims made for them by some scholars who should have known
better had died down, it became gradually clear that here was a
largely original tradition of scripture interpretation which in
certain respects bore a striking resemblance, in technique though
not in content, to that used by many New Testament writers.
Finally, in 1956, a complete copy of the 'lost' Palestinian Targum
on the Pentateuch was identified in the Vatican Library, the so-
called 'neofiti manuscript'. It has still to be published, edited and
translated in full, but it is already clear that it fulfils the hopes
that scholars had put in it. It contains much material apparently
uninfluenced by anti-Christian polemic, and therefore can often
give us a glimpse of Jewish exegesis of scripture during the period
when the New Testament was being written.

2   Most well-informed commentators on the New Testament
during the second half of the nineteenth century had abandoned
the belief in the inerrancy of the bible, even of the New Testa-

ment. But many of them, particularly in this country, still clung to the conviction that Christians of the nineteenth century could still take over largely intact most of the presuppositions of New Testament thought. This had the consequence that, far from actually adopting New Testament presuppositions, they tended rather to read their own presuppositions into the work of the writers of the New Testament. Nowhere perhaps was this more evident than in their treatment of the New Testament interpretation of scripture. We can test this by looking at those places where New Testament writers make claims about the scriptures which seem to us most bizarre. For example, in 1 Corinthians 10:1–11 Paul makes use of a piece of rabbinic *haggada* to the effect that Moses not only struck the rock to provide water, but that the rock followed the Israelites around to provide them with a perpetual supply of water as long as they were in the desert. How many Victorian commentators refuse to accept this bizarre idea! St Paul, they say, could not have accepted Jewish fables. Or turn to the nineteenth-century commentators on the Fourth Gospel, and see what they say about John 12:41, where John says in so many words that he whom Isaiah saw in his vision in the temple narrated in Isaiah 6 was the Word of God, Jesus Christ. An embarrassed silence, or an unconvincing attempt to explain it away is what we usually meet.

Today we have to a large extent freed ourselves from these inhibitions. We are coming to see that we must begin by discovering as far as we can what it was that the New Testament writers believed. After that we can tackle the task of hermeneutics proper, which is to ask what sense their belief makes to us today – and this is a side of the question which we do not ignore in this work. Since it is in their handling of scripture that the New Testament writers are in certain respects farthest from our modern point of view, it is important that we can now at last examine how they handled it without involving ourselves in at least some of the misconceptions of our forefathers of the last century. It is true, no doubt, that we have our own presuppositions, as everybody has; but we are in this epoch in a better position, I believe, to estimate with some impartiality what it was that the New Testament writers believed about the scriptures. In some ways this makes things more difficult for us, but we are at least trying to view things as they actually were.

3   The subject of the New Testament interpretation of scripture has a bearing on the ecumenical situation. One of the burning issues at the time of the Reformation was the relation of scripture to tradition. The Reformers tended to appeal back to scripture away from tradition, maintaining that scripture was self-interpreting and did not need the tradition of the Church to interpret it.

The Catholics claimed that without the tradition of the Church scripture was unintelligible, often going so far as to set up tradition as an alternative source of revelation. Modern exploration of the New Testament interpretation of scripture may be said on the whole to have vindicated the Catholic side in this debate, at least in the sense that it has shown one thing clearly: there never was a time when scripture occurred divorced from a tradition of interpretation. The New Testament writers expounded a scripture which was already modified by centuries of interpretation. Though they differed in certain vital respects from their Jewish teachers, they did not expound *sola scriptura*. They unconsciously took over an extensive tradition of interpretation. This does not of course justify the claims that were made on behalf of tradition by the Catholic party at the time of the Reformation. On the contrary, as we shall be seeing, biblical criticism has meant a far more radical dismantling of much of Christian tradition than ever the Reformers envisaged. But study of the subject of the New Testament interpretation of scripture must rule out any simplistic approach to the bible as a document that interprets itself, or as something which anyone can understand by the light of reason alone. The scripture which the New Testament writers expounded was a scripture born and maintained in the bosom of an exegetic tradition, and the Christian bible as a whole stands just as much in need of a tradition of interpretation today as did the Jewish scriptures in the first century AD.

I have referred above to the hermeneutic task which faces anyone who wishes to make sense and use of the bible today as always. I have not thought it right to ignore this question in this work. It would have been possible to write a textbook on the subject of the New Testament interpretation of scripture which might have been useful for those who restricted themselves severely to biblical studies. In that case there would have been no need to face the hermeneutic issue. But I have always believed that a Christian teacher of the New Testament at least has a duty to the Christian Church, which has after all furnished him with a Christian nurture and which provides him with most of his students. That duty in this case consists in attempting to say what sense we today as Christians can make of the New Testament interpretation of scripture in particular, and of the relation between the two parts of the Christian bible in general. I have therefore written three chapters at the end in which these questions are discussed. Those who are not Christians, or those who are modern Marcionites (by no means an extinct breed), or those who have an objection to theology, can omit these chapters. I have written them because I have a love and respect for theology.

Certainly the questions which they consider are profoundly theological ones.

I think a book such as this is needed. The only book in English which I know of which would seem to have the same intention is R. Longenecker's work *Biblical Exegesis in the Apostolic Period.* This is a valuable work in many ways and supplies much useful information. But it suffers, in my opinion, from an unnecessarily conservative outlook (e.g. he defends the Pauline authorship of the Pastorals; he seems to be unduly sanguine about the historical reliability of much of the Fourth Gospel), and it does not discuss in any great depth the hermeneutical problem, partly perhaps because the author's conservative presuppositions prevent him from viewing that problem in its full perspective. I have ventured therefore to try to fill the gap myself.

I will end this introduction with two purely occasional remarks. The first concerns the title. I have taken it from Acts 7:38, where the New English Bible somewhat freely renders *logia zōnta* with 'the living utterances of God'. The phrase seems to me to sum up very well what the writers of the New Testament believed the scriptures to be, and it may also serve as a challenge to us to decide how far, or in what sense, we can apply the phrase to our bible today.

The other remark is this: in this work I have never at any point given any countenance to the view that the New Testament writers sometimes accepted as scripture material taken from unknown apocryphal works. This is a favourite device with certain scholars (more popular perhaps with a past generation of commentators) when they encounter words cited as scripture whose source they cannot trace in any canonical or quasi-canonical work. I do not believe that any New Testament writer regarded as scriptural any work outside the canon of Judaism. There is one exception to this, the author of Jude. But even he does not quote an *unknown* apocryphon. And his example was not followed by the writer who took over and adapted his work.

1

JEWISH TRADITIONS OF EXEGESIS

The Interpretation of Scripture in Scripture

Since the Hebrew scriptures, and the intertestamental literature that followed them and to some extent overlapped with them in time, were probably composed over a period of nearly a thousand years, it is not surprising that within the body of scripture itself we can often detect early traditions being modified, corrected or even contradicted. This began to happen before any writings had been recognized by the Jews as sacred scripture, but it went on long after something like scripture had emerged. Even the strongest sentiment about the inerrancy of scripture did not prevent scripture being modified when circumstances seemed to require it.

An obvious example occurs in Hosea 1:4: 'For yet a little while, and I will punish the house of Jehu for the blood of Jezreel.' This refers to the incident narrated in 2 Kings 9, where Jehu, one of the army commanders in the northern kingdom, leads a coup against King Joram and murders him in Jezreel. The author of 2 Kings 9 obviously approves of Jehu's action and represents it as having been instigated by the prophet Elisha. But Hosea, who lived about a hundred years later, regards it as a crime to be punished by God. Of course this is probably not an example of written scripture being reinterpreted, since we have no reason to think that Hosea had read 2 Kings 9; but he is certainly contradicting a tradition which later became part of scripture.

Next we may point to a book by Professor J. Weingreen, *From Bible to Mishna*, in which he suggests that the whole book of Deuteronomy itself may have been intended to be a sort of Mishna to the older parts of the Torah. The Mishna is the collection of comments and elucidations on the Torah made by various rabbis and published about AD 200. It was intended to help the Jews of the Diaspora to apply the Torah to their own circumstances. Weingreen suggests that 800 years earlier the authors of Deuteronomy intended to issue a new edition of the Torah, applicable to their own day. If so, we have in Deuteronomy what is in effect a commentary on earlier law-codes, some of which are enshrined in what we now know as the Pentateuch.

Two good examples of scripture interpreting scripture can be drawn from the third division of the Jewish bible, the writings. The first is Psalm 78, which consists of a rewriting of sacred history in order to present it as 'a catalogue of the divine mercy' (Lindars p. 273). An equally good example is Psalm 106, which gives a similar review of Israel's history. Particularly remarkable is verse 16:

> When men in the camp were jealous of Moses and Aaron, the holy one of the Lord. . .

Earlier traditions represent Aaron as being anything but holy in view of his ambiguous conduct at the time of the episode of the golden calf (Exod. 32), or his rebellion against Moses (Num. 12). This psalm exhibits a very common tendency to glorify those who are remotest in history. Psalm 106 must have been composed at a time when Moses and Aaron were regarded as figures so remote in time as already to be surrounded with a halo of sanctity. The second example is best expressed in the words of T. C. Vriezen (p. 84): 'It seems as if the author of Job wants to combat the religious moralism of the Proverbs, which often shows strong leanings towards eudemonism.'

A particularly clear example can be found if we compare 2 Samuel 24:1 with 1 Chronicles 21:1. The first passage runs as follows:

> Again the anger of the Lord was kindled against Israel and he incited David against them, saying, 'Go, number Israel and Judah'.

The version of this event in 1 Chronicles is this:

> Satan stood up against Israel, and incited David to number Israel.

The Books of Chronicles were written at least 500 years later than this part of the Books of Samuel. In the meantime Israel's understanding of God's nature had been deepened and moralized, and the suggestion, implied in the 1 Samuel passage, that God could incite someone to sin, was quite unacceptable. So the part of the tempter was transferred from God to Satan, a figure who had become the very representative of temptation by the time that the Chronicles were written. Though the author of Chronicles probably regarded 2 Samuel as scripture, he did not hesitate to modify it. It is, however, very interesting to notice that the *Targum on Chronicles,* written centuries later still, renders this passage: 'Yahweh incited Satan against Israel' (see R. Le Déaut and J. Robert (1) in loc.). Is this an attempt at harmonization?

Our next example is taken from what was probably the latest book in the Hebrew bible to be written, the Book of Daniel. Daniel 9:2 runs:

> I, Daniel, perceived in the books the number of years which, according to the word of the Lord to Jeremiah the prophet, must pass before the end of the desolations of Jerusalem, namely, seventy years.

The reference must be to Jeremiah 25:11f. where Jeremiah says that seventy years must pass before the Babylonians are punished for their cruelty and injustice towards Israel. (Compare also Jer. 29:10.) But the author of Daniel has interpreted this prophecy in terms of weeks of years, i.e. seven years for every one of the seventy years, so as to bring it nearer to his own time when, he believes, the promised relief is to come. This would give us a period of nearly 500 years, a little too long in fact for the purpose, since Daniel was probably written about 400 years after Jeremiah's time. But the historical knowledge of the author of Daniel is confused and inaccurate about anything that occurred so long before his own day.

Our final example takes us out of the canonical books altogether into that penumbra of literature which can be called apocryphal or quasi-apocryphal. In 2 Maccabees 2:4–8 there is an account of how Jeremiah at the time of the capture of Jerusalem by the Babylonians in 587 BC was instructed by God to hide the ark of the covenant, and other items of the furniture of the temple, in a cave on Mount Sinai. This he did and the way to the cave was miraculously hidden. This contrasts remarkably with what the historical Jeremiah said about the ark in time to come. He tells us (Jeremiah 3:16) that 'in those days, says the Lord, they shall no more say, "The ark of the covenant of the Lord". It shall not come to mind, or be remembered, or be missed; it shall not be made again.' As James Moffatt remarks, commenting upon 2 Maccabees, 'Legend has no scruple in transforming a prophet who was radically indifferent, if not hostile to the ritual of the Temple, into a pious conservative.' (See his commentary on 2 Maccabees in Charles (2).) This is an excellent instance of a commentator, writing nearly 500 years later than Jeremiah, modifying Jeremiah's own belief so as to represent it as almost the opposite of what it actually was.

One could go on to give an extensive list of scriptural interpretations found in the intertestamental literature. Lindars, for example, describes the Testaments of the Twelve Patriarchs as 'a midrash on Genesis [a midrash is a piece of biblical commentary]

aimed at making out a case for Levi as the ruling tribe in support
of John Hyrcanus. The Book of Jubilees rewrites Genesis and
Exodus from the opposite point of view . . . it is thus a protest
against the Hasmonean claims' (p. 273). Or one could point to
the Book of Wisdom, written perhaps late in the first century BC,
which represents the patriarch Jacob as an innocent character
when he fled to Aramaean territory after deceiving his brother
over obtaining his father's blessing. See Wisdom 10:10:

> When a righteous man fled from his brother's wrath, she
> [Wisdom] guided him on straight paths.

Here again we see the tendency to cast characters in the remote
history of the race in the role of plaster saints. But we have surely
done enough to show that even within the history of the scriptures
themselves interpretation and comment had begun, and that
during the period between the testaments this activity continued
unabated. We must now turn to the various traditions of exegesis
that existed within Judaism at the time that the New Testament
began to be written.

The Greek Translators as Exegetes

The New Testament was written in Greek. All its writers were
therefore capable of reading the scriptures in Greek. Some of
them could probably read the Hebrew bible as well. This is
certainly true of Paul and probably of the author of the Fourth
Gospel. It is very likely indeed to be true of the author of the
First Gospel and the author of the Book of Revelation. On the
other hand some New Testament writers were probably wholly
dependent on Greek translations for their knowledge of the scriptures. There is no evidence that the author of the Epistle to the
Hebrews knew any Hebrew, and it is unlikely that Luke did,
though he may have known Aramaic. In any case, even those
who could consult the Hebrew did not always do so. Paul was
content normally to quote from his Greek version, and this is also
true of John. The ancients were not as sensitive as are we moderns
about the obligation to quote the original. Besides, the Septuagint
translation at least was held in very high esteem. Philo describes
the translators of the LXX as inspired prophets (*De Abrahamo*
258). It is therefore relevant to our theme to show the ways in
which the translators of the LXX modified their material in various
directions, thereby influencing those who accepted their translation as completely reliable. This is not to claim that every New
Testament writer used the Greek translation which we know as
the LXX. But we have no reason to think that the alternative
Greek translations which were certainly current during the first

century AD were any more free from the occasional tendentious rendering.

We begin with a few examples of places where the LXX has included *halaka* within its translation. *Halaka* means the process in Judaism whereby the scriptures are made applicable to every situation in life by means of comment and explanation. Genesis 2:2 is rightly rendered from the Hebrew by the RSV with:

> And on the seventh day God finished his work which he had done and he rested on the seventh day from all his work which he had done.

But the LXX offers:

> And God finished the works which he had done on the sixth day and rested on the seventh day.

God must not be represented as setting a bad example by working, even finishing his work, on the Sabbath. In Leviticus 24:7 the Hebrew means: 'And you shall put pure frankincense with each row', in connection with the weekly bread offering. But LXX has: 'And you will add to the offering pure frankincense and salt', presumably reflecting current practice. A third example of a halakic addition to the LXX occurs in Deuteronomy 26:12. The Hebrew says: 'When you have finished paying all the tithe of your produce the third year, which is the year of tithing, giving it to the Levite. . .' etc. But the LXX has altered this to read: 'When you have finished tithing all the tithe of the produce of your land in the third year, you shall give the second tithe to the Levite. . .' etc. The LXX translators therefore felt themselves free on occasion to alter or amplify the sense of the Hebrew in the interests of contemporary observance.

Next we can show examples of *haggada* in the LXX, though in this respect the translators are much more restrained than are the targums. *Haggada* is legendary enlargement and embroidery of scriptural narrative with a view to making it more informative or more convincing. We will cite four examples: Exodus 13:18 in the Hebrew runs:

> But God led the people round by the way of the wilderness towards the Red Sea. And the people of Israel went up out of the land of Egypt equipped for battle.

The LXX translators render the second sentence here with:

> And the children of Israel in the fifth generation went up out of the land of Egypt.

This could be a misreading of the Hebrew word for 'equipped for battle', but it is more likely to be a piece of quasi-historical calculation. Then in Joshua 24:30 we read in the Hebrew of the burial of Joshua in the hill country of Ephraim: but the LXX adds as an extra verse the following:

> There they placed with him, in the tomb in which they had buried him, the flint knives with which he had circumcised the sons of Israel in Gilgal when he led them out of Egypt, as the Lord instructed them, and there they are to this day.

As there is a Hebraism in the Greek of this addition at one point, it was probably taken from a Hebrew original. But in any case it is clearly a piece of *haggada*. Our third example is a very small one: in 1 Samuel 5:10 the ark of the Lord, captured by the Philistines, is passed on from Azotus to Ekron. The LXX has Ashkelon instead of Ekron. Is this a piece of local tradition, or does it indicate merely that Ashkelon was a more important town than Ekron during the Greek period? Finally we can point to quite a considerable addition at the end of the LXX translation of the Book of Job, of which there is no trace in the Hebrew. It begins with the words: 'And it is written that he will rise again with those whom the Lord raises up', and then goes on for fifteen lines to link Job with the lineage of Abraham and to connect Job and his friends with various Gentile peoples bordering Palestine. Here is *haggada* in abundance. These examples of *halaka* and *haggada* are only specimens drawn almost at random from a much larger store of instances.

The LXX translators will also on occasion alter expressions and ideas which they find unacceptable, unduly anthropomorphic language about God, for example, or language which suggests an unworthy conception of God. In other places they introduce into the original contemporary ideas which are really anachronisms. Here are three examples of the LXX toning down anthropomorphisms (all given in Sowers pp. 15–16): in Exodus 15:3a the Hebrew has: 'The Lord is a man of war.' The LXX offers: 'The Lord crushes wars.' In Numbers 12:8 it is written of Moses in the Hebrew: 'He beholds the form of the Lord.' The LXX has: 'He saw the glory of the Lord.' And in Deuteronomy 33:10c the Hebrew literally translated would run: 'They shall put incense in thy nostrils.' The LXX has altered it to 'they shall lay on incense in thy wrath'. Similarly in Exodus 4:24–5 we have a very primitive piece of tradition about Moses and his family. In the Hebrew it is narrated that the Lord met Moses and sought to kill him. But Zipporah his wife takes a flint, cuts off her son's foreskin, and touches Moses' feet with it; so God leaves Moses alone. This must contain echoes of some very early fertility rite, having passed through who knows how many modifications in the course of tradition. Not unnaturally, the LXX translators jib at reproducing this literally, so they attribute the attack not to the Lord but to the angel of the Lord, and instead of making the foreskin touch Moses' feet Zipporah is described as falling at Moses' (or the angel's) feet. Moreover, her enigmatic exclamation in the Hebrew, 'Surely you are a bridegroom of blood to me', is changed to 'the blood of the foreskin of my boy has been staunched'. Similar to this in sentiment is the LXX's treatment of Exodus 32:9: 'And the Lord said to Moses, "I have seen this people, and behold, it is a stiff-necked people".' The LXX simply omits this verse, presumably because it is too offensive to Israel's proper pride (see Farrar p. 122 for other examples).

As for the introduction of contemporary ideas in an anachronistic way, see Deuteronomy 32:8, which runs in the Hebrew:

> When the Most High gave to the nations their inheritance,
>   when he separated the sons of men,
> he fixed the bounds of the peoples according to the number of
>   the sons of God.

The LXX has rendered the last two lines thus:

> he fixed the bounds of the Gentiles according to the number of
>   the angels of God.

This reflects the notion that each nation had its guardian angel, an idea we first find in scripture in the Book of Daniel in the second century BC. We may quote two more examples of contemporary ideas infiltrating the LXX translation. The first is 1 Samuel 17:43, where in the Hebrew Goliath taunting David says: 'Am I a dog that you come to me with sticks?' The LXX inserts here David's answer: 'No, but worse than a dog', presumably reflecting anti-Gentile (or anti-Greek?) prejudice. The second example is 1 Samuel 19:13, 16, where Michal takes the *teraphim* and puts them in David's bed to simulate David's presence. *Teraphim* were some form of domestic idol. The LXX translators, according to the later iconoclastic tradition, strongly disapprove of idols, so they translate the word *teraphim* with *kenotaphia,* which is literally 'cenotaph', i.e. an empty tomb. They mean to indicate that idols are nothing more than empty tombs.

Finally the LXX can interpret simply by means of mistranslation. A famous example occurs in Psalm 40:6 (LXX 39:7; Masoretic Text 40:7). The literal rendering of 6ab is: 'Sacrifice and offering thou hast not desired, ears thou hast cut to me.' This does not make sense as it stands and it certainly needs emendation, but the correct sense is equally certainly not achieved by the LXX, which translates:

> Sacrifice and offering thou hast not desired,
>   but ears hast thou prepared for me.

But some early manuscripts read instead: 'but a body hast thou prepared for me'. This is indeed the translation reproduced in the Epistle to the Hebrews 10:5, where this text is made the basis for an exposition of the doctrine of the incarnation. Another striking mistranslation occurs in Habakkuk 3:2c. The Hebrew gives the sense: 'In the midst of the years renew it (thy work).' But the LXX has translated: 'Thou shalt be known in the midst of two animals.' Augustine took this as prophecy of the baby Jesus in the manger between the ox and the ass (see Farrar p. 124). A third example can be cited from Isaiah 51:20abc. The true sense of the Hebrew is:

> Your sons have fainted,
>> they lie at the head of every street
>>> like an antelope in a net.

The LXX translator has hopelessly misunderstood 20c and renders it 'like a half-cooked beet'. Anyone who regarded the LXX as an inerrant translation of the original, as many did in the Judaism of the first century and the Christianity of the first four centuries, would accept this as containing some hidden mystery inspired by the Holy Spirit.

Before leaving the LXX we should in all fairness observe that the Hebrew text itself, unaided by any mistranslation, is capable of misleading. An example occurs in the very verse after that which we have quoted above: Psalm 40:7b (MT 40:8b) is literally in the Hebrew: 'In the volume of the book it is written upon me.' This was apparently originally a marginal gloss which ran: 'One manuscript reads ᶜalai for bathi' (see Jellico pp. 323–4). The suggestion originated with Alfred Guillaume in *Prophecy and Divination*. But the author of Hebrews certainly regards this misunderstood text, which is faithfully reproduced by the Greek translator, as a proof that Christ in his coming to earth was fulfilling scripture.

The Qumran Method of Exegesis

The Qumran community was in all probability originally established in 142/1 BC when Simon the Hasmonean became high priest; 'the teacher of righteousness' who gave it its ideology probably flourished from about 110–75 BC, and the community was finally dispersed by the Romans during the Jewish War in AD 68. Most of its documents date from the first century BC and the first century AD. This estimate of its dating would not command universal assent, but would probably be accepted by an increasing majority of scholars. Though the documentary evidence is fragmentary, it is extensive, and we have certainly got enough material to be able to form a clear judgement about their methods of interpreting scripture.

They shared with all other Jews of the period a Torah-centric approach to scripture. They agreed entirely with the Pharisaic party that Israel was intended by God to obey the Torah in all its details with the utmost possible strictness. But they differed from the Pharisaic tradition in two respects: their method of obeying the law was different, notably, for example, in calendar observance; and they used a *pesher* method of interpreting scripture in terms of the history of their own sect. This method will be explained presently.

Kuss has neatly summed up their principles of scripture interpretation under two heads (p. 65): (a) prophetic scripture must refer to the end time, and (b) the present is the end time. We must bear in mind, however, that the word 'prophetic' could cover a wide range of meaning: in their view Moses was a prophet, so anything in the Pentateuch could be prophetic; and David was a prophet, so prophecies could be sought in the psalms. The *pesher* method referred to above means the method of identifying persons and events mentioned in scripture with persons and events connected with the history of the Qumran sect. The word *pesher* means 'meaning', and a Qumran commentary on a passage in scripture frequently introduces the interpretation with the phrase *pishro*, 'its meaning is . . .' etc. We give an example from their *Commentary on Nahum* (Vermes pp. 231–2). First comes the text from Nahum 2:11:

> Whither the lion goes, there is the lion's cub (with none to disturb it).

Then comes the interpretation (when Vermes writes 'Interpreted this concerns . . .' he is translating *pishro*):

> Interpreted this concerns Demetrius king of Greece who sought, on the counsel of those who seek smooth things, to enter Jerusalem. (But God did not permit the city to be delivered) into the hands of the King of Greece, from the time of Antiochus until the coming of the rulers of the Kittim.

This refers to an incident during the reign of the Hasmonean monarch Alexander Jannaeus. When the contemporary Seleucid king, encouraged by the Pharisees, attempted to take Jerusalem, he failed to do so (Horgan p. 161). Here is another example, this time from the *Commentary on Habakkuk*. The text is Habakkuk 1:4e: 'for the wicked encompasses the righteous'. The commentary runs: '*The wicked* is the Wicked Priest, and *the righteous* is the Teacher of Righteousness' (Vermes p. 235). Again at Habakkuk 1:6: 'For behold, I rouse the Chaldaeans, that bitter and hasty

nation' the interpretation runs: 'Interpreted, this concerns the
Kittim (who are) quick and valiant in war, causing many to perish'
(Vermes p. 236). The Kittim certainly indicates the Romans
(Horgan p. 13). We have in these passages the two characteristics
of *pesher* interpretation clearly exhibited: prophecy in scripture is
interpreted in terms of contemporary events and as applying to
the history of the sect.

The nearest parallel to this method of scripture interpretation
is to be found in the Book of Daniel. In that book we find much
talk about divine secrets (the Hebrew word is *rāz*, a Persian loan-
word) whose meaning *(pesher)* is to be earnestly sought. In Daniel
the secret is entrusted to one person and the interpretation to
another. Thus the secret is communicated to Nebuchadnezzar by
means of a dream, but the interpretation is supplied by Daniel.
In the Qumran scheme of interpretation the secrets of God are
communicated to the canonical prophets, who wrote them down,
and the interpretation centuries later is given to the Teacher of
Righteousness and his disciples. (See Longenecker p. 42; Horgan
pp. 252–3.) We have this scheme clearly set out in the *Commentary on Habakkuk* (Vermes p. 239): 'And God told Habakkuk to
write down that which would happen to the final generation, but
he did not make known to him when time would come to an end.
And as for that which he said, *that he who reads may read it
speedily* (Hab. 2:2), interpreted this concerns the Teacher of
Righteousness, to whom God made known all the mysteries of
the words of his servants the prophets.' We notice here that the
original recipient of the secret, Habakkuk, did not receive full
information as to what his words meant. That was only revealed
to the Teacher of Righteousness. We shall be encountering a
similar scheme when we come to consider the interpretation of
scripture in 1 Peter.

The *pesher* method of interpretation can be extended so as to
merge into allegory. This is well illustrated by the interpretation
of the Song of the Well in Numbers 21:17–18:

Spring up, O well! – Sing to it!
the well which the princes dug,
which the nobles of the people delved,
with the sceptre and with their staves.

In the *Damascus Rule* this passage is interpreted thus:

The well is the Law, and those who dug it were the converts
of Israel who went out of the land of Judah to sojourn in the
land of Damascus. God called them all *princes* because they
sought him. . . . The Staff is the interpreter of the Law of whom
Isaiah said, *He makes a tool for his work* (Isaiah 54:16), and

the *nobles of the people* are those who come to dig the well with the *staves* with which the *Staff* ordained that they should walk in all the age of wickedness. (Vermes pp. 102–3, slightly emended)

Here is full-blown allegory, and here is a clear example of scripture interpreted in terms of the sect's own history.

Sometimes there is remarkable coincidence between the Qumran interpretation of a text and that found in the New Testament. Thus in a Qumran *pesher* on Isaiah 54:11–12, a passage which describes the precious stones which are to be used in the rebuilding of Jerusalem, the stones are identified with various members of the sect (Horgan p. 125). This is very like Revelation 21:10–14. Again it seems possible that the text applied to Jesus in Mark 14:27, 'I will strike the shepherd and the sheep will be scattered', is applied by the sectaries to the Teacher of Righteousness, though this is by no means certain. (See *Damascus Document* VII, p. 104 in Vermes and IX, p. 3 in Charles; see also France p. 176; for the opposite view see Waard p. 40.)

It is possible that sometimes New Testament writers are using the same text of scripture, or even the same collection of proof-texts, as the Qumran people use. For example Amos 9:11 is quoted in Acts 15:16 and also in 4Q Flor. 1:12 (a collection of texts made by the Qumran sect). Waard writes (p. 25): 'The text form of the Amos quotation in Acts differs from that of the MT and the LXX, but is exactly identical with that of 4Q Flor.' Similarly, the Qumran sectaries make use of a 'stone' quotation from Isaiah 28:16 which is also very popular with New Testament writers; see 1 QS 8:7–9; Romans 9:33, 10:11; 1 Peter 2:6. The best explanation of this phenomenon is perhaps that there was a stock of scripture texts current in apocalyptic circles during the first century before Christ and the first century of the Christian era which would naturally come to mind if anyone was interpreting scripture eschatologically. With this we may put the suggestion, which seems to me to be a reasonable one, that there was one tradition in the Judaism of that period which interpreted much of the psalms and certain passages in the prophets in terms of a suffering or persecuted saviour figure who was to come. See Michel p. 82, where he puts forward this suggestion.

We may sum up by briefly comparing the Qumran method of *pesher* interpretation with that which we will be studying in the New Testament. The two have in common an eschatological approach and a belief that much prophecy in scripture is fulfilled in the events of contemporary history. The Qumran sectaries see the fulfilment in terms of the history of the sect, Christians in terms of the events of the career of Jesus Christ. The actual *pesher* method is found in the New Testament; compare Romans 10:6–8, which is exactly the *pesher* technique. But the only writer in the New Testament who seems to claim that he is revealing mysteries is John the Divine in Revelation, and his revelations are more concerned with salvation history than with scriptural fulfilment. The content of what is fulfilled is therefore very different in the two traditions; there is far more theology in the New Testament tradition because the writers are ultimately declaring a revelation of God's nature. There is much more secular history in the Qumran tradition because they were deeply concerned with recent and contemporary Jewish history. Perhaps we might say that the early Paul in 1 Thessalonians (and 2 Thessalonians if that is his) is most like the Qumran tradition, but this is the letter in which his interpretation of scripture is least significant for his thought.

Philo's Technique of Interpretation

Philo is almost the only example that has survived of the Jewish allegorical school of interpretation of scripture, but he certainly did not invent the technique. We know of an Alexandrian Jew called Aristoboulos who flourished about 160 BC; he is represented as having claimed that Greek philosophy derived from Moses, and this can only be defended by means of the extensive use of allegory (Farrar p. 128). There are also some traces of allegorizing in the Letter of Aristeas in the second half of the second century BC, cf. 144f. Philo, however, is the great champion and exemplar of the allegorical method. He was concerned both to defend the Jewish scriptures, which he regarded as inerrant, and to deduce from them a whole system of philosophy, psychology and ethics. See *De Abrahamo* 258: 'The testimonies for this are to be found in the holy books, which may never be convicted of false witness.' Philo certainly casts the mantle of inerrancy over the LXX, since he was unable to use the Hebrew text owing to his infinitesimal knowledge of that language. In any case he uses, and etymologizes, the LXX so freely that he must have regarded it as completely reliable. Williamson (p. 523) neatly summarizes the reasons why Philo used this technique of allegory: (a) it enabled him to explain away anthropomorphisms, and to avoid trivial, unworthy, offensive or incredible meanings in scriptures; (b) it helped him with historical difficulties in the scriptures and (c) it enabled him to read into the scriptures the philosophical and other doctrines which he believed he could find there. We should remember that Philo does not normally deny the literal sense of scripture, though he can do so on occasion, as we shall be seeing (Kuss p. 62). This comes out very clearly in his *Questions on Genesis* and *Questions on Exodus,* where he normally first expounds the literal sense of the text, sometimes in a very reasonable and commonsense way, and then gives what he calls the 'deeper' sense, i.e. the allegorical. He does, however, protest against those who had no use for the literal sense of the text. (See Sowers p. 28.)

We will now give a number of examples of Philo's allegorizing treatment of scripture. We begin with a very simple example of how Philo rejects anthropomorphisms: 'Again, some on hearing these words (Gen. 6:7) suppose that the Existent feels wrath and anger, whereas he is not susceptible to any passion at all. For disquiet is peculiar to human weakness, but neither the unreasoning passions of the soul, nor the parts and members of the body in general have any relation to God' (*Quod Deus Immortalis Sit* 52). And here is a good instance of how Philo defends his allegorizing technique: he is considering the phrase in Genesis 4:16, 'Cain went away from the presence of the Lord' (in the LXX 'from the face of the Lord'). He argues that God is no more in one place than another and anyway he does not have a literal face. He concludes 'the only thing left for us to do is to make up our minds that none of the propositions put forward is literally intended and to take the path of figurative interpretation *(allēgoria)* so dear to philosophical souls' *(De Post. Caini* 7). Similarly in *De Plant.Noe* 32–7 he deals with the statement in Genesis that God planted a garden in Eden. This, he says, cannot be literally true: God has no need of a garden and man, who might need it, had not yet been created. He categorizes such literal interpretations as 'utterly monstrous inventions of men who would overthrow great virtues like piety and reverence by representing (God) as having the form and passions of mankind. So we must turn to allegory, the method dear to men with their eyes opened.'

Finally we give some appropriate examples of Philo's exegesis from his *Questions on Genesis* and *Questions on Exodus*. Noah's three sons, Shem, Ham and Japheth represent the good, the bad and the indifferent *(Quest. in Gen.* 1:88). God closing the ark on Noah in Genesis 7:16 means that God enclosed the human body within a skin. He allegorizes the structure of the ark so as to make it represent the human body *(Quest. in Gen.* 2:19). 'Do not eat any of it raw' in Exodus 12.9 can hardly be intended literally: 'Accordingly, he appears to allegorize all this, for he says that those who change from wickedness to virtue shall not eat of repentance when it is raw and crude but (shall do so) by heating it, that is with hot and ignited principles' *(Quest. in Exod.* 1:16). Again, 'What is the meaning of the words "Thou shalt not sacrifice with leaven the blood of the victim"? (Exod. 23:18). . . He indicates through two necessary symbols that one should despise sensual pleasures, for leaven is a sweetener of food but not food itself' *(Quest. in Exod.* 2:14). Philo allegorizes the furniture of the tabernacle so as to make it represent the universe. The two poles by which the ark is carried represent the intelligible and the sensible worlds (*Quest. in Exod.* 2:57).

It is very difficult to detect any logical scheme according to which Philo invents his allegories. Sowers in fact argues, against C. Siegfried, that no such scheme exists (p. 26n). It is possible to discern dimly a sort of method behind the way in which he allegorizes names, a favourite technique of his (see an article of mine, 'Philo's Etymologies' in *JTS* 18, ns (1969), pp. 128–39). This lack of principle is surprising in view of the confidence with which Philo applies his allegorizing exegesis. Does he perhaps regard himself as acting under divine inspiration when he allegorizes, and thus deserve the epithet 'charismatic' which some scholars have applied to the scripture interpretation of the New Testament writers?

Philo's influence on the scriptural exegesis of the Church fathers has been very extensive indeed, but he cannot be said to have been a major influence on the New Testament. On the whole it does not seem likely that Paul had read him, though Paul certainly knew something of the Alexandrian Jewish interpretation of scripture. I believe myself that the author of Colossians (whom I regard as a disciple of Paul, but not Paul himself) had read Philo and does use his Logos doctrine, though not the name (see my *Image of the Invisible God,* ch. 4). Despite the learned and valuable work of Dr R. Williamson, it is difficult not to conclude that the author of Hebrews had read some Philo, even though he is no uncritical follower of his. The author of the Fourth Gospel also must surely have known his Philo. Different though his doctrine of the Logos is from Philo's, he can hardly have been unaware of his great predecessor. And John's scriptural exegesis does on occasion merge into allegory.

The Rabbinic Tradition of Exegesis

We have come to this last in order, not because it is less important than the other traditions, but because most of the evidence for it comes from a period considerably later than the first century AD. The rabbinic tradition of scriptural exegesis developed after AD 70 from what had been the Pharisaic tradition. The Pharisees' approach to scripture was based on the conviction that the changing problems of contemporary life must somehow find their solution in scripture. Hence scripture had to be manipulated so as to provide an answer (Kuss p. 63). This tradition differed from the Qumran approach in that it was not eschatological and was not therefore interested in prophecy as prophecy. The prophets were regarded as furnishing additional witness to the Torah. It differed from Philo's tradition in that it had no interest in philosophy. It did not therefore need to use allegory on the same scale as Philo did, though allegory was certainly one of the tools in the rabbinic equipment. Our evidence for the rabbinic tradition is not usually found in any documents earlier than the third century AD, though there are one or two earlier than this, e.g. the Pseudo-Platonic *Biblical Antiquities*. But for the most part we must rely on the Mishna (compiled *c.* AD 200) and the Talmud (compiled *c.* AD 400). There are various midrashes which may have been written down in the third century. There is also the *Pesikta Rabbati* and the *Pesikta de Rab Kahana,* collections of homilies delivered on festal occasions by distinguished rabbis at any period between AD 200 and 700. Some of them probably contain earlier material. The targums we discuss below.

In assessing the value of this material we must bear in mind that most of it was not primarily intended to be purely scriptural exegesis. It is mostly law-material or case-material. But in the process of drawing out *halaka* from scripture the rabbis have given us a good idea of how they interpreted scripture. Sometimes indeed they give a very full exegesis of one passage or another. We know that by the end of the first century AD Hillel had drawn up his famous *middoth,* seven rules to be observed when interpreting scripture. They were later much extended and elaborated. An account of these seven rules is given in Farrar (p. 184), Ellis (p. 41), Kuss (pp. 64–5), and Longenecker (p. 34). We may summarize them briefly thus: scripture can be interpreted by the following methods:

1 One may argue from the greater to the smaller and vice versa (the latter would be *a fortiori*).
2 Analogous or equivalent expressions may be applied interchangeably.
3 One may argue from the particular to the general and
4 Vice versa.
5 An inference may be made by putting several passages together.
6 A difficulty in one text may be resolved by comparing it with another text which has points of resemblance.
7 The meaning of a passage may be established by its context.

Using these methods, scripture could be interpreted with considerable latitude. Thus many characters which appear in scripture to be ambiguous or disreputable could be whitewashed; e.g. Reuben did not commit incest; the patriarchs only tried to murder Joseph because he attempted to lead them into Baal worship; David and Bathsheba were completely innocent, etc. (examples from Farrar p. 63). In the same way characters who in scripture

appear neutral or even benevolent acquire sinister reputations in
rabbinic tradition; examples are Esau and Baalam. An excellent
instance of whitewashing occurs in *Bereshith Rabba,* c 65 (quoted
by Farrar p. 15): Jacob did not lie to Isaac in order to secure his
blessing. What he said to his father was not 'I am Esau your firstborn' (Gen. 27:19), but 'I am Jacob, but Esau is your first-born.'
Bereshith Rabba is a commentary on Genesis. On the whole the
rabbis respected the literal sense of scripture more scrupulously
than did Philo, but they could on occasion evade the obvious
sense if it caused embarrassment. Thus in *Megillah* 11b (p. 67)
Rabbi Nahman does not like the implication of Isaiah 45:1: 'Thus
says the Lord to his anointed, to Cyrus', and he interprets it as
meaning: 'Thus says the Lord to his Messiah regarding Cyrus.' In
a similar way, some of the rabbis were understandably concerned
about the implications of Isaiah 45:7b, which the RSV renders 'I
make weal and create woe', but which literally translated would
be: 'I make good and create evil.' In the *Sifre to Numbers* (a
commentary of the Tannaitic period, AD 100–200) this line is
paraphrased, 'who has made peace and created the universe'
(K. G. Kuhn p. 126). This is explained in *Berakoth* 11b (p. 63)
thus: 'Rabbi Jacob said "It is written *evil*, and we must say 'all
things' as a euphemism".'

This is not to suggest that the rabbis were incapable of profound
exegesis. They certainly could on occasion show a very impressive
grasp of the full dimensions of a passage or book in scripture.
Consider, for example, this comment on Isaiah 40:1: 'Comfort,
comfort my people, says your God.' It comes from *Pesikta
Rabbati,* Piska 29–30b.

> God speaks to Israel like a brother, as Joseph spoke to his
> brethren, forgiving them. All the prophets came before the
> Holy One, blessed be he, saying to him: 'Master of the universe,
> we sought to comfort Zion, but she would not heed.' The Holy
> One, blessed be he, replied: 'Come with me. You and I shall
> go to her and comfort her' . . . If a man owns a vineyard, and
> robbers come and cut it down, who needs comforting? The
> vineyard or the owner of the vineyard? It is God who needs
> comforting for the desolation of Israel.

Another instance could be found in the rabbis' treatment of the
Book of Job. Perhaps because they read it in Hebrew, they understood what it was really about far better than did either the New
Testament writers who quote it or the early Christian fathers who
followed them.

When we turn to the targums, we find ourselves in a different
atmosphere but the same tradition. A targum is an Aramaic paraphrase of scripture for synagogue use. It used to be believed that

no targum was actually written down until well into the Christian era, but the discovery of a fragmentary targum on Job, and another on Leviticus, among the Qumran documents has caused this opinion to be revised. The targums are essentially popular literature; their aim was not only to make scripture comprehensible, but also to apply it to contemporary conditions. We may appropriately quote Stenning's comment on the purpose of the *Targum on Isaiah*: 'To gloss over or modify everything which seemed inconsistent with the accepted view of the history of the nation, to magnify and expound everything which redounded to the credit of the heroes of the past, whether patriarch or prophet, priest or king; to explain away the unworthy and to emphasize the pious motives which guided their conduct – is the ruling principle alike of the Chronicler and of the targumist' (Stenning p. xi). As an example of contemporary application we may cite the targum rendering of Isaiah 1:3. The RSV translates:

> The ox knows its owner,
>   and the ass its master's crib;
> but Israel does not know,
>   my people does not understand.

The Targum offers:

> The ox knoweth his owner and the ass his master's crib, but Israel has not learned to know the fear of me, my people has not considered how to return to my law.

The targumist was living in an age when the law was central to Israel's religion in a way which was not characteristic of Isaiah's time.

Two other features of the targum tradition should be observed. The first is a messianic emphasis. This is very noticeable in the *Targum on Isaiah,* and this is all the more significant in view of the big part which the Book of Isaiah plays in New Testament scriptural quotations. From many instances cited by Stenning (p. xv) we select three, all chosen from passages which are not overtly messianic. In Isaiah 10:27b the Hebrew has 'his yoke will be destroyed from your neck' but the Targum adds 'from before the anointed one'. Isaiah 16:1 in the Hebrew has: 'They have sent lambs to the ruler of the land.' The Targum renders: 'They shall bring tribute to the anointed one of Israel.' And Isaiah 28:5 runs in the Hebrew: 'In that day the Lord of hosts will be a crown of glory', but the Targum paraphrases: 'At that time the anointed one of the Lord of hosts shall be a diadem of joy.'

The other characteristic is a tendency towards the addition of *haggada* or legendary embroidery of scriptural narrative. This could be freely illustrated from all the targums on the Pentateuch.

We will content ourselves with one striking example. This is how the *Targum of Pseudo-Jonathan* reproduces Genesis 2:7:

> And the Lord God created man in two formations; and took dust from the place of the house of the sanctuary, and from the four winds of the world, and mixed from all the waters of the world, and created him red, black, and white; and breathed into his nostrils the inspiration of life, and there was in the body of Adam the inspiration of a speaking spirit, unto the illumination of the eyes and the hearing of the ears. (Etheridge p. 162)

We have here two leading characteristics of *haggada*, legendary details of narrative (the dust comes from the site of the temple), and supplementary 'information' (the ingredients of man's constitution).

Though the rabbis regarded the whole of scripture as inspired and inerrant, they were quite ready to admit degrees of inspiration among the authors of scripture. Thus in *Hagiga* 13b Raba is recorded as comparing Ezekiel with Isaiah: Ezekiel, he says, is like a villager compared with a townsman, as far as regards knowledge of the meaning of his message. The townsman is educated, so his testimony will be accepted at once. The villager has to give much more detail in order to be believed, hence the greater length of the description of Ezekiel's vision of God compared with Isaiah 6. Generally speaking, Moses would be regarded as having received most insight, then would come David; after that Isaiah and perhaps Jeremiah. The other prophets received varying degrees of insight. All of course recorded correctly what they had heard or seen; the variation consisted in the extent to which they understood it.

In this work we cannot go into the very technical details of the text of scripture used by the various persons who interpreted it according to their various traditions. But it should be said that all the representatives of all the last three traditions mentioned were quite relaxed in their choice of the text of the scripture they were expounding. Alternative readings, both in the original and in translations, are sometimes used. Relatively small adaptations of the text to suit the context are made; a paraphrastic or targumic rendering of the text is sometimes found. There was in the period we are concerned with no universally agreed text of the Hebrew, though what we call the Masoretic Text seems to have been fairly well developed. There was a LXX text, but it was competing with other Greek versions, and in some parts of scripture, e.g. Job, Jeremiah and the Book of Daniel, the LXX version differs so much from the Hebrew that it suggests that there must have been two widely accepted versions of these books current in Greek.

Hence, when we find that New Testament writers can on occasion cite scripture in versions which differ from the LXX, or from the MT, or which seem to follow a targumic version, we should not attribute this to the arbitrary fancy of the authors of the New Testament. In this respect they were only following the tradition in which they had been educated.

As we review the traditions of interpretation which we have traced in Judaism, we may well end by asking if there is anything which they all had in common. I think we may point to three things:

1   They all agreed that scripture is inspired by the Holy Spirit, is inerrant and therefore must be harmonized with itself. The only apparent exception to this would be those interpretations within scripture itself which are so ancient that they go back to a period before the writings later canonized as scripture had achieved canonization. For example, Hosea certainly did not regard the tradition which later produced 2 Kings 9 as inerrant. But this only means that scripture as such had not yet come into existence.

2   Scripture may be used out of context. By this I do not mean that proof-texts were used without any regard to the context in which they occur. On the contrary, the more I study the use of scripture in this period the more convinced I become that no deliberate quotation from scripture is made in complete disregard of the context. Almost always a close study of the context in scripture in which a passage quoted occurs will throw light on the interpretation put forward. But none of the writers with whom we are concerned shows the same desire to establish first the historical and literary circumstances in which any passage of scripture was composed before proceeding to interpret it, as a modern commentator would. Thus a verse of scripture can be applied to an event long after the period in which it was written, or, what is more surprising, long before. Because the Holy Spirit is the ultimate author of all scripture, the scripture itself is not bound by the circumstances of time, place or culture. Scripture was intended to be used by the people of God (see Rom. 15:4; 1 Cor. 10:11), and its use cannot therefore be restricted to the age or occasion on which it was uttered.

3   The third principle really follows this: any passage of scripture may have an extended significance, different from the literal one. This does not mean that the literal significance can be disregarded, though both Philo and Paul (cf. 1 Cor. 9:9) are capable of saying this in effect on occasion. Since, however, scripture was regarded as inspired by the Holy Spirit, the devout exegete has every reason for seeking as many meanings in any text as he thinks it can bear. The limit of significance will be determined not by consideration of culture, history or etymology, but by the

theological presuppositions with which the exegete approaches the text. As these differed considerably from one tradition to another, we have obviously reached the limits of what all the traditions of interpretation had in common.

2

THE NEW TESTAMENT INHERITANCE

We may now go on to examine the way in which each author in the New Testament uses scripture. But scripture was being applied to Jesus, we may be sure, before any word of the New Testament was written down. We must therefore devote a chapter to an examination of how Jesus himself used scripture, if we can discover this, and we must also make some attempt to decide what oral traditions about the application of scripture to Jesus were current in the early church before anything got committed to writing, and how far these traditions have influenced the authors of the New Testament. In addition, we may make some comments about New Testament interpretation of scripture as a whole.

Jesus' Interpretation of Scripture

It is by no means easy to decide what parts of scripture Jesus made use of. Up until about thirty years ago there was widespread agreement that Jesus did see himself as fulfilling the role of the suffering servant of the 'servant songs' of Second Isaiah in general, and of the fourth 'servant song' (Isa. 52:13—53:12) in particular. But since then there has been reaction against this view among scholars, chiefly because of the difficulty of finding any clear quotations from the fourth servant song among sayings that can be with any confidence attributed to Jesus. It is possible, however, that the question has been wrongly posed. Neither Jesus nor anyone else in antiquity thought in terms of 'servant songs', any more than they thought in terms of First and Second Isaiah. Moreover, if any of them did identify with the 'suffering servant' of Second Isaiah, he would not distinguish this figure from the righteous sufferer of the psalms. When we ask whether there is any evidence that Jesus identified himself with the righteous sufferer of the psalms and Isaiah, we may be able to achieve a clearer answer.

First, however, we should revert to one feature of one of the Jewish traditions of scripture interpretation which we have already examined. In the *Hodayoth* or Songs of Thanksgiving of the Qumran sect, the author of a hymn will sometimes identify himself with both the righteous sufferer of the psalms and the suffering servant of Isaiah. We begin with examples from the psalms: in *Hodayoth* 7:4 he quotes from Psalm 22:14 'my bones were out of joint', and this is a hymn in which, as we shall be seeing, he has already quoted from Isaiah 53:7. Psalm 22 is of course the psalm of the righteous sufferer *par excellence* in the New Testament. Then in 5:23–4 the author of the hymn writes:

> Al(so they that) eat my bread
> have lifted up their heel against me.

This is a direct citation of Psalm 41:9 (41:10 in MT). Mansoor comments (p. 136, n. 2) 'It appears likely, therefore, that in this and the following passage the author referred to unfaithfulness and rebellion by members of the sect who had turned against him.' Psalm 41:9 is of course applied to Judas' betrayal in Mark 14:18; John 13:18, 17:12; Acts 1:16. A third quotation from a psalm of the righteous sufferer occurs in *Hodayoth* 4:11; the author quotes Psalm 69:21 (MT 22): 'For their thirst they made them drink vinegar.' The author applies it to the false teachers who misled the members of the sect. The fourth evangelist sees a fulfilment of this verse in the action of the bystanders giving Jesus vinegar to drink on the cross; see John 19:28–9. It is likely that the three other evangelists record this incident because it was part of the traditional proof that Jesus was the righteous sufferer of the psalms, but none of them explicitly quotes the psalm.

We can trace five echoes of the servant passages of Second Isaiah in the *Hodayoth*. In *Hodayoth* 8:36 the author describes his God-given task as 'to revive the spirit of the stumbling and to sustain with words him that is weary', which is a citation of Isaiah 50:4, itself part of a servant song. Then in 4:8 the author claims that 'they esteem me not', a tag from Isaiah 53:3. In 2:8 he describes himself as 'a healing unto all that turn from transgression', which appears to be a conflation of Isaiah 53:5d and 59:20b. In 7:1, which is a much damaged part of the manuscript, he says of himself: 'I have become dumb (as a ewe lamb).' The 'ewe lamb' is restored by Mansoor (p. 148, n. 2) who says that 'the lower halves of the letters *caph* and *resh* (in the word k^erahel, which means "as a ewe lamb") are clearly visible in the manuscript.' This is a quotation from Isaiah 53:7. Finally, in *Hodayoth* 18:14 the author describes his task as being, among other things, 'to bring good tidings to the meek'. Mansoor (pp. 191–2, n. 13) quotes another scholar as saying 'the mission of the anointed prophet Isaiah is assumed by the author of the *Hodayoth*'. The quotation is from Isaiah 61:1, also cited by Luke of Jesus in Luke 4:18.

We must not make too much of these occasional quotations in

the *Hodayoth*, but we may certainly conclude that the author or authors of the *Hodayoth* can use the language of the righteous sufferer in the psalms and in Isaiah about himself and about the attacks of his opponents on him. He can even cast himself in the role of the anointed prophet of Isaiah 61:1f. This does not imply that he made any messianic claims, but it shows that there would be nothing inappropriate or anachronistic in suggesting that Jesus could use similar quotations in a similar way. We do not know whether any or all of the *Hodayoth* are written by the 'Teacher of Righteousness', but they are certainly composed by someone who regarded himself as entrusted by God with an extensive group of disciples. This was exactly Jesus' position. We do not need to read into Jesus' use of them any official messianic claim, though we can well understand how the early church, taking its cue from Jesus' usage, would proceed to make more specific the significance of the righteous sufferer. Perhaps the early church read into these quotations a messianic element, but no doubt the atoning element was already in Jesus' mind in view of his approaching death.

One of the leading features of all four Gospels is the conviction that Jesus had to suffer. They all represent him as teaching his disciples that his suffering and death was necessary and that it was in accordance with scripture. When we have made full allowance for the way in which the early church played up this element, it is very difficult to avoid the conclusion that it must in some form have gone back to Jesus himself. But if so, the only scriptural source from which he could have derived this conviction was the psalms and Second Isaiah. We can put with this those passages where Jesus is represented as describing himself as a servant: Mark 10:44–5 and parallels; Luke 22:26–7; John's account of Jesus serving the disciples (13:1–11). We can say of these passages also that they can hardly derive from anywhere else than Second Isaiah. Thirdly we might mention the 'cup' passages, Mark 10:38–9 (par. Matt. 20:22–3); 14:36 (par. Matt. 26:39; Luke 22:42; cf. John 18:11). The cup here means 'destiny of suffering ordained by God'. The most obvious passage where the cup appears in scripture is Isaiah 51:17–23, though the image also appears in the psalms (e.g. Ps. 11:6, 16:5, 75:8, 116:13). In the psalms the cup can also mean 'happy destiny ordained by God'. But, if the cup figure goes back to Jesus (and there seems no reason to deny that it does), then he did interpret as applying to himself those passages in scripture where drinking God's cup means accepting God's hard destiny of suffering.

Some scholars detected other echoes of Isaiah in Jesus' teaching. Barnabas Lindars believes that Jesus' reference to the lost sheep of the house of Israel (Matt. 10:6; cf. Mark 6:34) is an echo of Isaiah 53:6: 'All we like sheep have gone astray' (Lindars

p. 128). Bruce Chilton has recently advanced the theory that some of Jesus' teaching is based on the *Targum on Isaiah*. Chilton would see links with Isaiah 31:6, 53:1, 60:1, 22; 61:1–2 in the targumic version (Chilton pp. 86, 92, 95, 159–72). This theory has yet to be tested, but it may well point in the right direction. In the next chapter we shall be referring to a paper by Professor Otto Betz on Paul's application of Isaiah 52:13—53:12 to Jesus. Here it will be sufficient to point out that Betz believes that the application goes back to Jesus himself.

Other likely references to the psalms could be found: it is very probable that Jesus' cry on the cross, 'My God, my God, why hast thou forsaken me?', was a conscious citation of Psalm 22:1 (Lindars p. 89; cf. also Manson pp. 326–7; France p. 56). Gundry believes that Jesus' words at Gethsemane, 'My soul is very sorrowful, even to death', are an authentic echo of Psalm 42:6 (Gundry p. 59); and Lindars (p. 173) suggests that the citation of Psalm 118:26 in Luke 13:35; Matthew 23:39 was originally a prophecy of the coming Kingdom. There is a whole series of references to the later chapters of Zechariah in the Gospels. It is not easy to distinguish which go back to Jesus and which are the interpretation of the early church. Vincent Taylor (in loc.) claims that the quotation of Zechariah 13:7 in Mark 14:27 is authentic: 'To trace the quotation to later Christian reflection . . . is unnecessary in view of the frequent use by Jesus of imagery connected with sheep and shepherds.' France (p. 92) believes that Jesus' clearing the temple of traders was in conscious fulfilment of Zechariah 14:21: 'And there shall no longer be a trader in the house of the Lord of hosts on that day.' We should also notice Lindars' claim that Jesus foresaw his vindication by God and expressed it in the words of Hosea 6:2: 'After two days he will revive us, on the third day he will raise us up'; he compares Luke 13:32: 'Behold, I cast out demons and perform cures today and tomorrow, and the third day I finish my course.' This may be a translation of a Hebrew phrase *temōl šᵉ lōšōm*, which means no more than 'in the near future' (Lindars pp. 60–1).

It is also possible to trace a whole series of scriptural echoes in Jesus' ethical teaching. Thus Gundry (p. 69) considers that Jesus' blessing on the poor (Matt. 5:3; Luke 6:20) echoes Isaiah 61:1–2; and that Matthew 24:3–4 is based on Psalm 24:3–4 (p. 133), the blessing on the pure in heart. It is also possible that he is right in connecting Matthew 10:29 (Luke 12:6) with Amos 3:5 (p. 135). We may also point out an interesting link between Matthew 5:44 (Luke 6:27–8) and Psalm 109:4–5. For all the bloodthirsty cursing of enemies which this psalm contains, the author claims to have returned good for evil in just the way that Jesus enjoins. There may well also be an echo of this teaching in 1 Corinthians 4:12–13, which opens up all sorts of interesting possibilities. Gundry also claims (p. 72) that 'for your reward is great in heaven' in Matthew 5:12 (Luke 6:23) is an echo of Genesis 15:1. And he is probably right in saying (p. 72) that Matthew 5:39 (Luke 6:29) is based on the action of the suffering servant in Isaiah 50:6, where he turns the other cheek. There seems no reason to regard any of the above extracts from Jesus' teaching as anything but authentic.

There are also a number of more debatable passages where some scholars have seen authentic instances of Jesus using scripture. One of the most remarkable is the two places in which Matthew represents Jesus as quoting Hosea 6:6: 'I desire steadfast love and not sacrifice.' These are Matthew 9:13 and 12:7. Most scholars regard these citations as an interpretation of Jesus' message by the author of the First Gospel, though very many agree that the verse from Hosea represents very accurately an important element in Jesus' teaching. But Stendahl (p. 128) believes that the citation may go back to Jesus himself. He notes the authentically rabbinic formula: 'Go and learn what this means.' France may be correct in claiming that the quotation of Jeremiah 22:5, 'Behold your house is forsaken and desolate', in Matthew 23:38 (Luke 13:35) is authentic. Nor should we necessarily deny to Jesus the very significant echo of Exodus 3:6 in Mark 12:26 (Matt. 22:32; Luke 20:37): 'I am the God of Abraham, and the God of Isaac, and the God of Jacob.' Jesus' argument is that, if God had made himself known to these ancestors of Israel during their lives, he could not have abandoned them at death. It is essentially an argument from Israel's experience of God through the ages, and as such the quotation from the episode of the burning bush, the beginning of God's mighty acts of redemption, is extremely appropriate and fits in with the rest of Jesus' teaching about salvation history. Gundry also claims with a good deal of plausibility (p. 81) that the sentence of judgement on Capernaum in Matthew 11:23 (Luke 10:15) is authentic. It echoes Isaiah 14:13, 15, a denunciation of judgement upon Babylon. We might finally refer to the quotations from Deuteronomy with which Jesus is represented as answering Satan in the temptation narratives of Matthew 4:1–11 and Luke 4:1–13. Some scholars would defend these as authentic scriptural references on the part of Jesus, but it is more in accordance with the evidence to accept Birger Gerhardsson's conclusion in his scholarly treatment of the temptation narratives, *The Testing of God's Son* (p. 80): 'Jesus of Nazareth in his attitude of life and in the central themes of his teaching was the dominating influence on our scribe' (i.e. the Christian scribe who composed the narrative).

From this evidence can we draw any general conclusions about Jesus' interpretation of scripture? If we are right in claiming that

Jesus did see himself as fulfilling the role of the righteous and persecuted servant in scripture as a whole, then this in itself constitutes a very significant piece of scriptural interpretation, one which was taken up and elaborated by the early church. We might go on from this to say that the advent of the Kingdom, according to Jesus, demanded servant-like behaviour on the part of those who were preparing to enter the Kingdom. In as far as the coming of the Kingdom fulfilled God's design, it must have been in accordance with the scriptures; so we can say that there was a strong element of salvation history in Jesus' message, which of course necessarily implies a reference to scripture. Finally we might suggest that the stress on God's mercy as constituting his essential characteristic also implies a certain understanding of scripture. Thus, though we must beware of being too dogmatic about details, we can reasonably claim that Jesus did present a certain interpretation of scripture which was normative for the early church.

Scriptural Interpretation during the Oral Period

We now have to determine as best we can what happened to the scriptural interpretation of Jesus' career during the period between Jesus' resurrection and our earliest surviving written records. This is in fact not exactly the same as what scholars call 'the period of oral transmission', because in the first place surviving written records (Paul's letters, for example) and oral transmission must have existed side by side for a certain time; and secondly because there may have been written records during this period that have not survived (the document called Q, if it was a document; Pauline letters that have not survived). But we have used the phrase 'the oral period' as the shortest way of referring to this space of time.

We immediately come up against the question of *testimonia*. *Testimonia* are lists of christological proof-texts, strung together for the benefit of Christian apologists, primarily for use in controversy with the Jews. The earliest surviving Christian *testimonia* date from the third century. In 1916 and 1920 James Rendell Harris published two short books in which he argued that virtually all the quotations from scripture to be found in the New Testament are based on a book of proof-texts which he called 'the Testimony Book'. This book, he believed, was current in the early church before any word of the New Testament was written. He even persuaded himself that he had discovered a manuscript which contained this book (written as it happened some 1500 years later than the original). Rendell Harris pushed his theory to absurd lengths, claiming that Jesus used *testimonia*, and attributing even the most obviously idiosyncratic scripture citations (such as that

in John 10:34, for instance) to his hypothetical Testimony Book.
Some scholars, however, have suggested that the famous quotation from Papias about the composition of the Gospels really
refers to a written compilation of *testimonia*: 'So Matthew put
together the sayings in the Hebrew language, and each man interpreted them as he was able.' Rendell Harris did not succeed in
convincing very many people of the truth of his theory; most
scholars preferred C. H. Dodd's suggestion that, though there
were certain parts of scripture from which early Christians drew
most of their proof-texts about Jesus, there was nothing like a
written *testimonia* list. But since then there has turned up among
the Qumran documents a *florilegium,* or collection of texts from
scripture which the sectaries believed were especially applicable
to the history of their own community. This has given some new
life to the *testimonia* theory, though no one as far as I know has
accepted it in the form in which Rendell Harris originally put it
forward.

Thus Lindars (p. 127) believes there was an oral store of *testimonia* in use in the early church. Stendahl (p. 51, 145) thinks that
the conflated citation of Exodus 23:20; Malachi 3:1; and Isaiah
40:3 in Mark 1:2–3 may have come from an (oral?) *testimonia* list;
though Gundry (p. 165) is sceptical about the existence of written
testimonia books, and claims that Papias' phrase, 'the sayings' (*ta
logia*), could not apply to them anyway. Kilpatrick actually
suggests, on not very convincing evidence, that some of Luke's
scripture citations in Acts are drawn from a *non-Christian* collection of proof-texts (p. 91). Wilcox believes that the citation of
Psalm 89:20 in Acts 13:22 may come from what (pp. 22–3) he
calls 'a testimonium-fragment'. Similarly Holtz (p. 50) holds that
Psalm 16:8–11 cited in Acts 2:25f belongs to a set of *testimonia*
on the subject of the resurrection which was among Luke's
materials when he wrote the book, and he thinks that the christological citations in Acts 13:33–5 are taken from a *testimonia* list
(p. 87), chiefly because of vague methods of reference to scripture.
I have summed up what I believe to be Paul's position with regard
to *testimonia* lists in *Studies in Paul's Technique and Theology,*
pp. 191f.

Thus we may reasonably conclude that lists of proof-texts from
scripture were current in the early church, some of which may
have been written rather than oral. But we are certainly not
justified in speaking of 'the Testimony Book' as Rendell Harris
does, and the greatest exponents of scripture in the New Testament, Paul, the author of the First Gospel, the author of Hebrews
and the author of the Fourth Gospel were all capable of going
direct to scripture themselves when they wished to make a point,

without being dependent on *testimonia* lists for their knowledge of scripture.

It is possible certainly to point to various parts of scripture that were drawn on by the very earliest Christians in their preaching of the message about Jesus. We know from 1 Cor. 15:3–4 that both the atoning death and the resurrection of Jesus took place 'according to the scriptures' in the very earliest preaching, earlier even than Paul. From a study of the New Testament we can gain a pretty good idea of which scriptures these were. First and foremost, perhaps, came various passages from Isaiah. We have already argued that the 'servant' passages were cited from the first, and in particular the early church used the fourth servant song, Isaiah 52:13—53:12 as a quarry for proof-texts about Jesus' career (Lindars p. 88). Then as it became clear that most Jews were not willing to accept the Christian message, Isaiah 6:9f., about the unbelief of Israel, came into increasing use (H. Anderson pp. 297–8; see also Suhl p. 149, though I cannot agree with his idea that Mark 4:12 is not an example of prophecy fulfilled, but that Mark is only clothing present action in scriptural language). Then there are the two 'stone' passages in Isaiah 8:14 and 28:16, so often combined with other 'stone' citations such as Psalm 118:22 and Daniel 2:34 (the 'stone cut out by no human hand'). Waard actually concludes that the quotation of Isaiah 28:16 in Romans 9:33, 10:11; 1 Peter 2:6 must be referred to 'a midrash concerning the stone based on a *verbum Christi*', since we now have an example of just such a midrash in 1Q 8:7–8 (Waard p. 58; Suhl (p. 53) believes that Mark knew of the Psalm 118:22 citation because of its use in Q). Other uses of Isaiah would be 56:7, the prophecy of the temple as 'a house of prayer for all peoples' (H. Anderson pp. 288–9), and 29:13, the condemnation of the purely formal worship which Israel offers. Anderson believes this citation (in Mark 7:6–7 and Matthew 15:8–9) must have come from the early church and not Jesus because it deviates markedly from the MT. It is quite true that Isaiah 29:13d as cited in Mark 7:7 is much closer to the LXX than it is to either MT or the Targum. But this does not necessarily imply that it does not go back to Jesus, whose attitude towards the *halaka* it probably reflects. Mark (or his source) was no doubt dependent on a Greek translation for his citations (see Stendahl p. 58). Finally we should note Isaiah 40:3, 'In the wilderness prepare the way of the Lord', etc., cited in all four Gospels (Mark 1:3; Matt. 3:3; Luke 3:4f.; John 1:23) as a prophecy of the ministry of John the Baptist. This must have been a very early application of scripture, found by the earliest Christians to be most appropriate to the forerunner.

Next we must note a number of passages from the psalms which the earliest Christians found remarkably applicable to Jesus. The two psalms which seem to refer to the humiliation and exaltation of Jesus, Psalms 8 and 110, go back to very early usage. They are already conflated in 1 Corinthians 15:25–7; and see Hebrews 2:6–8, where both these psalms also appear (Lindars p. 50). Then Psalm 41:9 must have been applied to Judas' betrayal: 'Even my bosom friend in whom I trusted, who ate of my bread, has lifted his heel against me'; see John 13:18 (Lindars pp. 98–9; Waard p. 65). It seems likely that the incident in which Jesus was offered vinegar while on the cross, though no doubt historical, is seen by all four evangelists as a fulfilment of Psalm 69:21b: 'For my thirst they gave me vinegar to drink' (Mark 15:36; Matt. 27:48; Luke 23:36; John 19:29). This is very much a psalm of the righteous sufferer; verse 9 is quoted by both Paul and John (Rom. 15:3; John 2:17). Another psalm with a very early christological application is Psalm 2. Verse 7 is quoted in all our accounts of Jesus' baptism. Again, Jesus cites Psalm 22:1 on the cross and this psalm is much echoed by the Synoptic writers in their account of the passion: the wagging of heads by Jesus' mockers (Ps. 22:7), and the parting of the garments among the soldiers (Ps. 22:18) are both seen as fulfilments of this psalm (for this last detail see also John 19:24). We have already alluded to the part which Psalm 118:22 plays in the collection of 'stone' prophecies. The psalms therefore must very early on have been understood as providing a prediction both of Jesus' exaltation at the right hand of God and of his sufferings and atoning death.

Another group of scripture passages used by the early church comes from Second Zechariah. This comprises Zechariah chapters 9–14, and is one of the most obscure parts of the prophets. Scholars agree that it must have been written during the post-exilic period, but are by no means agreed as to when in that period it should be placed. It presents a picture of a martyred leader and this certainly appealed to early Christians. We have already suggested that Jesus himself began this tradition of interpretation. Lindars (pp. 112, 116, 123, 127, 132) points to a whole series of details in the passion narrative that the evangelists believed were foretold in Zechariah. Zechariah 9:9 is linked with Jesus' entry into Jerusalem; 9:11 with the 'blood of the covenant' mentioned in the narrative of the Last Supper; 11:12 with the incident of Judas selling Christ for thirty pieces of silver; 12:10 with the dead Jesus in the presence of those who killed him; 13:7, as we have noted already, is applied to the arrest and execution of Jesus. And Zechariah 12:12 is applied in Matthew 24:30a to the mourning of the unbelieving world at the parousia (France pp. 104f.). Swete (pp. xxxvif.) believes that Zechariah 13:7 belonged to a *testimonium* originally applied to Jesus' death, but was later extended to refer to the desertion of the disciples. (See also Suhl p. 63.) Zechariah must therefore have been regarded by the early church as a mine of information about Jesus.

There were no doubt other passages in scripture seized upon by the earliest Christians as throwing light on Jesus' career. Habakkuk 2:3–4, the passage in which occurs the famous sentence 'the just shall live by faith', is expounded by Paul in Romans 1:17 and Galatians 3:11; and also by the author of Hebrews in Hebrews 10:37–8; verse 3 is also echoed in 2 Peter 3:9. As we shall be seeing, the author of 1 Peter probably refers to this passage also. We may therefore conclude that Habakkuk 2:1–4 was regarded in the early church as a prophecy of the coming of Christ, who was to be recognized by those who had faith. (See Lindars pp. 230–2.) There are also several references to the Book of Daniel which seem to go back to an early period. We have already seen that Daniel 2:34 provides one of the collection of 'stone' quotations. There is a citation of Daniel 7:13 in a very prominent position in Mark 14:62: 'You will see the Son of Man sitting at the right hand of Power, and coming with the clouds of heaven.' Vincent Taylor defended this as an authentic utterance of Jesus, but subsequent scholarship has tended to see it as an application made by the early church on the grounds that the use of the phrase 'Son of Man' as a title is a development which had not yet taken place in Jesus' day. H. Anderson (pp. 288–9) believes that Jeremiah 7:11 (the temple has become 'a den of robbers') was already joined with Isaiah 56:7, referred to above, in the early church in order to prove that the temple was doomed. Some debate has occurred among scholars as to why. Matthew and Luke omit the echo of Malachi 3:1–2 from the composite citation about the Baptist which they presumably took from Mark 1:2–3 (see H. Anderson p. 282; Suhl p. 135). These three were certainly combined when Mark first met them; H. Anderson may even be right in suggesting that the group of citations goes back to the disciples of the Baptist. Possibly Matthew and Luke omitted the Malachi citation because they knew it did not come from Isaiah, as Mark in his context of quotation implies it does. But the same could be said for Exodus 23:20. Both Matthew and Luke quote Malachi later of the Baptist (Matt. 11:10; Luke 1:76). Stanton (p. 76) sees in Acts 10:39, a citation of Deuteronomy 21:22 'you hang him on a tree', an early Christian *testimonium* and not just an example of scriptural application on Luke's part. We know from Galatians 3:13 that this text from Deuteronomy was early employed in Christian apologetic.

Last of all, we should give some attention to the application of 'the sign of Jonah' to Jesus in the early church. Both Luke and Matthew represent Jesus as saying that no sign will be given to this generation but the sign of Jonah the prophet (Matt. 12:39–41, 16:4; Luke 11:29–32): the Ninevites, being Gentiles, repented at the preaching of the Hebrew prophet, whereas the Jews of Jesus' day do not. There may well be the implication that the Gentiles during the period in which the Gospels were being composed were listening to the message about Jesus. But Matthew 12:40 adds another interpretation of the sign of Jonah: 'As Jonah was three days and three nights in the belly of the whale, so will the Son of Man be three days and three nights in the heart of the earth.' Mark 8:11 records only an absolute refusal on Jesus' part to give a sign. Now the most probable conclusion from this evidence is that Mark gives us Jesus' actual position: he would not accredit himself by a sign. The explanation of 'the sign of Jonah' common to Matthew and Luke, that the accession of the Gentiles to the church corresponds to the repentance of the Ninevites, is a product of the successful Gentile mission. And the explanation peculiar to Matthew, that Jonah's sojourn in the belly of the whale is a type of Christ's lying in the tomb is – what? Most scholars, e.g. Stendahl (pp. 132–3) regard this as a later accretion to the tradition taken from some typologizing tradition known only to the author of the First Gospel. But now evidence has turned up which shows that this interpretation of 'the sign of Jonah' is at least a generation earlier than Matthew's Gospel. In Romans 10:6–9 Paul gives us an exposition of Deuteronomy 30:12–13, the passage in which the law is described as being neither hidden away in heaven nor beyond the sea. Paul explains this in Christian terms: 'Do not say in your heart, "Who will ascend into heaven?" [that is, to bring Christ down] or 'Who will descend into the abyss?" [that is, to bring Christ up from the dead]' (Rom. 10:6–7). Scholars have been very much puzzled as to how Paul can justify altering the language of scripture 'beyond the sea' to 'down in the abyss'. But now a complete copy of the Palestinian Targum on the Pentateuch has been discovered, which paraphrases Deuteronomy 30:12–14 in such a way as to bring in a reference both to Moses bringing the law down from Sinai and to Jonah descending into the depths of the sea (the passage is most easily accessible in Etheridge p. 654). Some scholars would deny any influence from the targum tradition here, and point instead to 1 Baruch 3:29–30 and 4 Ezra 4:8 (e.g. E. Schweizer in *Paul and Paulinism* (London 1982), p. 116). Certainly the 1 Baruch passage is based on Deuteronomy 30:12–13, but it does not provide an explanation for 'who will descend into the abyss?' (Rom. 10:7) as does the passage from the Jerusalem Targum. The verse from 4 Ezra occurs in a context which has nothing to do with searching for wisdom, which the 1 Baruch passage at least has. Hence Paul already knew the tradition which saw Jonah's experience inside the whale as a type of Christ's death. Matthew is not purveying late speculations; he is giving very early Christian tradition.

Some Conclusions

As we review the way in which the very earliest Christians used scripture, a homogeneous picture begins to emerge. Jesus is presented as the suffering servant, representative of faithful Israel, coming in the last days to be the Messiah in a mode which Israel had not expected. He is the humiliated, rejected Messiah, who by his sufferings and death brings redemption both to Israel and to all the world. He is God's delegate and as such the bearer of salvation. Everything he said and did was in fulfilment of scripture. He is not only the rejected and murdered servant, climax and exemplar of all the prophetic line, but also the exalted saviour, whose resurrection by the power of God shows him to be the clue to God's whole design towards the world. He now, according to God's plan, appeals to the Gentiles and, as the Spirit-filled prophet, offers the gift of the Spirit to all who believe. Faith is indeed now the distinctive feature of Israel in the new age, for the old ethnic distinction is now abolished and the Kingdom of God that Jesus inaugurated is open to all men everywhere. What is lacking from this early account of Jesus, as compared with what we find in Paul, in Hebrews and in the Fourth Gospel, is any suggestion that Jesus is personally God, or any hint of pre-existence. The Christology of the earliest church was strictly functional.

Since in this chapter we are not only summarizing the content of the earliest interpretation of scripture, but also giving a preview of some of the leading characteristics of New Testament scriptural interpretation as a whole before going into detail in the subsequent chapters, it is relevant to point out one feature of that interpretation which has not always received the emphasis it deserves. New Testament writers did not ignore the context from which their scriptural citations were taken. It is often claimed by scholars that they did ignore the context, because they did not have our sense of history and of the relativity of culture. And it is quite true that they did not concern themselves about the context of their quotations in the way we do; e.g. they did not try to fix the date of the utterance, or the audience to which it was originally addressed, etc. But they did pay attention to the verses preceding and following their citations, and often we cannot appreciate the point they are making unless we study the context also, but always of course from their point of viewing, not being misled by our modern presuppositions (see Lindars p. 17). Lindars cites a good example in Acts 2:24f. (p. 39). Peter quotes Psalm 16:8–11, but in verse 24 he refers to the last verse of the psalm, when he declares that it was impossible that Jesus should be held by the cords of death. Lindars (p. 266) gives another example in John 10:34 where the citation of Psalm 82:6 cannot possibly be understood without a reference to the rest of the psalm, as we shall be seeing when we come to examine John's use of scripture.

By way of illustrating this point further, we will give two instances from Paul, both from 2 Corinthians, a letter in which Paul makes extensive and subtle use of scripture. The first example is 2 Corinthians 4:13, where Paul quotes Psalm 116:10, 'I believed, and so I spoke'. When we look at this psalm as a whole, we see that from Paul's point of view it would seem to recount the main points of Christ's life: his cry for aid in the face of death is echoed in verse 8: 'For thou hast delivered my soul from death.' (See also verse 4: 'O Lord, I beseech thee, save my life!') Verse 15 would refer to his atoning death: 'Precious in the sight of the Lord is the death of his saints.' Verse 16c would be seen as a reference to Christ's resurrection: 'Thou hast loosed my bonds.' Then when we turn back to the context in 2 Corinthians 4 we see that Paul is speaking of the way in which he and his fellow workers reproduce the career of Christ's life, sufferings, death and resurrection in their own lives. The RSV slightly alters the sense of the Greek in 4:13. Literally it should be 'having the same spirit of faith, according as it is written. . .' Paul is not suggesting he has the same spirit of faith as David, who is merely the organ of the Holy Spirit, but of Christ, who was prophesying his incarnate career through the mouth of David. Paul goes on to say 'we too believe, and so we speak', and immediately follows it with a reference to the resurrection both of Jesus and of Christians. Thus a careful study of the whole psalm looked at through Paul's eyes greatly illuminates our understanding of 2 Corinthians 4:7–15.

Our other example comes from 2 Corinthians 5:21—6:2. In 5:21 Paul has made the striking statement that God made Christ to be sin, and he follows it up in 6:2 with a citation of Isaiah 49:8: 'At the acceptable time I have listened to you, and helped you on the day of salvation.' When we turn to this passage in Isaiah 49 the whole meaning of Paul's exposition becomes clear. We have to read 49:1–8 if we wish to understand Paul's allusion. In this passage the servant of the Lord (whom Paul would certainly identify with Jesus) complains that his labour has apparently been in vain and appeals to God for vindication: 'I have laboured in vain . . . yet surely my right is with the Lord, and my recompense with my God' (49:4). In the ensuing verses God assures the servant that he will be vindicated. The climax of this assurance comes in the verse quoted by Paul: 'In a time of favour I answered you, in a day of salvation I have helped you.' When we turn back again to the passage in 2 Corinthians, we can see that God's making

Jesus, who was without sin, to be sin corresponds to the death of Jesus on the cross, condemned as a criminal, though not by God. He appeals to God for help (Gethsemane? the cry on the cross?), and God vindicates him by means of the resurrection. The same process is (mystically, sacramentally) to be carried out in the lives of those who are 'in Christ'. This is why Paul can apply the citation to himself and his fellow Christians, in just the same way as he does in 2 Corinthians 4:13f. We can even trace an echo of the text of scripture in 2 Corinthians 6:1: 'We entreat you not to accept the grace of God *in vain*.' This takes up 'I have laboured *in vain*' in Isaiah 49:4a. Once again a study of the context of the citation throws a flood of light on Paul's exposition.

Next we must be prepared for considerable differences between the ways in which the various authors of the New Testament used scripture. Some of these no doubt go back to a difference of tradition about the use of scripture. The examples we have cited above of the use of scripture during the oral period must not be regarded as representing a uniform tradition throughout the early church. Not all early preachers of the gospel used exactly the same texts. Even in the case of those traditions which can be traced back to Jesus himself, we cannot be sure that all his disciples were acquainted with all of his teaching (it is very unlikely that they were). Add to this the difference of milieu, cultural background and literary intention among the authors of the New Testament and we must see that there is plenty of room for diversity. Perhaps the most obvious distinction is that between those who can go to scripture for themselves and those who are content to purvey what they have received in the way of traditional exegesis. Some scholars would express this by saying that some New Testament writers are skilled authors of midrash and others are not. Among those who obviously can go to scripture for themselves and use it to bring out the significance of Jesus we must number Paul, the author of Hebrews, the author of the First Gospel and the author of the Fourth Gospel. Mark and Luke on the other hand seem content on the whole to hand on the scriptural interpretation of others. We could also make a distinction between those who have a profound approach to scripture, so that they can make it effectively illuminate the figure of Jesus, and those who are more simple and even naive in their usage. In the latter category we might number the author of the Epistle of James and also the author of Jude. Then again there are differences of technique. Matthew, for example, has his own peculiar way of using scripture whereby he gives one the impression that everything said or done by Jesus was said or done primarily in order to fulfil scripture. (I use 'Matthew' to indicate the author of the First Gospel without suggesting that it was written by the

apostle Matthew, just as I use 'John' for the author of the Fourth
Gospel without implying apostolic authorship either.) The author
of the Book of Revelation has a technique of scripture-usage
which is strikingly unlike what we meet in most of the rest of the
New Testament. And finally we might point to idiosyncrasies of
each New Testament author in his use of scripture, Matthew's
'formula quotations', for example, or Paul's daring use of the
words of the Torah in order to show that the Torah is now obsolete
or ineffective (Gal. 3:10–11; Rom. 10:5–9); or, best of all, John's
hidden echoes of the language of scripture in the middle of his
narrative (to be illustrated in Chapter 6). The New Testament is
a book of occasional writings, not a uniform presentation of an
articulated system of thought, and this is demonstrated as much
by its usage of scripture as by any other feature.

Longenecker at one point in his book (pp. 93, 95) outlines what
he regards as the four presuppositions of Christian exegesis. They
are as follows:

1 Corporate solidarity
2 Correspondences in history
3 Eschatological fulfilment
4 Messianic presence.

This is a fair presentation of the case, though we cannot say that
every New Testament writer shares all of these presuppositions.
For example, 2, which I would prefer to call typology, is not
prominent in James and is hardly present at all in Mark. It is
interesting also to note that of these four presuppositions only
one, the last, cannot be found in some tradition of contemporary
Judaism. Corporate solidarity was of course claimed by everyone.
Both the Qumran sectaries and the rabbis believed that their
group was the true Israel of which scripture speaks. Correspondence in history was in some sense claimed by Qumran also,
though they tended more towards allegory than does the New
Testament on the whole. Eschatological fulfilment again was also
claimed by Qumran; the end time was already come, they
believed, though not yet the Messiah. And here of course we put
our finger on the grand distinguishing mark of all Christian
exegesis: it was christocentric from first to last as no other tradition
was.

I would prefer therefore to rephrase the expression of what all
New Testament exegesis has in common and to put it thus, and
sum it up under three heads:

1 The end time has come, the time to which all scripture is
   looking forward.
2 Scripture can therefore be freely applied to Jesus Christ

and through him to the Christian church, which is the true
inheritor of the promises made in scripture to Israel.

3   From this it follows that the authors of scripture knew a
great deal about Christ. Much information about Jesus may
therefore be found by studying the scriptures. Indeed it is
no exaggeration to say that the Jewish scriptures constituted
the theological textbook of the New Testament church.

Everyone in the Jewish world agreed that it was a pious and
profitable occupation to 'search the scriptures'. But each tradition
had its own notion as to what one ought to search the scriptures
for. The Pharisaic party, founders of the rabbinic tradition,
searched them primarily in order to find guidance as to the application of the Torah to daily life, though in the process they believed
that they learned a great deal about God and his ways. The
Qumran sectaries searched the scriptures in order to discover
prophecies about the past history and contemporary destiny of
their own sect, though they also used them in order to confirm
their own interpretation of the *halaka,* especially at those points
where it differed most sharply from that of the Pharisees or of
the Saducean party. Philo searched the scriptures in order to find
allegorical expressions of philosophical, moral and psychological
principles which bore a remarkable resemblance to those of the
Greek philosophical schools of his day. This was no coincidence,
he believed, since Moses had known of these principles long
before they had been enunciated by the various pagan authors,
and had incorporated them into the Pentateuch, hiding them in
allegorical form so as to stimulate the ardour of pious (and well-
educated) souls. Philo could also use the scriptures as providing
examples of godly life in the careers of such men as Abraham and
Moses. And this no doubt is what Josephus most valued the
scriptures for.

Christians on the other hand searched the scriptures in order
to find prophecies of Jesus Christ and to learn from them about
his relationship to themselves, to God and to the world. In order
to do this they did not have to use allegory very much, though
they did not repudiate its use altogether. Typology, or correspondence in history, they used to a greater or lesser degree. They
refrained on the whole from using scripture as proving examples
of godly life (though Hebrews 11 is an exception) because they
believed that they had the supreme example in the life of Jesus
himself. They were not at all interested in using scripture to
provide *halaka*, since they did not take the Torah as their guide
in life and therefore did not need a *halaka*. This does not mean
that scripture is never used in order to provide guidance in morals,
but it is never used in a halakic way. Above all there is a remark-

able absence of laying down of rules, a feature so universal in the Talmud, for example. This is not to say that we never encounter rules in the New Testament: we do in such places as Matthew 18:15–17 and 1 Timothy 5. But these are exceptional passages and probably constitute the beginnings of a system of canon law which, however necessary for the continued life of the Church as a legally constituted body in the world, had very little to do with inspired scripture. They represent a tendency to regulate the Church by means of legal principles derived illegitimately from scripture, and in the very long run were to culminate in a form of institutionalism in the Western Church from which it is only beginning to free itself in our generation.

3

PAUL'S INTERPRETATION OF SCRIPTURE

Paul is of primary importance to any student of our subject. He is the earliest Christian writer whose works have survived. He is also a first-class intellect, constantly wrestling with the theological as well as practical problems in connection with his faith. He is one of the greatest exponents of scripture in the New Testament, but he has perhaps been more misunderstood in this aspect of his work than any other New Testament author, because his technique seems to us so strange that we are constantly tempted to make him say what we think he ought to have meant, rather than what he did mean. It is convenient to sum up his treatment of scripture under six heads.

1 Paul's Debt to Jewish Exegetical Tradition

We intend in this section merely to demonstrate that, for all his deeply christocentric understanding of scripture, Paul's primary approach to it was strongly influenced by the Jewish exegetical tradition in which he was educated, some of the presuppositions of which he never abandoned. We shall give a number of instances of how Paul takes for granted what for convenience we may call rabbinic traditions of interpreting certain passages in scripture.

We begin with a very simple one: in Galatians 4:29 Paul writes: 'But as at that time he who was born according to the flesh persecuted him who was born according to the Spirit, so it is now.' He is referring to an incident narrated in Genesis 21:8–14, where Abraham makes a feast in order to celebrate the weaning of his son Isaac. Sarah, Isaac's mother, sees Ishmael, Abraham's son by Hagar, playing with her son Isaac (v. 9). Sarah subsequently out of jealousy persuades Abraham to send away Hagar and Ishmael into the wilderness. Traditional Jewish exegesis disliked the suggestion that Sarah behaved like a capricious jealous wife, so they interpreted the Hebrew here correctly rendered 'playing' as meaning 'attempting to hurt'. Various theories were put forward, one of which was that Ishmael fired arrows at Isaac (for references see my *Studies in Paul's Technique and Theology*, pp. 98–9). This piece of *haggada* Paul simply takes for granted: Ishmael 'persecuted' Isaac, and is therefore a type of the Jews persecuting Christians in Paul's day.

Another clear example comes in 1 Corinthians 10:4 (which occurs in a passage which will concern us again later). Paul is drawing a typological comparison between the events of the exodus and sojourn in the wilderness on one hand and the experiences of the Corinthian church in his day on the other. He writes: 'For they drank from the supernatural Rock which followed them, and the Rock was Christ.' There is nothing in the scriptural narrative about a rock following the Israelites in order to provide them with a constant supply of water, but we know from rabbinic writings much later than Paul's time that there was a *haggada* to the effect that God provided Israel with a moving rock which followed them throughout the wilderness wanderings and gave them water. Christian commentators have struggled hard to dissociate Paul from this 'Jewish legend', this 'puerile fable', but honesty compels us to admit that Paul did accept this story as part and parcel of the wilderness history, and that he brings it into his exposition of the narrative without any apparent hesitation. It was an element in the tradition of scriptural exegesis he had been taught which he never had occasion to question. (For references see my *Jesus Christ in the Old Testament*, pp. 22–3.) Ellis (p. 58) points out that Paul, in quoting Exodus 32:6, 'the people . . . rose up to dance', is following the rabbinic tradition which taught that the Hebrew word rendered 'dance' here (ṣāḥaq) meant in this context 'commit idolatry' (see 1 Cor. 10:7).

A third example comes from 2 Corinthians 11:3, 14: Paul refers to the serpent deceiving Eve and then says that Satan can disguise himself as an angel of light. This detail is found in a book called *Vita Adae et Evae* of uncertain date, but probably belonging to the first century AD (for details see my *Studies in the Pastoral Epistles*, ch. 6). It is not to be supposed that Paul had read this book, but he certainly knew the *haggada* which it contains and uses it without scruple.

A final example of a slightly different nature can be found by comparing Romans 12:9–21; 13:8–10 with a passage in the Mishna. The passage is to be found in the tractate *Aboth* of the Talmud, chapter 2, 10–11. It is a description of what is the 'good way' for a man to follow as outlined by various rabbis. The parallels between these verses in Romans and the Mishna passage may be set out as follows:

Romans	*Mishna*
12:9 Hate what is evil, hold fast to what is good.	The good way unto which a man should cleave . . . the evil way from which a man should remove himself far.

12:13	Contribute to the needs of the saints.	a good eye, i.e. generosity; cf. Proverbs 22:9.
12:17	Take thought for what is noble in the sight of all (cf. Prov. 3:4, LXX).	One who looks ahead.
12:18	Live peaceably with all men.	Be not easily provoked to anger.
12:19	Never avenge yourselves . . . by so doing you will heap burning coals upon his head.	Warm thyself before the fire of the wise. And beware of their glowing coals.

The last parallel is obscure because it is not clear what exactly the Mishna means, but I have argued that it refers to the conversion to law-observance of one who stood in need of instruction. Paul's phrase seems to envisage the enemy being converted by the gentle treatment which he encounters (for details see *Studies in Paul's Technique*, pp. 129–34). Thus Paul has used a piece of homiletic material, partially based on scripture, and adapted it for the needs of the church in Rome. Paul therefore never hesitates to take over unaltered the tradition of scriptural exegesis in which he was educated as long as it is not inconsistent with his christocentric interpretation. To that interpretation we must now turn.

2   The Pre-Existent Christ

We begin with the claim that Paul traced the activity of the pre-existent Christ in Israel's history. He did this by identifying Christ with either the angel of the Lord or with 'the Lord' in the narrative of scripture. The most obvious passage to illustrate this is 1 Corinthians 10:1–11 to which we have already referred, and to which we will have to refer again. But the obvious conclusion after reading that passage is that, according to Paul, Christ was present during the sojourn in the wilderness to supply the Israelites with water. And not only so, he is in all probability regarded as the source of the manna as well, and no doubt also as being present as the angel of the Lord in the pillar of cloud when the Israelites crossed the Red Sea. This conclusion is rendered very probable indeed by the consideration that in 10:9 the right reading is 'We must not put Christ to the test, as some of them did' (see Zunz pp. 126–7). This speculation seems to us today so bizarre that it has been strongly resisted by some scholars, and we must give attention to this presently.

The identification of Christ with a pre-existent being is also attested by Paul's presentation of Christ as the 'Second Adam' in 1 Corinthians 15:45–9. We know from the writings of Philo that there was a tradition in Alexandrian Judaism at least that the two distinct accounts of the creation of man in Genesis 1:26–7 and 2:4 following referred to two distinct men. The first account referred to an ideal, heavenly man, who belonged to the sphere of mind; the second to empirical physical man, the figure we moderns would call *homo sapiens*. Now Paul certainly makes use of this tradition in the passage in 1 Corinthians 15 just referred to. But he alters it in that he says the heavenly Adam came after the earthly one: 'The first man was from the earth, a man of dust; the second man is from heaven' (v. 47). It seems very unlikely, however, that Paul meant that the Second Adam only first came into existence when he appeared on earth. We know from other passages, such as Galatians 4:4; Romans 8:3; Philippians 2:6–8, that Paul believed that Christ pre-existed and was sent from heaven. In saying therefore that Christ was the Second Adam, he meant that he appeared on earth second to empirical Adam, not that he was created second. Here then is another passage where Paul is finding the pre-existent Christ referred to in scripture.

My next two examples of Paul's belief in the pre-existent activity of Christ are more debatable, but are worth mentioning. The first is 2 Corinthians 3:7–18. This is a difficult passage in which Paul is arguing with his opponents in Corinth in strictly scriptural terms. They must have been playing up the role of Moses, perhaps in contrast to that of Jesus Christ: Moses, they claimed, was a man of amazing spiritual powers, the recipient of divine mysteries, and this is proved by the quasi-transfiguration which he is recorded as having undergone in Exodus 34:29–34. Perhaps they even suggested that Moses put a veil on his face on that occasion in order not to disclose those divine secrets, which were, they may have hinted, accessible to those who studied the law correctly. Paul replies that, great as was the glory that Moses experienced, the glory of the Messiah, and therefore of the messianic era, was even greater; and, far from being a carefully guarded secret, it was accessible to all who accepted in faith Paul's open preaching of the gospel. Now my interpretation of this midrash on scripture goes one step further. Paul believed that he whom Moses met in the tabernacle was the pre-existent Christ. It follows that Moses put the veil on his face in order that the Israelites should not witness the messianic glory, even though it was the lesser glory of the pre-incarnate being. His veiling was thus a prophetic or typological gesture, very much the sort of thing we might expect Paul to believe about Moses. This interpretation depends on understanding 3:16 as meaning 'Now when a man turns to the Lord Jesus Christ the veil is removed'. I have expounded this argument fully in my article 'The Midrash in 2 Corinthians 3', pp. 2–28.

The other reference is to Romans 11:34–5, where Paul gives a remarkable combination of a passage from Isaiah 40:13 with one from Job 41:11 (in the English versions). Paul quotes the same passage from Isaiah 40:13 in 1 Corinthians 2:16, though he does not reproduce exactly the same part of it (he quotes 13ab of the LXX in Romans 8:34 and 13ac of the LXX in 1 Corinthians 2:16). We cannot understand what Paul sees in this composite quotation in Romans 11:34–5 unless we realize that the Job citation could only have been regarded as relevant by Paul because when he encountered it the passage had already been interpreted as a reference to God's creative work, which it certainly was not in its original context in Job. The to us apparently rhetorical question in Isaiah 40:13 'who has been (God's) counsellor?' was not regarded as rhetorical in Jewish tradition. God, they believed, had a counsellor, his divine wisdom (the evidence for all this is to be found in my book *The Interpretation of Scripture*, pp. 77–89, 92–3). Paul identifies the pre-existent Christ with this counsellor, and with the mind (or spirit) of God. Thus a careful examination of what lies behind Paul's scriptural citations often throws a great deal of light on his Christology.

I have mentioned that the counsellor was identified with the divine wisdom. This indeed provides us with the clue for understanding how Paul could interpret scripture in what must seem to us so strange a manner. He was an inheritor of the wisdom tradition in Judaism. We can indeed point to a book, probably written not very long before Paul's day, in which the divine wisdom carries out very much the same activity in Israel's history as Paul attributed to Christ. In chapters 10 and 11 of the apocryphal Book of Wisdom the author conducts us through the history of mankind, of the patriarchs and of Israel in the wilderness, describing how at each crisis the divine wisdom was present to guide and command. For example, this is how he describes Jacob's flight after his deception of Esau (Genesis 28):

> When a righteous man fled from his brother's wrath,
>   she guided him on straight paths;
>   she showed him the kingdom of God,
>   and gave him knowledge of angels. (Wisdom 10:10)

And this is how he describes the exodus:

> She gave to holy men the reward of their labours;
>   she guided them along a marvellous way,
>   and became a shelter to them by day
>   and a starry flame through the night.
> She brought them over the Red Sea,
>   and led them through deep waters;

> but she drowned their enemies,
> and cast them up from the depths of the sea.
>
> (Wisdom 10:17–19)

Paul has not explicitly identified Christ with the divine wisdom but he has attributed to the pre-existent Christ the activities and attributes of the divine wisdom. The figure of wisdom was, so to speak, waiting in his scriptural tradition to be used, and he has used it in order to explicate fully a thoroughly christocentric interpretation of what were after all the only scriptures that he knew.

3 Typology and Allegory

We should now examine Paul's use of typology in greater detail. Typology means the process of tracing a parallel between a set of events in the old dispensation as recounted in scripture and a set of events in the new Christian dispensation. The new dispensation can mean either the events of Christ's life, death and resurrection, or the present experience of the Christian church, though that experience is always related to Christ. Paul did not invent typology; it is to be found within the scriptures themselves. The Second Isaiah, for example, uses the typology of exodus events in order to describe the events of Israel's liberation from Babylonian exile that God is ready to bring about; see Isaiah 44:27; 50:2; 51:10. The Qumran sectaries used a sort of typology when they interpreted the utterances of the prophets as applying to the history of their own community, though they showed much less interest in the historical events to which the scripture passages they quote originally referred, and consequently their typology constantly passes over into allegory. Nor is a typological interpretation of scripture confined to Paul in the New Testament. It is also used by the author of Hebrews, the author of the Fourth Gospel and the author of 1 Peter.

We have already mentioned several passages where Paul uses typology. Galatians 4:28–30 is one: Ishmael persecuting Isaac is a type of the synagogue persecuting the church in Paul's day. Then comes 1 Corinthians 10:1–11, by far the most elaborate piece of typology in Paul's writings. The Israelites crossing the Red Sea under the guidance of the pillar of cloud is a type of Christians being immersed in baptism into Christ (the presence of Moses under the old dispensation is a crucial distinction which, Paul believes, marks the old as inferior because a mediator had to be used; see Galatians 3:19–20). The giving of the manna in the wilderness and the supply of water from the rock are types of the sacrament of the Eucharist wherein bread and wine are

supernaturally blessed. Further, the failure of many Israelites in
the wilderness to appreciate the generosity and mercy of God and
their subsequent unhappy fate is a type of what could happen
(perhaps did happen in view of 1 Corinthians 11:30) to Christians
who take for granted the presence and power of the Lord Christ
in the Eucharist. Then there is certainly typology in the midrash
in 2 Corinthians 3. Moses veiling his face so that the Israelites
should not see the glory of the pre-existent Christ reflected in it
is a type of the unbelief of the Jews at the present day, who, even
though the scripture is read to them every week in the synagogue,
do not see that Christ is spoken of in it. Paul presses his 'veil'
type rather too strongly here, so that it virtually becomes an
allegory. There is plenty of typology also in Romans: we have
already pointed out that Adam is a type of Christ, though in fact
he is an imperfect type. He shares with Christ an aboriginal,
corporate archetypal existence, but in all other respects he offers
a contrast to Christ. Where he disobeyed, Christ obeyed; where
he inaugurated death for mankind, Christ inaugurates life. His
very origin is from the earth, Christ's is from heaven. In Romans
4:23 Abraham is a type of the believing Christian: Abraham
believed before he was circumcised, thereby showing that faith in
Christ is what God requires, not circumcision. Then in chapter 9
of Romans we have a series of typological interpretations of scripture: God's choice of Jacob rather than Esau before they were
born is a type of his choice of the Gentiles in Paul's day, who are,
like Jacob, children of promise (9:7–13). Then follows a typological treatment of Pharaoh: he was a 'vessel of wrath' in that by
his obduracy he demonstrated what happened to those who
oppose God's design in history. To him and the Egyptians whom
he instigated to oppress Israel at the time of the exodus correspond
the unbelieving Jews in Paul's day (see my article 'Vessels of
Wrath or Instruments of Wrath', pp. 433–43). In the previous
chapter we have already referred to Paul's treatment of Deuteronomy 30:12–14. In his handling of the text is clearly implied
the typological treatment of Moses and Jonah: Moses bringing
the Torah down from heaven is a type of Christ descending from
heaven for our redemption. Jonah descending to the abyss and
returning is a type of Christ's death, *descensus ad inferos*, and
resurrection (Rom. 10:6–9). See p. 37 above. We know that the
type of Jonah was not peculiar to Paul, and hence he probably
did not invent it; and we may conjecture that the type of Moses
was not his invention either, since elsewhere in his works he does
not use the figure of Moses in this way. In the next chapter
another piece of typology follows (11:1–5): Elijah finding himself a
member of a persecuted minority in Israel in Jezebel's day is a

type of the Christian church in Paul's day, partly made up of a minority of Jews.

Occasionally, as we have seen, Paul strays into allegory. The difference between typology and allegory is that, whereas typology is concerned with parallel series of events, in allegory one takes a person or feature in the old dispensation and more or less arbitrarily declares that it corresponds to some person or event in the new. For example, the author of the Epistle of Barnabas interprets Exodus 33:3, 'Go up to a land flowing with milk and honey', allegorically: the 'land' is the Lord's flesh in his incarnation, and the 'milk and honey' are Christians newborn in baptism (Ep. Barnabus 6). There is no obvious connection between the various terms of the comparison here, though the author of the Epistle ingeniously makes one. Paul, we feel, has almost reached a similar position in his elaborate piece of attempted typology in Galatians 4:21–7. He begins with a fairly straightforward comparison between Ishmael and Isaac: Ishmael corresponds to the unbelieving Jews in Paul's day and Isaac to Christians. But then further comparisons and contrasts are introduced: Ishmael's mother Hagar and Isaac's mother Sarah. Then appear two events: the covenant on Sinai, and, presumably, the new covenant made in Jesus' blood, though this side of the comparison is never made explicit. Not content with this, Paul has to bring in two mountains as well, one in Arabia and one presumably consisting of Mount Zion, though the figures have become so confused by now that this cannot be said with certainty. Paul crowns the confusion by suggesting a third comparison, two Jerusalems, the empirical Jerusalem and 'the Jerusalem above'. But by this time the terms of the comparison have become so complicated that the original point has been lost. Paul is confounded by the very richness of his imagery. Like Leigh Hunt, who intended an ode but it turned out a sonnet, he intended a piece of typology but it has turned into an allegory. Another much more straightforward allegory is found in 1 Corinthians 9:9: Paul wishes to show that scripture commends the support of ministers by the congregations, so he quotes Deuteronomy 25:4: 'You shall not muzzle an ox when it is treading out the grain.' This cannot be intended literally, for God is not interested in oxen ('Is it for oxen that God is concerned?'). It must therefore mean that those who devote themselves to the work of the gospel have a right to expect support from those who receive it. This is certainly allegory: if Paul needs any defence for this particular piece of exegesis, perhaps it can be found in the fact that this text was well thumbed already when Paul handled it. He was certainly not the first to give it an allegorical meaning (see my *Studies in Paul's Technique*, pp. 161–6).

Some scholars, however, challenge this account of Paul's use of typology. Paul, they say, was not interested in what happened in past history, even salvation history. He uses these past figures as ciphers to refer to the present. In fact he is really a crypto-allegorist. Of such is Suhl, who claims (p. 176) that Paul in 1 Corinthians 10:1–11 is interested only in the contemporary relevance of what he narrates, not in the historicity of the scriptural narrative. He would describe apparently typological language in the New Testament as 'illustrative' (p. 178). Thus all Paul is saying in 1 Corinthians 10:1–11 is that the behaviour and experiences of Israel in the wilderness are a good illustration of the relation of the Corinthian Christians to Christ.

A more recent exponent of the same theory is Dr J. D. G. Dunn. In his book *Christology in the Making* he argues that in the passage in question Paul is not saying anything about what happened in the past, only about what the actual words of scripture indicate concerning Christ now. He regards the situation described in scripture as being in Paul's view 'a typological allegory of the spiritual realities now experienced by the Corinthians' (pp. 183–4). And he adds: 'Paul's readers should see the rock then as the type of Christ now.' It is true that one phrase in Paul's typological exegesis might seem to be evidence against Dunn's theory: in 10:4 Paul writes 'and the Rock was Christ'. Paul's use of the past tense strongly suggests that he is interested in what took place in the past and does not treat it as a mere cipher in an allegory about the present. But Dunn has an answer for this: in all other cases where this sort of typology is used (he calls it 'allegory') the object designated is present to the writer there and then, whereas the rock belonged exclusively to the past. His other instances are Galatians 4:24f.; 2 Corinthians 3:17; and CD (the so-called 'Zadokite Document' of Qumran) 6:4. In this last source, of the well mentioned in Numbers 21:17–18 they write: 'The well is the law, and those who dug it were the converts of Israel.' (See Dunn, op. cit., p. 330, n. 78.) Thus Paul is to be understood as having used the past tense not because he really thought Christ was there in past history, but because the figure that indicates Christ in the present is completely a matter of the past.

But it is difficult to appreciate that there is any real difference between the well in the Book of Numbers; the rock in Exodus 17:1–6 and Numbers 20:10–11; Hagar in Genesis 21; and the veil in Exodus 34:29–35, as far as pastness is concerned. They are all equally in the past. It is true that in 2 Corinthians 3:15 Paul does project the veil into the present. But this is not allegorizing the veil that Moses used: a literal, historical veil (as Paul believed) in the old dispensation points to a metaphorical veil in the new. Paul is therefore not allegorizing scripture, but the present position of unbelieving Jews. We have therefore no reason to believe that when Paul writes 'the Rock was Christ' he means this in anything but a straightforward sense, strange though his interpretation of scripture must appear to us. As we have already pointed out, the reading in verse 9, 'let us not tempt Christ', must surely give the *coup de grâce* to any theory that Paul is not referring to what happened in the past. The Israelites tempted Christ during their sojourn in the wilderness because he was present to them in pre-existent mode (I have argued this out at great length in Chapter 4 of my book *The Image of the Invisible God*).

We must therefore accept the conclusion that Paul so interprets scripture as to find in it not only the figure of the pre-existent Christ with the attributes of the divine wisdom, but also evidence for the activity of that pre-existent being in Israel's history. In other words, Paul is fully committed to a doctrine of salvation history: God in Christ, he believes, has been active from the first for salvation in the history of Israel. Naturally we feel inclined to challenge Paul's method of interpretation. How does he know that the pre-existent Christ was present in the wilderness? In any case, what does it mean to say that Jesus Christ, who lived in Palestine for thirty years, was present on various occasions in the past history of Israel, hundreds of years before he was born of Mary? These are very relevant questions which must be faced, and are faced later on in this work. But for the moment we must be content to continue our study of how Paul does actually interpret scripture, without stopping to ask what sense we can make of it.

4   The Problem of the Law

For Paul perhaps the first problem that presented itself after his conversion was the question of the Torah. This was essentially a scriptural as well as a practical problem, since in scripture, especially in Deuteronomy, Torah-observance is commanded as God's will for Israel. How was he to reconcile this commendation with his conviction that the death and resurrection of Jesus had abolished the need for Torah-observance? He achieves this end by an argument drawn from scripture itself which he sets out in Galatians chapter 3 and Romans chapter 4. He points to the figure of Abraham, and he shows that Abraham was justified by his faith in God before he was required to do anything in the way of obeying God's commands. The key text is Genesis 15:6: 'And he (Abraham) believed the Lord; and he (God) reckoned it to him as righteousness.' God had promised Abraham that he should have an heir through his wife Sarah. Abraham believed God's promise. Paul, therefore, takes Abraham as the great model of faith: Abraham could only know by faith that he would have an heir, so his faith preceded his works. In Galatians the promise seems rather to be that made in Genesis 12:3: 'In you all the families of the earth shall be blessed' (RSV mg), and Abraham's faith is shown in his leaving his homeland at God's bidding. But Paul draws the same conclusion from both incidents: faith precedes law, therefore law is inferior and temporary. In this respect Paul is markedly diverging from rabbinic tradition. The rabbis, with their conviction that God always intended the Torah to be Israel's guide through life, could not believe that Abraham had known nothing of it. They therefore represent him as having been, so to speak, orally instructed in the Torah centuries before it was engraved on stone tablets on Sinai. They did not ignore Genesis 15:6, but they interpreted it as meaning that his faith was manifested in his works, very much the way it is understood in James 2:20–3.

Paul thus presents a schematized version of salvation history. It proceeds in a series of stages or epochs: first God creates man, and man sins. Death enters the world through Adam's sin: men are now mortal, liable to death because they follow in Adam's footsteps. But their sin has not yet been made absolutely clear to them because the law has not yet been given. Then comes God's promise to Abraham, and Abraham is justified by faith. One might say that the era of faith had begun, but it is more likely that according to Paul's scheme of things God had always desired faith in those who obey him; only at the time of Abraham was this made clear. Compare the schema of the author of Hebrews: he sees faith as having been exhibited from the very first, beginning with Abel, Enoch and Noah. At any rate, from Abraham onwards, according to Paul, God had revealed to those who listened to him that he desired men to live by faith rather than works. Works (symbolized by the acceptance of circumcision in the case of Abraham) were a 'seal' of faith or a confirmation of faith. They were not a saving ordinance. Then, 400 years after Abraham, came the giving of the Torah. This was marked, in Paul's view, by clear signs that it was both inferior and temporary or provisional. It was issued by means of a double mediation: God gave it to angels, who gave it to Moses, who gave it to Israel. (See Gal. 3:19–20.) Incidentally, the belief that the law was 'ordained by angels' is itself a piece of Jewish *haggada*. Paul does not mean that the law was invented by angels, but that it was transmitted by them. The giving of the Torah, says Paul, was not intended to supersede the era of faith. The Torah was given in order to bring out the full sinfulness of sin and thus reduce all, Jew and Gentile alike, to the point where they had no recourse but in the mercy of God. It was only in force until the Messiah should come. When he came he was according to prophecy to live by faith. It seems likely that Paul understood Habakkuk 2:4, 'the just shall live by faith', to mean 'the righteous one [i.e. the Messiah] shall live by faith' (for all this see *Studies in Paul's Technique*, pp. 42f., 52f.).

Professor Hans Hübner seems to have shown very clearly that by the time Paul came to write Romans he had to some extent modified the rather extreme view of the Torah which he took in Galatians. (See *Das Gesetz bei Paulus*.) It was not to be completely abolished: it had a normative function. In default of a faith relationship one had sometimes to fall back on it. But the essential schema of salvation history remained intact: there had been an era of faith before the era of law. The faith era had never been completely displaced, and was now, with the coming of the Messiah, in full force. Certainly God does not require that anybody, whether Jew or Gentile, should base his relationship to him on the Torah. We cannot of course accept Paul's account of scriptural history exactly as he sets it out in Galatians and Romans. Adam is a purely mythical figure; it is very doubtful whether any historical figure corresponding to Abraham ever existed; Moses, though no doubt there was a real person of that name, is very largely legendary as far as any positive historical facts about him are concerned. But in one respect the critical study of the Hebrew scriptures has resulted in vindicating Paul's schema of a faith era followed by a law era. We now know that the religion of the Jews only became Torah-centred after the exile. In the period of the great prophets, roughly 750–550 BC, the Torah as a law-code written out in all its details was not the centre of Israel's religion. There were various traditions concerning the law, there were priests one of whose functions was to give torah or instruction about how God wishes his people to behave, and there were some written codes, though nothing like what we know as the Pentateuch. The great prophets, in recalling Israel to obedience towards God, do not appeal to the Torah. Their attitude is much more that of Paul: what they ask for is 'the obedience of faith'. Thus it could be said that the era of the great prophets was an era of faith, and that the Torah-centric era only came later. Christianity is in this sense a 'back to the prophets' movement, and it is no coincidence that all the great writers of the New Testament quote extensively from the prophets, especially Isaiah. So we have here an example of a situation in which we can say that the point about scripture which Paul was making is valid, even though we cannot endorse the precise historical terms in which he made it.

5   Christ as Suffering Servant

But Paul did not see the pre-existent Christ only as a heavenly being, surrogate for God on many occasions in Israel's history. He saw him also as the suffering servant mentioned in Isaiah 40—55, and particularly in Isaiah 52:13—53:12. With this he connected the righteous sufferer of the psalms, representative of faithful Israel. This point must be vigorously asserted, because there is an influential school among English New Testament scholars who claim that the identification of Jesus with the suffering servant is a relatively late development, first found in Luke–Acts and elaborated in 1 Peter. I have always tried to show that the Pauline evidence is entirely incompatible with this theory; see *Studies in Paul's Technique*, pp. 35, 36, 211. I do not think that anyone who has studied Paul's use of scripture in any depth will be disposed to deny that he did see Jesus as the suffering servant. But I will not use my own arguments here. I shall give instead an outline of a paper on the subject delivered by Professor Otto Betz of Tübingen at the annual conference of the Society for New Testament Study at Rome in August 1981. As far as I know, it has not been published anywhere.

He begins from Romans 15:21; Paul declares his intention of refraining from preaching the gospel in any place where it has already been preached; his aim is to preach only to those who have not heard it before, and in confirmation of this he quotes Isaiah 52:15:

They shall see who have never been told of him,
and they shall understand who have never heard of him.

Paul interprets this verse as applying to the gospel which he preaches. But in Isaiah the verse refers to the suffering servant. Betz reasonably concludes that Paul believed the suffering servant was Jesus Christ, since his gospel was certainly about Jesus Christ. Next Betz turns to Romans 10:15–16. Here we have a quotation from Isaiah 52:7 followed by one from Isaiah 53:1. The first refers to the gospel, the good news proclaimed by Christians, Paul wishes us to understand. The second refers to the unbelief of the Jews. The prophet, according to Paul's interpretation, knows about the content of the gospel of Jesus Christ and also knows beforehand that it will meet with a large measure of unbelief in Israel. We might point out incidentally that in the material between these two citations occurs a clear reference to the suffering servant. We are certainly not justified in claiming that Paul must have ignored this material. We have already claimed that New Testament writers, least of all Paul, did not normally make citations in total disregard of their context. Paul must therefore have regarded Isaiah 52:13–15 as applying to Jesus Christ.

Betz then steps aside in order to show that this identification of Jesus with the figure of the fourth servant song was not Paul's invention. It is pre-Pauline, because it is presupposed by the hymn which Paul quotes in Philippians 2:6–11, and he backs this up with an examination of Romans 4:25, which echoes Isaiah 53:4–5.

Next he points to Romans 1:16: 'For I am not ashamed of the gospel: for it is the power of God for salvation to every one who has faith, to the Jew first and also to the Greek.' This, says Betz, is Paul's answer to Isaiah's question already mentioned in connection with Romans 10:16: 'Lord, who has believed our report?' 'I have', says Paul, and he goes on to echo the second half of Isaiah 53:1, which is 'And to whom has the arm of the Lord been revealed?' The phrase 'the arm of the Lord' means 'the power of the Lord' and that is what Paul is implying when he says the gospel is the 'power of God'. The Targum renders Isaiah 53:1b with 'the power of the arm of the Lord, to whom has it been revealed?' Betz also compares Isaiah 52:10:

> The Lord has bared his holy arm
>   before the eyes of all the nations.

Betz says that Romans 3:21f. also contains references to the prophecy of Isaiah. Isaiah 56:1 is implied in 3:21: 'But now the righteousness of God has been manifested apart from the law, although the law and the prophets bear witness to it.' The verse he has in mind runs thus:

> for soon my salvation will come,
>   and my deliverance be revealed.

When we read on in this passage from Romans 3, we encounter verse 26: 'It was to prove at the present time that he himself is righteous and that he justifies him who has faith in Jesus.' This echoes Isaiah 53:11, which runs in the LXX:

> to justify the righteous one who well serves many.

Betz agrees that Paul takes 'the righteous one' as the Messiah, in accordance with our interpretation of Habakkuk 2:4 above. He also sees a reference to the next verse, wherein the servant intercedes for many, in Romans 8:34, where Christ is described as interceding for us.

He sums up by claiming that the last servant song as a whole is a description of how the sentence pronounced on mankind by God because of sin has been removed by the voluntary self-offering and death of the servant; the curse has been changed into blessing. That is precisely the kernel of Paul's doctrine of the atonement as set out in Galatians, 2 Corinthians and Romans, particularly of course in Romans 3. Betz ends by connecting Romans 5:1–11 with Isaiah 53:5. This verse in Isaiah is the clearest expression in the fourth servant song of the substitutionary and vicarious nature of the servant's suffering, and it must be behind such verses as Romans 5:6–8, 10.

It is important to realize that all these intricate and detailed references to the servant passages in general and Isaiah 52:13—53:12 in particular cannot be dismissed as just so many instances of Paul clothing his thought in appropriate language drawn from scripture, like Mr Stiggins in Dickens, who could never refer to a girl except as a 'handmaiden', and so on. That was not the way in which Paul used scripture. When he quotes it or echoes it, he means the quotations to be significant. For him, as for all the writers of the New Testament, scripture was not just a useful source book for exalted, familiar and inspiring language; it was a source of information about Jesus. The prophets, they held, knew a great deal about the coming messianic age, and when they wrote about it they intended their writings to be noted and to be referred to for confirmation when the events prophesied actually happened; cf. John 2:17; 12:16, passages which exactly express this early Christian belief.

Ellis at one point (p. 126) makes the statement that Paul was not interested in predictive prophecy as such, but in typology. There is some truth in this, since, as we have seen, Paul does not have the complete lack of interest in the context of the scripture citation evinced by the Qumran sectaries. But it is hardly true to say that he never cites a scripture passage simply as a prediction. What are we to make, for example, of Romans 15:3, where Paul quotes Psalm 69:9: 'The reproaches of them that reproached thee fell upon me'? Paul understands this psalm verse as uttered by the pre-existent Christ (or at the very least concerning the pre-existent Christ by the prophet David), who prophesies his vicarious sufferings during the period of the incarnation. Other examples of this use of the psalms are not far to seek: I have interpreted the catena of quotations in Romans 3:10–18 in this sense (see *Studies in Paul's Technique*, pp. 16f.). Romans 8:36, when carefully analysed, can be shown to treat Psalm 44 in a similar way (ibid., pp. 36f.). Compare also Romans 11:8–10, and there are three clear examples in Romans 15:9–11. In most of these citations Paul regards the pre-existent Christ as the speaker, prophesying either his sufferings, or the behaviour of his persecutors, or the way in which the church should react. The element of prediction cannot be excluded, though no doubt Paul was chiefly interested in these passages as affording information about Christ's career and his relation to the church.

Paul can of course use passages from the prophets in this way. He would not have felt inclined to make the clear distinction between psalmist and prophet that we would insist on. He would have regarded all this material as coming from the same source, the Holy Spirit. Thus we find him in Romans 10:19–20 making very effective use of Deuteronomy 32:21 and Isaiah 65:1–2; these two verses are uttered by Christ, he believes. The Deuteronomy quotation refers to the fact that the Gentiles were to accept the message of the gospel, thereby inciting the Jews to emulation; the Isaiah citation is applied in the first verse to the same theme, the unexpected accession of the Gentiles; and the second verse applies to the unbelieving Jews. It is even possible that Paul actually has the appeal of the cross in mind. Incidentally, only three verses earlier in 10:18 Paul has made what appears to us to be a most extraordinary use of Psalm 19:4: the universal range of the sun's rays indicates the universal range of the gospel. Commentators have shied away from the conclusion that Paul really thinks that Psalm 19:4 refers to the spread of the gospel, and tend to suggest that he is merely taking a scriptural illustration. It is more likely, however, that Paul means this reference to be taken seriously: the rabbis applied this verse to the universal range of the Torah. Paul will not claim less for the gospel. Another example in this genre is Paul's use of Isaiah 45:23, which he quotes twice in his writings: it occurs at the very end of the 'hymn of the incarnation' in Philippians 2:9–11, and is in my opinion Paul's addition and not part of the original hymn. It also occurs in Romans 14:11. A careful study of the context of this citation in the LXX of Isaiah 45 tells us a great deal about Paul's theology (consider the relevance of 45:21, for example). But we have not time to examine this in detail.

6   Other Usages in Paul

We will conclude our review of Paul's usage of scripture by referring to two other characteristics of his. The first we may call 'the hidden influence of scripture'. Sometimes in a passage where Paul is not explicitly citing scripture one can nevertheless detect the influence of the words of scripture as if he had been meditating on one particular passage and it had influenced the train of his thought and even the words he used. We can give one instance from Romans 8:19–21. It looks as if when Paul wrote these verses he had Psalm 89:46–8 in mind. The parallels are not very obvious if one compares the two passages in the English version, but if one compares Paul's Greek with the LXX (still more with what we know of the other Greek versions accessible to New Testament writers in the first century AD), the parallel is quite striking. Paul

writes about the *expectation* of the *creation*, and about *hope*. The
creation is subjected to *vanity*. All the words in italics have got
some correlate in the LXX of Psalm 89:46-8 (in LXX 48:47-9) or
in some other Greek version. There is also the thought of the
creation being *liberated* from *corruption*: there is a non-verbal
equivalent to this in the LXX of Psalm 89:48. We must remember
that the Greek translators often misunderstood the Hebrew and
imported nuances and overtones that were not there in the
original. Paul would see in this passage in the psalms a reference
to the vicarious suffering of the Messiah, which his faithful disciples are to share with him. For details, see *Studies in Paul's
Technique*, pp. 32f.

Another example of this unacknowledged use of scripture is to
be found in Romans 11:17-24, the famous parable of the olive
tree. The olive tree represents Israel both old and new: the
Gentiles, like shoots from a wild olive, have been grafted into the
stock of the domestic olive carefully tended by God. It is surprising
that Paul should use the figure of an olive tree. The obvious tree
to choose is the vine. That figure has plenty of precedents in
scripture, from the 'song of the vineyard' in Isaiah 5:1-7 to the
vine that has been uprooted by the wild boar of the forest in
Psalm 80:8-19. The answer to this question is to be found in a
passage from Jeremiah. It is Jeremiah 11:16: 'The Lord once
called you "A green olive tree, fair with goodly fruit"; but with
the roar of a great tempest he will set fire to it, and its branches
will be consumed.' God is of course addressing Israel. But the
LXX has misunderstood and mistranslated the Hebrew and
produces the following:

'The Lord has called thy name a beautiful olive tree, in appearance, affording good shade. At the voice of its circumcision fire
was kindled on it; great was the affliction on thee; its branches
have been damaged.' It is by no means clear how the motif of
'circumcision' has crept in. It is certainly not in the Hebrew. But
this LXX mistranslation is probably what Paul used. As such the
verse would make excellent sense to Paul: it would suggest to him
that it was at the instigation of the Jews (whom he describes as
'circumcision' in Romans 15:8; cf. also Galatians 2:7-12) that the
fire of God's judgement was kindled, manifested in the cross. It
would also indicate that the branches have not been wholly
destroyed, as the Hebrew conveys, but only 'damaged'. This
would allow him his concept of a new Israel made up partly of
Jews and partly of Gentiles, and the reference to 'affliction',
another importation of the LXX, would speak to him of the
affliction which was to be expected in the messianic era which,
Paul believed, had been inaugurated. (This is worked out in
greater detail in *Studies in Paul's Technique*, pp. 121f.) There are

no doubt other places in Paul's letters where the hidden influence of scripture could be traced. We shall encounter a similar phenomenon in the Fourth Gospel.

The other feature to which we would draw attention can be best introduced by posing the question: does Paul ever use scripture in a simple, non-typological, illustrative manner? Does he ever say in effect: 'What I wish to say can be illustrated by the words of scripture'? Or we could express it differently by asking whether Paul ever uses scripture in a non-theological way. The answer must of course be: yes. To take a very simple instance: in 2 Corinthians 13:1 Paul is threatening the Corinthian church that if he has to visit them again before they show any signs of repentance for their bad behaviour, he will have to discipline them sternly. He quotes a well-known text from Deuteronomy 19:15: 'Any charge must be sustained by the evidence of two or three witnesses.' This is used in a perfectly straightforward way, and was obviously part of the disciplinary machinery of the early church, as we can see from the use of (or reference to) the same text in Matthew 18:16 and 1 Timothy 5:19. But it is worth observing that Paul at this point is not dealing with the Corinthians on a strictly Christian basis. Their conduct has been so bad that he can no longer deal with them on the basis of mutual faith and love, but must fall back on a legal text literally applied. Again, in an earlier part of 2 Corinthians, where Paul is chiefly concerned with encouraging the Corinthians to give generously to his special fund for poor Christians in Judaea, he seems to use scripture in a purely exhortative way. For example, in 2 Corinthians 9:7 he writes: 'Each one must do as he has made up his mind, not reluctantly or under compulsion, for God loves a cheerful giver.' This looks like a scriptural tag: 'God loves a cheerful giver' and it probably is so. We cannot help noting, however, that this tag is found only in the Greek, not in the Hebrew, of Proverbs 22:8c. He uses in this passage a number of other texts connected with giving, e.g. Proverbs 3:4 in 8:21; Psalm 112:9 in 9:9 and Exodus 16:18 in 8:15. Not all of these are straightforward, however, and there is probably hidden typology in the citation from Exodus 16:18 (see the discussion in *Studies in Paul's Technique*, pp. 174f.) Another scripture text used apparently in a purely illustrative manner is Isaiah 52:5 in Romans 2:24: 'The name of God is blasphemed among the Gentiles because of you.' Paul is at this point addressing Jews and does not seem to have any *arrière-pensée* about salvation history. On the whole, it must be said, we would be wise to examine carefully any alleged examples of texts used in a purely illustrative manner by Paul. His mind had a strongly theological bent, and he usually cites scripture in order to prove something rather than merely in order to illustrate his theme.

As we look back over our account of Paul's interpretation of scripture, we must be deeply impressed with the impetus which he gave by means of his writings to the Christian interpretation of scripture. He did not of course invent the discipline. As we have seen, the earliest Christians had already given a definite orientation to the Christian interpretation of scripture. It was the prophets, notably Isaiah, the psalms and the main outlines of Israel's historical (or quasi-historical) records that interested Christians, not the details of the Torah or the story of Esther (so much beloved by rabbinic exegetes). But Paul gave to Christian interpretation a much deepened christological character. His Christology was more far-reaching and exalted than that which he received, but it was thoroughly scriptural. Unlike John, Paul draws all his christological vocabulary from scripture. The very concept of pre-existence, which one would imagine might seem to have been imported from philosophy, was expounded in terms of Israel's history and hence the activity of the pre-existent Christ was detected in scripture. Whatever he might seem to us, Paul must have believed himself to be a biblical theologian. He would have been surprised if he could have known of the accusations that were made against him by scholars in the last century, that he imported pagan speculations into the originally Hebraic gospel. He genuinely believed that everything he taught was based on scripture. He was constantly quoting scripture in support of what he said. His interpretation of scripture may not indeed be ours, and we have to turn our attention to this question later in this work. But no one who studies Paul in depth can doubt that he believed himself to be drawing his Christology and ecclesiology from scripture and nowhere else.

Paul in fact claimed the Jewish scriptures for Christ and in this he set a model for the early church. We must not lay at Paul's door the blame for the extensive allegorical exegesis that later Christian theologians used in order to Christianize the Jewish scriptures. Paul is much more restrained in his use of allegory than are many of the fathers. But he certainly orientated the church in this direction. It was his claim that salvation history is fulfilled in Christ that enabled later Christians to connect the Jewish scriptures with the New Testament. Without Paul's strong conviction that the scriptures are full of references to Christ, the Christian church might have set off on its career in history without a bible.

4

THE USE OF SCRIPTURE IN THE SYNOPTIC GOSPELS

In Chapter 2 we attempted to distinguish those scriptural allusions which went back to Jesus himself and also those which the earliest Christian community made use of in their preaching about Jesus after the resurrection. This was necessarily a difficult and precarious operation with an inevitable element of subjective judgement in it. The same conclusion applies in our treatment of the scriptural usage in the Synoptic Gospels. There is nothing remotely approaching a consensus of scholars on this topic, and we must be content to state our conclusions, giving such reasons for them as seem to us convincing. What we are trying to do in our handling of the Synoptics is to decide (a) which scriptural allusions come from their own peculiar sources, as contrasted with a more general usage throughout the early community (dealt with in Chapter 2), and (b) what allusions, if any, have been actually composed by the evangelists themselves.

The Use of Scripture in Mark's Gospel

These remarks apply with greatest force perhaps to Mark's Gospel. It is extraordinarily difficult to distinguish between the use of scripture which was already embedded in whatever sources Mark used and his own original use of scripture. Indeed it would appear at first sight that Mark may not have quoted scripture on his own initiative at all. If one takes up almost any commentary on Mark's Gospel, it is very unlikely that one will find a section devoted to Mark's use of scripture. Swete's commentary is an exception here, but Swete wrote before the modern form-critical analysis of the Gospels had been invented, and much of what he regards as Mark's own use of scripture would today be attributed to Mark's sources. A generation later than Swete, T. W. Manson wrote an article on Jesus' use of scripture which throws some light on Mark's way of dealing with scriptural quotations. Manson comments: 'When Mark records our Lord's quotations from the Old Testament they usually agree with the Hebrew or the Targum against the LXX in cases where the witnesses are divided'

(p. 318); and he lists a number of passages where Mark seems to have his own version of scripture, which indicates, he believes, that Mark is using free quotation or relying on his memory. But even Manson might be regarded today as over-sanguine about the possibility of distinguishing what is authentic to Jesus, what comes from Mark's sources, and what is Mark's own usage.

One scholar, A. Suhl, has however devoted a whole monograph to the scriptural quotations and allusions in Mark's Gospel. He has very decided and indeed radical views about the nature of Mark's Gospel. He thinks it was written during the Jewish War of AD 68–70, that it was influenced very strongly indeed by a belief in the imminence of the parousia, and that this belief meant that Mark abandoned all sense of history. Jesus' life was seen as a contemporary drama to be reproduced in the life of his disciples. As far as Mark's use of scripture is concerned, Suhl maintains that Mark has no idea at all of the fulfilment of scripture; he has repudiated the notion of salvation history: all is swallowed up in the apocalyptic present. Consequently, all Mark's conscious scriptural references are to be seen as illustrative, not predictive. Because the last great events are taking place, they may be appropriately described in scriptural language, but this does not mean that scripture is being fulfilled. Suhl therefore sides with W. Marxsen against H. Conzelmann in claiming that the attitude towards the parousia reflected in chapter 13 is Mark's own attitude. Conzelmann had maintained that the highly apocalyptic attitude of the 'little apocalypse' came from Mark's source, and did not reflect the opinion of Mark himself, who wished rather to discourage the expectation of an immediate parousia (see Suhl pp. 18–21). Thus Suhl argues that, with the arrival of Paul at Rome, the gospel was to be regarded as having been thereby preached to the whole world, a belief he attributes also to Paul (see Mark 13:10). This seems an unjustified conclusion, especially in the light of the fact that Paul, when he wrote Romans 15:24, 28 apparently hoped to reach Spain. Suhl is therefore compelled to interpret all Mark's allusions to the fulfilment of scripture as being general statements, not referring to any specific passages of scripture: 'the general tenor of the scriptures', a belief which Mark inherited more or less unexamined from the early preaching (p. 38). Mark's use of *dei*, 'it is necessary', as applying to Jesus' death is, he says, 'apocalyptic-eschatological' rather than suggesting any idea that Jesus had to fulfil the scriptures (p. 43). It was the belief of the early church, he says, that everything about Jesus happened according to the scriptures. But we may well point out that, even if this were the case, it would not follow that no particular passage in scripture need ever be indicated or intended. Thus in Mark 14:49 Jesus indicates that his arrest in Gethsemane took place in accordance with scripture: 'But let the scriptures be fulfilled.' If we ask which, we surely have an answer to such a passage as Mark 12:10–11, where a citation from Psalm 118 is applied to the death and resurrection of Jesus. It is quite true that we have in Chapter 2 attributed this quotation to the common stock of the early church, but there is no reason to doubt that Mark accepted it and understood it as applying to Jesus: by his death and resurrection he fulfilled the scriptures. Suhl writes: 'It is not a question of prophecy and fulfilment, but of exposition of the events of Jesus' life by the help of the Old Testament' (p. 47, my trans.). But this bypasses the real issue: how can the scriptures throw light on the events of Jesus' life unless he is regarded as fulfilling scripture? So also Suhl says of Mark 7:6–7 that the position of Jesus' opponents can suitably be described in the words of Isaiah 29:13, but that Isaiah 29:13 is not regarded as a prophecy fulfilled in the behaviour of the opponents (p. 81). This is to go against the whole tenor of the formula with which Mark introduces the citation: 'Well did Isaiah prophesy of you hypocrites, as it is written . . .' In the same vein Suhl claims that the description of the division of Jesus' clothes is narrated by Mark in scriptural language, but is not regarded as prophecy fulfilled (p. 48). We may well ask why Mark goes out of his way to use scriptural language if he does not regard it as being the fulfilment of prophecy. Of all the evangelists he is the one who shows least capacity to investigate and apply scripture for himself, and is therefore least likely to lapse into scriptural language. If, therefore, he uses the language of scripture it must be because he (or conceivably his source which he consciously accepted) believed that the events he described happened in fulfilment of scripture.

Suhl is not content to describe Mark as one who used scripture for illustration, and not to point to fulfilment; he also includes Paul in this category (pp. 176–7). This, I believe, indicates his fundamental misunderstanding of the way in which New Testament writers generally use scripture. If our study of Paul in Chapter 3 has demonstrated anything, it has shown that for Paul scripture was a source of information about Jesus Christ because it was prophetic and indicated the course of salvation history according to God's design. Mark is no scripture expert, as Paul is, and he certainly uses scriptural language in an illustrative way in non-christological contexts, as we shall see later, but he shared the universal conviction of the early church that the events of Jesus' life, death and resurrection took place in fulfilment of scripture, and that a whole series of specific passages from scripture could be quoted to prove that this was true. To attribute to Mark a purely 'illustrative' usage of scripture is, in the last analysis, to commit a major anachronism.

We will therefore run rapidly through Mark's Gospel, commenting on those places where scripture is quoted or alluded to. But first we should perhaps give separate attention to the passages in which Mark claims explicitly that scripture has been fulfilled. These are three: 9:12; 14:21, and 14:49 (verse 15:28 is not found in the best manuscript authorities). In 9:12b Jesus is represented as saying: 'And how is it written of the Son of Man, that he should suffer many things and be treated with contempt?' Though the attempt to find a verbal link between this text and some text in Isaiah 53 has not been very successful, there can be little doubt that the reference is to the identification of Jesus with the righteous sufferer of the psalms and of Isaiah. As we have seen, this was a basic conviction of the earliest community. H. Anderson discusses this question (p. 295) without any reference to the psalms at all. Suhl (p. 133) regards Mark 9:11–13 as a pre-Marcan complex, but this does not of course imply that Mark did not believe that Jesus' death fulfilled scripture. A more difficult question is posed by the implication in this passage that the death of John the Baptist was also a fulfilment of scripture (see 9:13). We may, with Suhl, dismiss Jeremias' suggestion that there is an allusion to an unknown apocryphal work regarded as scripture. This is only a highly speculative way of disguising our ignorance (though Anderson appears to regard this as a possible solution). Anderson has an alternative solution: it is an allusion to 1 Kings 19:2–10, the passage in which Jezebel threatens to kill Elijah (but, be it noted, does not actually do so). Is this meant to be a sort of unfulfilled type? Much more likely, in my opinion, is the suggestion that the fate of the Baptist is wrapped up in the fate of all the prophets: they were destined to be rejected and killed; cf. Matthew 23:34–7; Acts 7:52. If we want a type we are more likely to find it in the death of Zechariah in 2 Chronicles 24:20–2 than in anything that happened to Elijah. We should also bear in mind that in the death of Jesus the servant of the Lord the deaths of all God's servants are foretold. Compare the way in which Paul in 2 Corinthians 6:2 can apply to himself as Christ's servant the language of Isaiah 49:8 which he must have regarded as originally applying to Christ. This is well expressed by E. Best in *Following Jesus*: 'The sufferings of Jesus and John go together; John's is a minor passion . . . foreshadowing what was to happen to Jesus; what was to happen was itself foretold in scripture (v. 13)' (p. 63).

In Mark 14:21 we read: 'For the Son of Man goes as it is written of him.' This must refer to Jesus as the righteous sufferer of the psalms and Isaiah; only three verses earlier Mark has alluded to Psalm 41:9, the betrayal of Jesus by one of his closest disciples, who shares his covenant meal. H. Anderson follows Suhl's lead here in saying that this does not refer to any particular passage in scripture, but merely indicates God's intention (p. 290). This seems most unlikely: we only know God's intention because it has been declared in scripture. Otherwise the reference to scripture seems pointless.

The third passage is 14:49, which we have already looked at in connection with Suhl's interpretation. As in the case of 14:21, H. Anderson follows Suhl here also, describing the sentiment as the equivalent of 'let God's will be done' (p. 290). We may reply as above that God's will was only known because it had been recorded in the scriptures.

Having vindicated, as we hope, Mark's belief, shared with the earliest Christian community, that Jesus' death and resurrection took place in accordance with a number of specific prophecies in scripture, we may now turn our attention to some other passages where we can find light on Mark's use of scripture. At the very opening of the Gospel we are faced with something of a problem since Mark gives us a composite quotation from Exodus 23:20, Malachi 3:1 and Isaiah 40:3, introduced by the words 'as it is written in Isaiah the prophet'. The alternative reading 'in the prophets' indicates that there was perplexity about this in ancient times. Stendahl believes that the compilation came to Mark already made up in the form of a *testimonium*. Suhl agrees (p. 135). D. Moody Smith conjectures that Mark 'does not know where it comes from' (p. 40). H. Anderson (p. 282) suggests that the two quotations peculiar to Mark have been taken over from the disciples of John the Baptist, which seems an unnecessary conjecture. We may certainly put it down to a source peculiar to Mark, since both Matthew and Luke confine themselves to quoting Isaiah. But the text Isaiah 40:3 must have been part of the armoury of scripture texts used by the early community, since it is quoted in all four Gospels. It requires, of course, some readjustment of the original context to make it fit the Baptist, since what the prophet who made this utterance meant was that God would prepare a path for Israel in the wilderness, whereas the evangelists take it to mean that a voice was crying in the wilderness that a way for the Lord should be prepared.

Next we note the scriptural allusions at Mark's account of Jesus' baptism in 1:10–11. Stendahl (p. 144) actually describes verse 11 as 'a Christian hymnic translation (sc. "of Isaiah 42:1") coined *ad hoc*'. It is not clear whether he thinks Mark did the coining, but it seems unlikely. Gundry (p. 128) claims that the phrase in verse 10, 'the heavens opened', goes back to the Hebrew text of Isaiah 63:19 (Evv 64:1). Matthew 3:16, he thinks, has adapted the quotation so as to echo Ezekiel 1:1. We move on to 4:12, where Mark quotes Isaiah 6:9–10 with the ostensible signification that Jesus utters his teaching in parables in order that the people should not understand. The citation itself is a very popular one in the New Testament and belongs to the earliest stock of scriptural texts (see our reference to it in Chapter 2). Stendahl (p. 144) points out that Mark's rendering of the last three words of the quotation ('and to be forgiven') seems to be influenced by the Targum's rendering of the last two words of the Hebrew of Isaiah 6:10. Suhl is no doubt right (p. 147) in rejecting Manson's claim that this quotation goes back to Jesus himself, but Mark undoubtedly believes that the use of parables by Jesus was in accordance with scripture. Compare Matthew's comment on Jesus' teaching in parables in Matthew 13:35.

We have an interesting echo of Joel 3:13 in Mark 4:29 at the end of a little parable of seed sown in a field: 'Put in the sickle for the harvest is ripe.' This parable is not found in either Matthew or Luke, but in Revelation 14:15 we have a paraphrase of this verse from Joel in the course of a vision of angels reaping the harvest of contemporary history perhaps. Could this be Mark's own scriptural allusion? If so, it is possible that Mark is applying it to the Neronian persecution and John the Divine perhaps to another persecution a generation later, or indeed to persecution generally. We should also notice Mark 4:32, which appears to be modelled on Ezekiel 17:22–4. There is no reason to deny that this parable is authentic to Jesus. In Ezekiel the small shoot that grows great is Israel among the nations. Vincent Taylor sees an echo of Daniel 4:12, Nebuchadnezzar's vision of a great tree. He writes: 'In these passages the tree symbolizes the protection given to subject peoples by a great empire. It is reasonable therefore to suppose that Jesus had Gentile nations in mind.' This seems unduly sanguine as to our ability to divine Jesus' intentions. It is more likely perhaps that the detail of the birds nesting in the tree's branches is the addition of Mark or Mark's tradition.

In 6:23 Herod's offer of half his kingdom is an echo of Ahasuerus' offer to Esther in Esther 5:3; 7:2. No doubt, as Taylor remarks, the story of Esther has influenced Mark's narrative. This must be scriptural allusion, and not deliberate typology, on Mark's part, as there is no Christology involved here. On the other hand, at 6:34, where Jesus is described as taking pity on the crowd because they were like sheep without a shepherd, Mark is suggesting the typology of the shepherd-king of Ezekiel 34:5, 11. The shepherd is God himself. Best sees in 8:38 a use of the imagery of Daniel 7:13f., but believes it is pre-Marcan (p. 42). In 9:48 we have an echo of Isaiah 66:24, a description of Gehenna. Taylor suggests that Mark may have added this; it is not reproduced by Matthew. This would therefore be another instance of Mark using biblical language; but once more we note that it is not in a christological context. In a similar context, 10:27, Jesus uses a text from scripture: 'For all things are possible with God.' Best comments (p. 110): 'The logion of v. 27 is a theological maxim based probably on certain Old Testament passages (Zech. 8:6; Job 10:13, 42:2; Gen. 18:14).' He concludes that the reference comes from Mark himself.

The quotation from Psalm 118:25–6 in 11:9–10 is certainly part of the earliest tradition. (For a suggestion as to why Mark put it here, see Suhl p. 53.) The 'stone' quotation from the same psalm (vv. 22–3) in 12:10–11 belongs to the same category, but Best is fully justified when he comments that this does not mean that it was not very meaningful to Mark (p. 219): 'Quite clearly they form the climax of the pericope.' Here certainly is a belief in the fulfilment of scripture. The scripture quotation in 12:32 is interesting: 'You have truly said that he (God) is one and that there is none other but he.' This is not paralleled in the account of this incident in the other two Synoptics. Deuteronomy 4:35 is echoed; in that context the unity and uniqueness of God is demonstrated by the Sinai revelation and the deliverance from Egypt. Perhaps Mark is implying that the still greater saving act of God in Jesus Christ demonstrates his unity and uniqueness even more clearly. The reference in verse 33 to the unimportance of sacrifices emphasizes the new situation which the coming of the Kingdom precipitates.

Chapter 13 is full of scriptural allusions, many of them to apocalyptic passages in Daniel. But this chapter is surely taken by Mark from a special source or sources, so, though he certainly approves the conviction running through it that the parousia is to be expected and will be indicated by traditional signs, we cannot safely conclude that the scriptural allusions are his work. This leaves us with a number of allusions in chapter 14. In 14:7, 'you always have the poor with you' (reproduced in Matthew 26:11, and also found in John 12:8) there is an echo of Deuteronomy 15:11 (see Gundry p. 56). But this may well go back to Jesus himself. The reference to the blood poured out in 14:24 is part of the community tradition; Gundry (p. 59), believes it is an echo of Isaiah 53:12. Similarly, Jesus' description of his own state of mind in 14:34: 'My soul is very sorrowful, even to death' echoes Psalm 42:6f. Gundry holds that this is authentic (p. 59); the psalm would still be in Jesus' mind, since it formed part of the Hallel (see 14:26). If it is Mark's way of describing the event, it is certainly significant: he sees Jesus as the righteous sufferer of the psalms. Mark 14:62 is a very important passage in the context of the Gospel. Lindars (pp. 48–9) points out that it is a conflation of two texts, Psalm 110:1 and Daniel 7:13. It originally meant 'I am the Christ, and am to be declared so at my resurrection', and the second text is a reference to the parousia. Lindars does not regard either as authentically the utterance of Jesus. Suhl (p. 55) believes that Mark has joined the two texts together. No doubt Psalm 110:1 was used of the risen Jesus by the community from the earliest times. Mark has added the Daniel citation in order to point to the parousia. This usage is very far from being merely illustrative: Mark is here using scripture as a source for Christology.

Finally, we should ask whether there is any trace in Mark of a typological use of scripture in his narrative. It looks very much as if there is: in a recent article, 'The Good News of the Miracle of the Bread' (pp. 191–219), S. Masuda has argued that in both his accounts of Jesus miraculously feeding the multitude, Mark 6:31–44 and 8:1–10, Mark is consciously using scriptural typology. Jesus is the new Moses, who gives his people food in the wilderness. He is also the new Elisha, who provides his disciples with miraculous food (see 2 Kings 4:42–4). This, Masuda claims, is Mark's own interpretation. It seems hard to deny that there is an element of typology here, especially in view of the fact that a very similar typology is found in 1 Corinthians 10:1–14; Hebrews 3–4, and John 6. We may therefore safely conclude that Mark was quite capable of going to scripture himself in order to bring out the full significance of Jesus Christ.

As we review our examination of Mark's use of scripture, we must surely be impressed with the large part which scripture does in fact play in Mark's account of Jesus. Though he has nothing like Matthew's explicit scheme of scripture fulfilment, or John's subtle use of scripture as an undergirding of his exalted Christology, he does accept and use scripture freely, not only for purposes of illustration, frequent though this is, but also typologically and christologically. For all his lack of formal parade of scripture learning, and despite his remarkable ability to conceal his own personality behind his material, Mark stands squarely in the main tradition of the New Testament interpretation of scripture.

The Use of Scripture in Matthew's Gospel

When we come to examine the First Gospel we find a situation markedly different from that which we encountered in Mark. In Mark it was difficult to distinguish the work of the evangelist as far as use of scripture is concerned. In Matthew the signs of the evangelist's peculiar interpretation of scripture are perfectly plain to see. When we say it is the evangelist's peculiar interpretation, we do not mean to rule out Stendahl's theory that in fact he represents a school of interpretation; we merely wish to maintain that this interpretation is peculiar to Matthew's Gospel and is not part of the general inheritance of the early church. In particular, scholars have distinguished a series of scripture citations running all through the Gospel, which they have called 'formula quotations'. This is because all, or nearly all, are introduced by the same formula: 'All this took place to fulfil what the Lord had spoken by the prophet. . .' There are eleven such quotations, as follows: 1:22–3; 2:5–6; 2:15; 2:17–18; 2:23; 4:14–16; 8:17; 12:17–21; 13:34–5; 21:4–5; 27:9–10. Of these 2:5–6 does not bear the formula. It is introduced instead by the words 'for so it is written by the prophet', perhaps because this one, unlike all the others, is not directly cited by the evangelist, but is put into the mouth of the chief priests and scribes whom Herod consults. In the case of two others in this list the formula is slightly varied. The passage 2:17–18 is introduced by the words: 'Then was fulfilled what was spoken by the prophet Jeremiah' and 27:9 has the same phrase. These 'formula quotations' show a remarkable freedom of citation. They do not correspond exactly to the MT or the LXX. Sometimes the original text has to be considerably modified in order to yield the sense which Matthew wished to find in them. Stendahl (p. 201) actually calls them 'targums'. We must look at them in detail.

We begin with 1:23: there is a deliberate change here; the MT text represents the young woman as calling the child's name 'Immanuel' in Isaiah 7:14. Matthew changes it because in fact the parents did not call Jesus by this name. As for the propriety of using this text as a prophecy of the virgin birth of Jesus, Lindars (p. 215) suggests that the text may originally have been used in some tradition of Judaism for the Messiah, without any thought of a literal birth from a virgin. The virgin may well have been the virgin Israel. We now know that the Qumran sectaries could present the messianic community (their sect) in terms of a woman in travail. (See 1 QH 3:8–12.) But 'they shall call' could be a Semitic way of saying 'he shall be called', so perhaps the change is not so very great (Stendahl p. 98). Stendahl describes the next 'formula quotation', 2:5–6, as being markedly Christianized (p. 100). Matthew reads the word in the MT which the LXX (correctly enough) translates with 'thousands' as 'chiefs' in Micah 5:2b (Heb. 5:1). This means only a change of pointing in the Hebrew. The third special quotation is from Hosea 11:1: 'Out of Egypt have I called my son.' It is an accurate rendering of the text, but is very far indeed from what Hosea meant. The prophet refers to the calling of Israel out of Egypt by means of the exodus. Matthew uses it of the infant Jesus returning from Egypt after the death of Herod the Great. The only possible link between the two meanings is that Jesus should be regarded as the representative of obedient Israel, as indeed he may have understood himself to be.

But it is by no means clear that Matthew is concerned to establish the link. Next comes 2:17–18: the death of the firstborn, which Matthew sees as a fulfilment of a text from Jeremiah 31:15. Matthew's citation is markedly different from our LXX; he is probably translating direct from the Hebrew (Stendahl p. 102). The prophecy fulfilment referred to in 2:23 is so difficult that we keep it for separate treatment later. In 4:14–16 Matthew applies Isaiah 9:1–2 (8:23—9:1 in MT) to Jesus' ministry in Galilee. Lindars (p. 197) says that Matthew has adapted the quotation so as to show that Galilee was the place where the Messiah should first appear in public; he thinks it was originally used in order to show that the Messiah should be born there as well. Chilton (p. 111) concludes that neither the MT nor the Targum can account for Matthew's version of this quotation; he thinks that his differences from any text known to us are due to 'varieties with the LXX tradition'. He suggests that there is a certain element of 'Greek mission apologetic' in the quotation (p. 115). This reinforces the view, held by other scholars, that, though the 'formula quotations' are peculiar to Matthew, they were not simply invented by him, but were preserved in his 'school' though derived from various sources.

The next 'formula quotation', 8:17, comes from Isaiah 53:4: 'Surely he has borne our griefs and carried our sorrows.' Though this is in line with the tendency of the earliest community, going back to Jesus himself we believe, to see Jesus as the righteous sufferer, it is marked with Matthew's peculiarities. The LXX has spiritualized the text, making it refer to our sins; Matthew has probably translated the Hebrew for himself (Stendahl p. 106), and has in fact come nearer to the meaning of the Hebrew. He makes it refer to Jesus' healing powers, and rather finely suggests that the act of healing cost Jesus labour and perhaps pain. Now comes by far the longest of Matthew's special quotations: he cites Isaiah 42:1–4 in 12:17–21. Stendahl (p. 109) calls it Matthew's 'set piece' and describes him as moulding the text in a Christian direction, using such versions as were available to him. It is a 'targumizing translation of Christian origin'. Lindars (pp. 147f.) says that Matthew has adapted Isaiah 42:1f. so as to be a commentary on the Messiahship, ministry, death and resurrection of Jesus, and also on the accession of the Gentiles. It helped to explain why Jesus' ministry did not follow the expected messianic programme. Then in 13:34–5 Matthew explains Jesus' use of parables by a quotation from Psalm 78:2. It is, says Stendahl (p. 200), 'a reading created for the occasion from the Hebrew text'. The hidden things are not eternal truths but the revelation of Jesus' Messiahship (p. 116). McConnell (p. 125) believes that it was the use of the word *parabolai* in the LXX to translate the Hebrew singular *māšāl* that alerted Matthew to the possible significance of this text (LXX 77:2).

At Matthew 21:4–5 we find a prophecy which certainly belonged to the common stock of the earliest community being modified by Matthew and used in his series of 'formula quotations'. He cites Zechariah 9:9 in full and actually represents Jesus as having been seated on two animals. The Hebrew of 9:9ef is:

humble and riding on an ass,
on a colt the foal of an ass.

This is of course Hebrew poetic parallelism; the prophet refers to only one beast. Matthew has often been accused of crude literalism and of being ignorant of the nature of Hebrew poetry. But Lindars (p. 114) argues persuasively that Matthew does not mean to imply that Jesus rode on two animals: he mentions two in order to show that it really was an animal on which no one before had ever ridden, it was still with its mother. Last of all the 'formula quotations' comes 27:9–10, where a citation of Zechariah 11:12–13 is attributed to Jeremiah and applied to what the chief priests and elders did with the money which Judas returned to them. This is a famous problem for believers in the inerrancy of scripture. Stendahl (pp. 122–4) thinks it probably was 'a slip or rather a confusion of memory', but he points out that Jeremiah did have financial dealings about a piece of land, and we may add that he also uses the work of the potter to illustrate God's dealings with Israel. Matthew is aware of a possible double meaning of the Hebrew word for 'potter' in Zechariah 11:13: *yōṭēr*; it could be read *'ōṭār,* which means 'treasury', since he uses the word *korbanan* in 27:6, which means 'temple treasury'.

We must now consider the difficult reference in 2:23: 'And he went and dwelt in a city called Nazareth, that what was spoken by the prophets might be fulfilled, "He shall be called a Nazarene".' The difficulty lies in discovering what possible passage or passages of scripture Matthew has in mind. There is none that corresponds exactly, or even remotely, to the citation. The suggestions made by scholars may be reduced to three: (a) it refers to Judges 13:5: 'For the boy shall be a Nazarite to God from his birth.' Codex Vaticanus of the LXX at this point reads: *nazir theou,* 'a Nazarite of God', which could presumably be interpreted to mean 'a Nazarethean' or some such meaning. This (rather desperate) expedient is adopted by Longenecker (p. 146). But it must be confessed that Samson is an extraordinarily inappropriate type of Jesus, one met nowhere else in the New Testament. (b) It may refer to Isaiah: 'A branch shall grow out of his [Jesse's] roots.' The word for 'branch' is *neṭer.* This has at least the advantage of being a well-known messianic passage. Stendahl (p. 103) is inclined to favour this, though he suggests later (pp. 198–9) that it may be combined with texts from Judges about Samson the Nazirite. He remarks very justly that it would require a school of interpreters to produce anything so far-fetched. Gundry (p. 103) is content with the reference to Isaiah 11:1, and so is McConnell (pp. 114–15). (c) It has been suggested that the reference is to Isaiah 49:6bc, which runs in the RSV:

> to raise up the tribes of Jacob
> and to restore the preserved of Israel.

The Hebrew for 'preserved' is $n^e\underline{t}\bar{o}rey$, so that the two lines could be translated:

> to raise up the tribes of Jacob,
> and as a Nazorean of Israel to restore them.

Admittedly the phrase makes no sense in the context of Isaiah 49, but it is nearest in form to Matthew's word *Nazōraios* in 2:23. Lindars (p. 195) is attracted by this solution, but he does not rule out a reference to Isaiah 11:1. We may at least be allowed to observe that at this point Matthew's 'formula quotations' have reached the remotest point from anything that we today would regard as a reasonable interpretation of scripture.

Gundry attempts to some extent to modify the peculiarity of Matthew's 'formula quotations'. He denies that they are a textually distinct group (p. xi). He therefore questions Stendahl's theory that they issue from a 'school' (p. 157). He believes that Matthew wrote his targums himself (p. 173) and even suggests that Matthew's peculiar interpretations may go back to Jesus himself (p. 213), which seems extremely unlikely. Manson's suggestion (p. 233) that the 'formula quotations' come from a testimony list does not seem very likely either. Such a list must be capable of being used by a wide variety of Christian apologists, and Matthew's citations seem much too far-fetched to be used for such a purpose. McConnell remarks that Matthew found his special quotations useful as illuminating the life, ministry and teaching of Jesus, but not, for some reason, his death (p. 134). In fact, as we have seen, 12:17–21 is an exception to this generalization. But it is not difficult to guess why Matthew did not need special quotations to show that the death of Jesus was prophesied in scripture. The earliest church tradition had already supplied him with plenty of these. What he needed was scripture quotations to show that the birth, childhood, ministry and teaching of Jesus were also prophesied in scripture, and this function his peculiar scripture citations certainly supplied. At least we may say of them that they testify amply to the fact that Matthew was one with the early church in believing that Jesus' whole career was part of salvation history, and therefore scripture should be ransacked in order to find prophecies about it. Matthew's own technique (or that of his school – it does not matter very much which, as far as our purpose is concerned) is peculiar. He is quite unlike Paul, Hebrews and John, the other great exponents of scripture in the New Testament, in the way in which he presents his proofs. If we take him *au pied de la lettre* we must conclude that all the events of Jesus' life happened in order to fulfil scripture, as if scripture was more important than the events to which it bears witness. But Matthew can hardly have intended this. He was simply anxious to show how completely the career of Jesus followed the design of God. That design, he believed, had been recorded in scripture and therefore he was justified in going to scripture in order to find it there.

We now turn to a number of other passages in the First Gospel where scripture is used in a significant manner. Twice Matthew represents Jesus as explicitly quoting a text from Hosea 6:6: 'I desire steadfast love and not sacrifice.' This occurs in Matthew 9:13 and 12:7, and on both occasions the context is significant. In the first context Jesus is defending his habit of eating with outcasts and sinners, and appeals to the great prophetic tradition against those who would restrict the mercy of God to orthodox observants. The second occurrence is in the context of a dispute about Sabbath observance. Jesus appeals to the example of David and the teaching of the prophets about God's will for Israel. Stendahl, on the basis of the authentically rabbinic formula in 9:13, 'Go and learn what this means', believes that the citation goes back to Jesus himself. This may be unduly sanguine, but Matthew has certainly here used scripture very effectively in order to underline a genuine part of Jesus' teaching, the centrality of God's mercy.

In 11:25–9, besides quoting Jeremiah 6:16, 'Find rest for your souls', Matthew also seems to be echoing Ben Sira 51:23–6 (see Zarb p. 117). Jesus is here presented as a teacher of wisdom, says Stendahl (p. 141). This is the well-known passage, paralleled in Luke 10:21–2, where the Synoptic narrative seems to take a Johannine turn. But both the quotation from Jeremiah and the echo from Ben Sira are peculiar to Matthew. In 21:16 Matthew represents Jesus as quoting Psalm 8:2 in connection with the children in the temple acclaiming Jesus as the son of David, an incident peculiar to Matthew. He quotes the psalm in the LXX version, 'Thou didst perfect praise', whereas the Hebrew has 'Thou hast founded a bulwark'. It looks as if Matthew may have fitted the incident to the scripture passage. Much the same impression is given by the incident of the visit of the magi led by a star in 2:1–12. The star probably comes from Balaam's prophecy in Numbers 24:17 and the gifts they present from Psalm 72:10 (see

Gundry pp. 128–9). This confirms the view that a good deal of the infancy narrative in Matthew must be regarded as legend inspired by scriptural passages, i.e. prophecy turned into incident.

Other uses of scripture worthy of special notice in Matthew are 13:43, 'Then the righteous shall shine like the sun in the kingdom of their Father', a tag from Daniel 12:3, where it is a description of what will happen in the end time. Similar is 25:35, where the account of the deeds done by the righteous in their lifetime echoes Isaiah 58:7. Gundry (p. 142) calls it 'a targumic adaptation'. This may be an instance of Matthew using illustrative language from scripture. In 23:35 occurs the well-known crux which consists in the fact that Jesus is represented as making a mistake. He has confused the Zechariah, son of Jehoiada, whose death as a martyr is recorded in 2 Chronicles 24:20–1, with the Zechariah, son of Berechiah, who is one of the canonical prophets. It is very unlikely that the mistake goes back to Jesus. It probably ought to be laid at Matthew's door. Gundry brings evidence to show that the mistake is also found in rabbinic sources (p. 87). (See also Strack–Billerbeck (1) pp. 940 and 941 for references to other passages where the rabbis have made the same confusion.) We should also note the interesting fact that Matthew borrows the language of Daniel 10:6 in order to describe the appearance of the angel at the empty tomb in 28:2–3. This is not surprising; no doubt his sources only mentioned an angel. For the description of what an angel looks like one would naturally turn to a book such as Daniel, where there are considerable details about angels to be found. Also the claim made by the risen Christ to his disciples in 28:18 echoes the language of Daniel 7:14 (Gundry pp. 146–7). This is no doubt an indication that Jesus is to be identified with the glorified Son of Man figure of Daniel 7.

As we did with Mark, so we should last of all ask the question whether Matthew shows any traces of scriptural typology in his narrative or the structure of his book. He does in fact do so much more clearly than Mark does. Ellis (p. 132) works out an elaborate Moses typology in the events of Jesus' life in the First Gospel: like Moses, Jesus is saved from the tyrant's slaughter, comes forth from Egypt, calls out the twelve sons of Israel, gives the law from the mount, performs ten miracles (corresponding to the ten plagues of Egypt of which Moses was the agent), and provides manna from heaven. Thus in the matter of typology Matthew clearly does share in the main New Testament tradition of scriptural interpretation.

Matthew is certainly one of the outstanding interpreters of scripture in the New Testament. Together with Paul, the author of Hebrews and the author of the Fourth Gospel, he is one of those earliest Christian writers who established the Christian tradition of scripture interpretation. Some of his exegesis, e.g. 1:22–3, was built into the traditional Christology and remained unchallenged for centuries. At the same time it would not be unfair to call him an extremist: at least he pushes to an extreme the technique of text manipulation which was a feature of some Jewish exegesis of scripture. Perhaps his actual interpretations are no more fantastic by our modern standards than are those of Paul or of the author of Hebrews, but he does not back them up, as these two do, by an explicit theology of salvation history. His understanding of Hosea 11:1 is no more bizarre, perhaps, than is Paul's understanding of Genesis 12:7 (see Gal. 3:16), but the point that Matthew is making is a much more trivial one. Paul uses Genesis 12:7 in order to show that God's promises were always intended to be fulfilled in the Messiah. Matthew uses Hosea 11:1 (theologically one of the profoundest passages in the prophets) to show that the return of Joseph and Mary with the child Jesus from Egypt was foretold in scripture. We must therefore regard Matthew as a more superficial exegete than Paul.

He reminds us, no doubt, of the writers of the Qumran sect. This comparison has been made by Stendahl (p. 195); in fact this is one of the main reasons why he thinks that Matthew is the representative of a school. McConnell goes into greater detail and gives us three things that Matthew has in common with the Qumran outlook as far as use of the scriptures is concerned (p. 139): both Matthew and the Qumran sectaries believed (a) that everything in the prophets bore a veiled or eschatological meaning, (b) that this meaning may be detected by means of the orthographical peculiarities of the text and (c) the application of the text may be determined by analogous circumstances in the present to those which obtained when the text was uttered. This is a fair summary, though we may add that the third point applies equally to other writers in the New Testament. Their difference from Matthew lies in the fact that they chose much more significant texts and circumstances as subjects of their exegesis. We can find certain principles in common with much of Paul's exegesis, though certainly we cannot accept his detailed interpretation. Too often in the case of Matthew's accounts of the fulfilment of prophecy we find ourselves concerned with trivialities. Perhaps Bultmann was right when he applied the epithet 'rabbinic' to Matthew's technique.

There are occasions, however, when Matthew's technique of scripture interpretation is more impressive: his application of Isaiah 53:4 to Jesus' acts of healing in 8:17 has great potential value. It suggests, as we have said above (p. 72), that his miracles of healing cost him something. Again, the verse from Hosea 6:6, 'I desire mercy, and not sacrifice', which he twice attributes to

Jesus (9:13; 12:7), is a brilliantly successful example of scriptural citation: it sums up one central element in Jesus' message. We may say the same about Matthew's 'set piece', the application of Isaiah 42:1–4 to Jesus' ministry in 12:17–21: it does express the significance of Jesus' career most impressively, and is entirely true to Jesus' own conception of his vocation. Thus we may reasonably conclude that Matthew's technique of scriptural interpretation, though capable of producing trivial and inept results when pressed to an extreme, could on occasion be a means of providing a profound and illuminating commentary on Jesus' message and ministry.

The Use of Scripture in Luke–Acts

Luke appears in his two writings more as a discernible personality than Mark does in his Gospel, but he shares with Mark the negative quality of not being an expert in the scriptures. Unlike Paul, the author of the First Gospel, the author of Hebrews and the author of the Fourth Gospel, he does not 'search the scriptures' in order to find prophecies of Jesus Christ. This means that, as in the case of Mark, it is not easy to distinguish those places where he is interpreting scripture for himself from those where he is reproducing the scripture interpretation of his sources.

However, it is possible to make some fairly accurate generalizations about Luke's use of scripture. Like Matthew, he sees the events of Jesus' life as foretold in scripture, but he uses a different technique to convey this (Barrett p. 399). He quotes directly or echoes scripture in his hymns. The infancy narratives, for example, are saturated with scripture references. Mary's song in Luke 1:46–55 (the Magnificat) is closely modelled on Hannah's song in 1 Samuel 2:1–10. Simeon's song (the Nunc Dimittis) echoes Isaiah 42:6; 49:6; see Luke 2:32. (Luke returns to this second passage in Acts 13:47, which we discuss below, pp. 80f.). Bovon (p. 92) claims that Luke had a cruder and more simplistic notion of the fulfilment of scripture than had Paul. This means, however, that we today can often go along with his interpretation in a way that we find difficult in the case of Paul and impossible with many of Matthew's examples of exegesis. Dupont (quoted in Bovon p. 94) points out that the programme outlined by the risen Lord in Luke 24:27 is not actually carried out in Luke's writings. He does not find 'the things concerning Jesus' in 'all the scriptures'. Like every other writer in the New Testament, he is selective in his use of scripture. We may add that a similar exaggeration occurs in Luke 1:70. Simeon says that God's holy prophets have prophesied God's salvation *ap'aiōnos*. The RSV renders this 'from of old' and the NEB 'age after age'. The impression is that there was no age without a prophet. In fact, however, Luke is only reproducing the common Christian (and indeed Jewish) belief that not only the canonical prophets but also Moses, David and (probably) Solomon had the gift of prophecy. See also Acts 3:24, where prophecy is traced back as far as Samuel. Bovon (p. 96) adds that Luke himself is not greatly interested in the Old Testament (*sic*) as such and that the citations in the early chapters of Acts 'reflect the tradition of the apostles more than that of the author of the book' (my trans.). It is quite true, as we shall see, that Luke uses sources; but it would be unfair to suppose that he was not fully aware of the implications of what was in his sources for the interpretation of scripture.

Conzelmann in his introduction to his commentary on Acts makes a number of statements about Luke's use of scripture which are worth examining (p. 11). He says, quite rightly, that Luke has a clear conception of salvation history. He adds that when Luke quotes the scriptures for himself he sticks to the LXX; where he differs, he is using sources, perhaps even *testimonia*. We shall find that this principle runs into difficulties when we try to apply it rigorously. He goes on to say that there are no Semitic sources for his quotations. Here too the work of Wilcox has challenged Conzelmann's thesis. Schneider agrees with Conzelmann that promise and fulfilment is the great theme of Luke–Acts. But salvation history, he maintains, continues into the period of the church according to Luke (pp. 136–7). Stendahl makes the illuminating remark (p. 159) that the scriptural hymns in Luke chapters 1 and 2 employ the same technique of biblical allusion without explicit quotation as we find very extensively used in the Book of Revelation. But we must not commit ourselves to the view that Luke himself composed these songs. It is more likely that he took them from a source.

A leading theme in both Gospel and Acts is Jesus as the righteous sufferer, and in particular as the subject of Isaiah 52:13—53:12. Indeed, the school of English scholars referred to in Chapter 2 maintained that Luke was the first to make this identification, though we have shown reason why we cannot possibly accept this view. The theme runs all through his writings, but we may look at a few examples. In his passion narrative at Luke 22:37 Luke alone among the evangelists attributes to Jesus a direct quotation of Isaiah 53:12: 'And he was reckoned with transgressors' (see Stendahl p. 94). His quotation differs slightly from the LXX text, since he reads 'with transgressors' whereas the LXX tradition has 'among the transgressors'. Holtz (p. 42) points out that in his extended citation of Isaiah 53:7–8 in Acts 8:32–3 he does not differ from the LXX text at all, and concludes that the variation in Luke 22:37 is simply an oversight on Luke's part. But we may suspect that Luke may have had a Greek translation that deviated from our LXX in verse 12. It is a verse in which the Hebrew is not altogether clear. Stendahl (p. 94) believes that Luke has introduced the citation of Isaiah 61:1–2 into Jesus' sermon in the synagogue at Nazareth in Luke 4:18–19. This would certainly be the view of the majority of scholars today, but if we follow Dr Chilton's theory that some of Jesus' teaching is based on the *Targum on Isaiah,* we may find reason to accept Isaiah 61:1–2 as a part of scripture which Jesus did see himself as fulfilling. (See above, Chapter 2, p. 30.) At least we may accept the Isaiah citation in Acts 8:32–3 as Luke's own work. Indeed, in view of the eunuch's question in verse 34: 'About whom, pray, does the prophet say this? About himself or about someone else?', we may reasonably conjecture that Luke was acquainted with some tradition of learned exegesis of this passage that took into consideration a number of possible views.

There is one quotation from Isaiah in Acts that has caused considerable perplexity, since Luke appears to be applying a servant prophecy directly to the apostles and missionaries, bypassing Christ. It is Acts 13:47, where Luke quotes Isaiah 49:6 in the following context: Paul and Barnabas are speaking to Jews in Pisidian Antioch. They encounter opposition and insult, and they reply:

It was necessary that the word of God should be spoken first to you. Since you thrust it from you, and judge yourselves unworthy of eternal life, behold, we turn to the Gentiles. For so the Lord has commanded us, saying,
'I have set you to be a light for the Gentiles,
    that you may bring salvation to the
    uttermost parts of the earth.'

Edgar (p. 53) accepts that Luke has applied a 'suffering servant' quotation directly to the missionaries and not to Christ. Rese (p. 77) accepts the same conclusion. The phrase 'the Lord has commanded us' must refer to the Lord Christ and the perfect tense of the verb must refer to a specific event, which Rese believes is Paul's conversion. Both Wilcox (p. 51) and Haenchen (p. 160) point out that Luke's rendering of Isaiah 49:6 here is closer to the Hebrew than is the LXX, which inserts the phrase 'for a covenant of a nation' from 42:6. Both conclude that Luke is using a source here for Paul's whole address. We may, however, challenge the conclusion of these three scholars that Luke is applying Isaiah 49:6 directly to Paul, bypassing Christ. In the first place Luke writes 'For so the Lord has commanded us', meaning Paul and Barnabas, who are the ostensible speakers. It is not the apostolic 'we' which Paul sometimes uses in his letters. Secondly, we must suppose that Luke and his source had studied the context in which this citation occurs. Any early Christian who read Isaiah 49:1–6 must have concluded that the passage applies primarily to Christ: 'The Lord called me from the womb' is applicable perhaps to Paul but not to Paul and Barnabas. 'And he said to me, "You are my servant, Israel, in whom I will be glorified".' This must surely apply to Jesus, the representative of obedient Israel. Next, in verse 4 the servant appeals to God for vindication in a way completely in line with the behaviour of the righteous servant throughout the scriptures. Other features in the chapter would seem to belong primarily to Christ, such as the task of 'restoring the preserved of Israel' (v. 6) or the description of the servant in verse 7 as 'one deeply despised, abhorred by the nations'. We may therefore very well conclude, as we did in our exposition of this very passage when it occurs in 2 Corinthians 6:2 (see above, Chapter 2, pp. 39f.), that the command to preach to the Gentiles comes through the Lord Jesus, but comes by means of the fact that he fulfilled the 'servant' prophecy of Isaiah 49:1–8, and that the commission of Paul and Barnabas, as of all the apostles, was to carry out his 'servant ministry', a theme which is by no means absent from Luke's Gospel. The Isaiah passage is applied to the missionaries because they are carrying out the ministry of the original servant of the Lord. Perhaps we may conjecture that the theology of the source from which this passage in Acts 13 comes is more profound than that consciously held by Luke himself. We may add as further evidence that in Acts 26:23 Paul is represented as applying a paraphrase of Isaiah 42:6 or 49:6 directly to Christ: 'By being the first to rise from the dead, he would proclaim light both to the people and to the Gentiles.' Also in Simeon's song in Luke 2:32 Jesus is described as 'a light for revelation to the Gentiles', an echo of these two passages in Isaiah.

We should perhaps pause at this point in order to emphasize that in the Book of Acts Luke does use sources, even in the earliest speeches. There has been a tendency among some scholars to suggest that Luke wrote at least the speeches in Acts so to speak 'off the cuff'. It is held that he did not have any sources for the speeches, certainly not any early sources. It is indeed very difficult not to conclude that the longest and most distinctive speech in Acts, Stephen's speech in Acts 7, is from a special source. It has so many features which are not paralleled in the rest of Acts (but some of which do find parallels in other parts of the New Testament, e.g. Hebrews), that it would require great credulity to believe that Luke simply invented it. And indeed most scholars treat Stephen's speech as an exception. But good evidence can be brought, mostly from the treatment of scriptural quotations, to show that other speeches also must have primitive sources behind them. Thus Professor Wilcox (pp. 22–4) has shown that there is some sign of the influence of the Targum on the psalms in the citation of Psalm 89:20 in Acts 13:22. He concludes that Luke was using sources in these places where he has scripture citations, which occur mostly in the speeches (pp. 51–2). Even more interesting are Professor Stanton's conclusions about the speeches in Acts 10 and Acts 13 (see Stanton pp. 70–83). He believes that Peter's speech in Acts 10:34f. originally began with a citation of Psalm 107:20; this helps to explain the strange construction in Acts 10:36. There is a reference to the same psalm quotation in Acts 13:26b in Paul's speech. Reverting to Acts 10, he points to the explicit citation of Isaiah 61:1 in Acts 10:38. It serves to link up the two scriptural echoes in 10:36, namely Psalm 107:20 and Isaiah 52:7. This linking of two citations by means of a third is a rabbinic technique. All this strongly suggests that Acts 10 comes from an already existing source. Another proof-text is 'hanging him on a tree' in 10:39, a common text in the early church, very unlikely to have been discovered by Luke. He concludes therefore that behind these speeches in Acts lie primitive exegetical traditions which must come from an early period in the church when the first missionaries were preaching the message about Jesus.

We now turn to four difficult citations of scripture in Acts, all of which when elucidated show that Luke had access to a sophisticated technique of scripture interpretation. The first is the double quotation applying to the death of Judas Iscariot in Acts 1:20. They are as follows:

Let his habitation become desolate,
    and let there be no one to live in it

from Psalm 69:25 (LXX 68:26), and

His office let another take

from Psalm 109:8b (LXX 108:8b). Luke's version of Psalm 69:25 is not identical with the LXX, nor is it any closer to the Hebrew (where it is Psalm 69:26); it looks like an abbreviated version of it, since Luke omits 'in their tents' of the original. The adjective he uses to translate the Hebrew word for 'desolate' is *erēmos,* which is frequently used by the LXX translators to render various forms of the Hebrew verb which the RSV translators have rendered 'desolate'. Luke reproduces exactly the LXX of the second psalm quotation. There seems therefore to be little justification for Haenchen's comment on this passage: 'The freedom with which the LXX text has been altered in this process is astonishing'

(p. 103, my trans.). We cannot take for granted that Luke had our LXX text before him. Holtz (pp. 44–6) points out quite truly that the psalm quotations are connected with the death of Judas, not with his replacement. He believes that the first citation comes from early Christian tradition, but that Luke has added the second himself, a view which we will presently challenge. Bovon (p. 109) holds that the citations are both Luke's own choice.

We can easily see why a citation from Psalm 69 should be applied to Judas. This psalm was a favourite messianic prophecy in the early church: it is quoted by Paul in Romans 15:3, and by John in John 2:17 (the same verse, though each quotes a different line). It supplied scriptural commentary on the giving of vinegar to Jesus on the cross (see 69:21). Verses 23–9 of this psalm are an account by the psalmist of what he would like to happen to his enemies, and must have been viewed by early Christians as a description of the fate of those who were responsible for putting Jesus to death, including of course Judas Iscariot. It is just possible that verses 24 and 25 are regarded as having been fulfilled in the fate which actually befell him according to Acts 1:18. The verses run in the LXX:

> Let their eyes be darkened so that they may not see,
>> and ever bow thou down their back:
> pour upon them thy wrath,
>> and let the fierceness of thy wrath seize them.

The second psalm citation, 109:8, leads us into deeper waters. Despite the terrible curses which it contains, it could be called the psalm of the man who returned good for evil. As we have already pointed out in Chapter 2, p. 30, it lies behind a logion in the Sermon on the Mount. Now this particular piece of teaching is also found in Luke, but not in Mark; compare Matthew 5:43–4 with Luke 6:27–8. But Luke has in fact a fuller version of this logion than has Matthew. Luke's version is:

> Love your enemies, do good to those who hate you;
>> bless those who curse you, pray for those who abuse you.

Now this is in fact an echo of Psalm 109:4–5:

> In return for my love they accuse me,
>> even as I make prayer for them.
> So they reward me evil for good,
>> and hatred for my love.

We have also noted (pp. 30–31) that Paul echoes this citation in 1 Corinthians 4:12–13. In fact all three New Testament writers are dealing with authentic teaching of Jesus. Thus we have established that Psalm 109 was an important one in the early church:

it contained some of the teaching of the Lord. It described how he had behaved to his enemies. It is not at all surprising therefore to find a verse from this psalm applied to Judas Iscariot. But we can point to another link with him: only two verses earlier than that quoted here we read:

> Appoint a wicked man against him;
> let an accuser bring him to trial.

The word for accuser in the Greek is *diabolos* (Hebrew *Šātān*), which is of course the word extensively used in the New Testament for the devil. Thus an early Christian would see in Psalm 109:6 the wish that the devil should deal with Judas. Now we observe the significant fact that only Luke and John record that Satan entered into Judas Iscariot: see Luke 22:3; John 13:27. We have here therefore a very interesting element in the tradition common to Luke and John (the existence of this tradition was noted by C. H. Dodd); that tradition must have had a special concern about Judas, which comes out in this citation of Psalm 109:8 in Acts 1:20. We conclude certainly that both these citations are part of Luke's special tradition, were not discovered *ad hoc* by Luke, and that their significance is fully understood by Luke as he uses them in this context.

We now look briefly at Acts 2:25–8, where Peter in his speech at Pentecost quotes Psalm 16:8–11. Dupont, quoted by Bovon (pp. 92–3), points out that the same text is cited in a speech attributed to Paul in Acts 13:35, and from this he draws the very reasonable conclusion that the citation comes from Luke's own tradition, since no one else in the New Testament cites it. Rese (p. 74) asks whether the citation is intended to prove both that Jesus' death was according to God's plan and that his resurrection was in fulfilment of scripture, or only one of these points, and rightly concludes that it is intended to prove both. In my book *The New Testament Interpretation of Scripture,* pp. 150–54, I have discussed this whole passage, including the strange phrase in verse 24, 'having loosed the pangs of death', and I conclude that both this phrase and the citation of Psalm 16 must come from a very early source, since the Messiah himself is represented as speaking in the psalm and expressing a confident hope that God would raise him from the dead. I compare the passage with 1 Peter 3:19, where the implication seems to be that Christ survived death because he was immortal spirit, a later conception than what we have here. Once more, therefore, a careful consideration of how Luke uses scripture has brought us to the conclusion that he is consciously using very early sources.

Two more passages call for special attention, in both of which Amos is quoted with a significance which on the face of it is not very clear. The first is Acts 7:42–3, where Amos 5:25–6 is cited. This occurs in the course of Stephen's speech, which we have already agreed constitutes a special source. The point of the citation seems to be to associate the idolatry of the wilderness period with the sacrificial worship in the temple at Jerusalem, suggesting that there was little to choose between them. The *skēnē* ('tent') of Moloch is meant to point forward to the *skēnē tou marturiou* of verse 44 ('the tent of witness'), and soon after comes the reference to the building of Solomon's temple, with the strong hint that this was a disastrous mistake (vv. 47–50). The more general aim of the speech is to show that the purest worship is not that offered in the temple but worship offered through Jesus Christ. For this purpose the LXX mistranslation of the Hebrew *sikkuth malkᵉkem* (literally 'the booths of your king') with *tēn skēnēn tou Moloch* ('the tent of Moloch') is very helpful, since it enables the author of Stephen's speech to associate idolatrous worship with the worship in the tabernacle. The speech must therefore go back to a Greek and not an Aramaic source. The only serious difference from the LXX lies in the substitution of 'beyond Babylon' for 'beyond Damascus'. Haenchen (p. 161) and Holtz (pp. 15, 18) may well be right in claiming that this is the work of Luke the historian. If so, he is editing his source, for it is most unlikely that Luke composed this speech himself. We have therefore in this passage an example of Luke effectively editing a source in which a significant scriptural citation occurs.

Our fourth example is in some ways the most perplexing of all: it is ostensibly a citation of Amos 9:11–12 made by James in the course of his speech to the council at Jerusalem in Acts 15:16–17. The difficulties it contains are as follows: (a) the very first phrase, 'after this I will return', does not belong to the Amos context and is not found in this form anywhere in scripture; (b) the Greek of the Amos citation differs markedly from the LXX, which in its turn differs from the MT; (c) Acts 15:18, 'says the Lord who has made these things known from of old', introduces a phrase which is in neither the MT nor the LXX. We may take these difficulties in order: (a) the notion of God turning back to have mercy on Israel is quite common in scripture: see Zechariah 1:3, 1:16, 8:3; Isaiah 63:17. The Hebrew verb used is invariably *šūb* and the LXX invariably translates with *epistrephein*, not *anastrephein*, as here. This in itself suggests that the citation comes from an alternative Greek version of the Hebrew. There is a passage in Jeremiah 12:15f. which conveys the sense, though hardly the language, fairly well: 'And it shall be after I have cast them out I shall turn *(epistrepsō)* and I shall have mercy on them' (my trans. of LXX). It refers to those peoples who have been seizing Israel's lands during the confusion caused by the Babylonian invasions of

Palestine. God promises that he will have mercy on them if they will 'learn the way of my people to swear by my name'. To an early Jewish Christian this might seem very appropriate as applying to those Gentiles who wished to join the church. God admits them on conditions similar to those on which Gentiles are to be admitted according to the Jerusalem council's decision. We may suggest therefore that this initial phrase comes from a citation which was believed to concern the admission of the Gentiles to the Christian church.

The second problem (b) was that the Greek of James's citation differs markedly from the LXX. In fact it differs much more markedly in Amos 9:11 than it does in Amos 9:12. In the second of these two verses the only difference between Acts and the LXX is that Acts has inserted 'the Lord' after 'seek', and of course that in Acts we have this addition: 'who has made these things known from of old', a problem which we deal with later. Acts 15:16 seems to be giving an abbreviated version of Amos 9:11; it omits altogether the clause 'and repair its breaches', and uses a different verb *(anorthōsō)* to render the phrase 'and rebuild it', nor does it agree exactly with the LXX rendering of 'and raise up its ruins'. On the other hand, it is impossible to believe that the citation from Amos has been translated directly from the Hebrew, since in Acts 15:17 it follows the LXX mistranslation of the Hebrew, and this mistranslation contains the whole point of the citation as far as James's purpose is concerned. Lake and Cadbury point out that Amos wrote: 'that the Israelites may inherit what remains of Edom'. The LXX read 'may inherit' as 'may seek' (substituting the verb *dāraš* for *yāraš* and 'man' (*'ādām*) for 'Edom' (*'edōm*). It also understood 'man' to be the subject of the verb, and thus got the sense 'that the remnant of mankind may seek'. Because of this variation between the first and the second verses of the citation Holtz suggests (p. 25) that the two halves of the quotation may have had different origins. This is difficult to believe: Amos 9:11 by itself would have no particular appeal to an early Christian; it merely expresses a belief in the restoration of the Davidic dynasty. Only when coupled with a prophecy of the accession of the Gentiles does it fall into place: the coming of the Messiah is to be marked by the admission of the Gentiles into Israel. On the other hand, can we suppose that an alternative Greek version, such as we are driven to conjecture lies behind Acts 15:16, would necessarily include the same mistranslation of the Hebrew as we find in the LXX of Amos 9:12? We may perhaps say that such a situation is possible if we remember that there was a tendency among some Jews of the Diaspora, who would be the main users of a Greek translation, to emphasize the missionary aspect of Judaism. Perhaps a translation such as we find in the LXX of

Amos 9:12 had by Luke's time attained the status of a sort of targum, and would therefore be reproduced in more than one Greek version. Or, conceivably, whoever put together this citation originally felt free to use the textual liberty we have already been indulged in by the Qumran sectaries and by the author of Matthew: he has compiled his prophecy from whatever versions of the text suited best the sense he wanted.

The third problem (c) is posed by the addition in Acts 15:17 to the LXX of Amos 9:12 of the words 'who has made these things known from of old'. Strictly speaking, the addition consists only in the words 'known from of old'. But the addition materially alters the sense of the verb. The LXX as it stands simply gives the sense: 'says the Lord God who does these things', a fair rendering of the Hebrew. The addition in Acts alters the verb from meaning 'does' to 'makes' and then adds 'known' so as to give quite a different sense. Lake and Cadbury can only suggest that the clause represents 'a confused memory' of the LXX's 'as in the days of old' at the end of Amos 5:11. This seems a desperate expedient. More probable is Haenchen's suggestion (p. 164) that the addition is a fragmentary citation of Isaiah 45:21cd: 'Who told this long ago? Who declared it of old?' The LXX version runs: 'that they may know (gnōsin) together who made these things heard from the beginning'. Only two verses later comes the declaration that every knee shall bow and every tongue confess God, which of course an early Christian would take to be a prophecy of the accession of the Gentiles.

From all this fragmentary evidence the best conclusion seems to be that in this passage in Acts Luke is drawing on a stock of scriptural passages all bearing on the accession of the Gentiles in the last days: Jeremiah 12:15–16; Amos 9:12; Isaiah 45:21–3 are all passages that would suit admirably the intention of James's speech in Acts 15, at least if they are quoted in a Greek version. Though that Greek version does not seem to have been identical with our LXX, it must have had some relation to it. The citation is not a translation of the Hebrew, and therefore Bovon is no doubt right when he insists (p. 93) that the historical James could hardly be the author of this speech. It looks as if Luke is drawing on one of his many sources for supplying him with suitable scriptural citations for a speech which he has composed himself. Once again, we cannot fail to be impressed by the extent of his sources and his ability to make effective use of his scriptural material.

Does Luke himself consciously use typology? Not very often and not with any great subtlety. But Bovon (p. 116) is surely right in saying that there is a general typology of Sinai in Luke's description of the descent of the Holy Spirit at Pentecost in Acts 2. There is of course plenty of typology in Stephen's speech in

Acts 7: the figure of Jesus is foreshadowed by both Joseph and Moses in their respective experiences of rejection (see Acts 7:9–10; 7:18, 35). But we have agreed that this comes from a source and cannot be attributed directly to Luke, though Luke no doubt recognized and accepted the typology.

There are undoubtedly some places, though not very many, in which Luke has gone directly to scripture himself in order to assist his narrative. One such is Luke 23:30, where Jesus on his road to the cross is represented as quoting Hosea 10:8: 'Then they will begin to say to the mountains, "Fall on us"; and to the hills, "Cover us".' Luke has transposed the two clauses, but otherwise agrees with the LXX. This addition of Luke's corresponds to Matthew's detail of the Jewish people saying to Pilate: 'His blood be on us and on our children' (Matt. 27:25). Both evangelists believe that the sack of Jerusalem in AD 70 was the consequence of the crucifixion of Jesus by the Jews; but Luke, true to the Dantesque description *scriba mansuetudinis Christi*, prefers to emphasize the horror of the event rather than its punitive significance. Holtz (p. 27) agrees that this is Luke's own addition. He likewise maintains (p. 53) that the citation of Psalm 2:1–2 in Acts 4:25–6 is Luke's own invention. Though verse 7 of this psalm is often quoted in the New Testament, this is the only place where verses 1–2 appear (we must except Revelation 11:18, 19:19, but, as we shall be seeing, these are not precisely citations).

We have already observed (pp. 82–3 above) that Haenchen accuses Luke of arbitrarily altering the scripture text to suit his meaning, and have attempted to defend Luke from this charge. Haenchen makes the same accusation apropos of Acts 3:25, where Luke quotes Genesis 22:18 as 'all the families of the earth' instead of the LXX, which renders the Hebrew with 'all the nations of the earth'. Haenchen (p. 166) claims that Luke makes this alteration because at this point in the narrative the Gentile mission had not yet begun. But once again we take leave to doubt this. In the first place, it is not quite certain to which text in Genesis Luke is referring. This promise to Abraham is made in Genesis 12:7, 18:18, 22:18 and 26:4. In 12:6 it is 'all the families of the earth' (LXX *phulai*). In 22:18 an alternative reading in the LXX is *phulai* for *ethnē* ('nations'). Le Déaut renders the neofiti manuscript of the *Targum of Palestine* at 12:6 with '*toutes les familles de la terre*'. When we consider the wider variety of alternative Greek versions now known to us through the Qumran finds, and the latitude of targumic citation that New Testament writers could allow themselves on occasion, we will be less willing to accuse Luke of having arbitrarily altered the text of scripture to suit his convenience.

After this investigation of Luke's method with scripture we will still no doubt stand by our original claim that he is more like

Mark than Matthew, in that he is more a purveyor of other people's interpretations of scripture than one who searches scripture for himself. But we must surely be impressed both by the range of scriptural interpretation which was available to him in his sources and by his own comprehension of their significance. Luke did not have the profound scriptural technique of a Paul or a John, but he was well able to appreciate and to utilize the scriptural exegesis of others.

In our exploration of the usage of scripture in the Synoptic Gospels we have ranged very widely. We have discovered that some of them had access to special sources of their own, and one of them, Matthew, used a technique that is peculiar to him in the Gospels. But our overall impression after a review of the evidence must surely be of how much they have in common: all witness to the common early Christian belief in salvation history, recorded in scripture. All of them seem to know a common stock of texts, going back to the earliest era of the church and in some cases reaching back to Jesus himself. All of them show a growing tendency to elaborate, to allow room for the interpretation of an individual or a school. And finally in all of them the same question is put to us today: what do we make of the New Testament interpretation of scripture? When we have looked at how the other traditions in the New Testament deal with the interpretation of scripture, we shall still be left with this question. To bypass it or to refuse to answer it would be a betrayal of the New Testament itself. If we cannot find any ground in common with the New Testament interpretation of scripture, we cannot claim that it is possible in any reasonable sense to hold the same faith today as did the writers of the New Testament.

5

THE INTERPRETATION OF SCRIPTURE IN THE DEUTERO-PAULINES AND THE EPISTLE TO THE HEBREWS

The Deutero-Paulines

I should make it clear that I do not regard Colossians or Ephesians as being directly Pauline. I believe there may be Pauline material in Colossians, especially in chapter 4; but that the bulk of the Epistle was written by a disciple of Paul, who knew his master's mind, but who was facing a different situation. In any case, all the scripture references which we examine occur in what I regard as non-Pauline material. Ephesians I believe to have been written somewhat later than Colossians, by a member of Paul's school indeed, but one who had a very distinctive style. But he was extending and amplifying Paul's teaching rather than striking out a line of his own. The Pastoral Epistles, I hold, have no connection with Paul at all, though their author admired Paul and could make use of Paul's writings.

Colossians

At first sight Colossians would seem to be devoid of any scriptural references whatever. A rough and ready method of assessing the scriptural content of any given writing in the New Testament is to go through the Bible Societies' version of the Greek text noting where lines or words in black letters occur. This is how the editors indicate scriptural citations. There are no black letters in the Bible Societies' edition of the Greek text of Colossians. This does not mean, however, that Colossians, like Philemon, is devoid of references to scripture. They can be found, and in fact they play a very significant part at certain points. We will confine ourselves to examining four passages.

The first is the great christological hymn of 1:15–20. We need not concern ourselves with the question of whether the author of Colossians composed this hymn himself or not, but will assume that the sentiments expressed there are his. All editors are agreed that behind this hymn lies the wisdom tradition of the early church, and this in turn derives from the wisdom tradition of scripture. But there is much debate as to which passages of scripture are actually echoed here. Perhaps we can best begin with Burney's article of 1926, in which he maintained that the passage in Colossians is a deliberate commentary on Genesis 1:1, interpreted in the light of Proverbs 8:22–30. The first word of the Hebrew bible is *bᵉrē'šīt*, 'in the beginning' and *rē'šīt* can mean 'principle, origin, creative power': the preposition *bᵉ* is interpreted as meaning 'in', 'by' and 'into', and *rē'šīt* is expounded as meaning 'beginning', 'sum-total', 'head' and 'first-fruits'. Burney holds that the meaning of Proverbs 8:22 is:

> The Lord begat me as the beginning of his way,
> the antecedent of his works of old.

So elaborate an interpretation of the Colossians passage has not been accepted by most scholars, though Houlden seems to think it is correct. Aletti in his monograph has rejected it on two grounds (p. 66): (a) the array of prepositions is more likely to come from popular Stoicism than from a rabbinic interpretation of Genesis 1:1; and (b) it is impossible to achieve the meaning which Burney holds is correct for Proverbs 8:22a without recourse to the LXX. But this is inconsistent with Burney's claim that the interpretation comes through rabbinic tradition. This latter objection does not seem to hold water; and it is very difficult to deny that Proverbs 8:22–30 stands behind this Colossian hymn in some way. Scott has suggested in an article (pp. 215, 222) that the original meaning of the word translated 'master workman' in Proverbs 8:30a was 'binding, uniting' and that this is in fact the inspiration for 'in him all things hold together' in Colossians 1:17b. In order to get this sense he has to change the pointing of the Hebrew word *'āmōn* to read *'ōmēn*. He well compares Wisdom 1:7: 'That which holds all things together knows what is said.' Several editors have drawn attention to another scripture passage in connection with 1:15b, 'the firstborn of all creation'. This is Psalm 89:27 (MT 89:28; LXX 88:28):

> And I will make him the firstborn,
> the highest of the kings of the earth.

J. B. Lightfoot believes this connection exists; and Scott sees in Colossians 1:15b 'a messianic interpretation of Psalm 89:28' (p. 218). Dibelius (ed. H. Greeven) sees a link between this whole passage and Proverbs 8:22–30. Late Judaism, he adds, had already identified the ideal Man with Wisdom. The use of *eikōn* in verse 15 certainly points in this direction: it is a continuation of Paul's doctrine of Christ as the second Adam (cf. 2 Cor. 4:4). Gnilka, following Lohse, claims that the use of *eikōn* implies a reference to Genesis 1:26. Moule is content to say that both Genesis 1:1 and Proverbs 8:22f. lie in the background. Another scripture passage that has been brought into connection with this hymn in Colossians is Psalm 132:14 (LXX 131:14):

> This is my resting place for ever;
> here I will dwell, for I have desired it.

Christ is seen as the true place of worship and therefore the place where God's full presence is to be found. (Compare our remarks on Acts 7:49–50 on p. 85 above where Isaiah 66:1 is quoted.) In both Isaiah 66:1 and Psalm 132:14 the word translated 'resting-place' is *menūḥah* in the Hebrew and *katapausis* in the LXX. We shall be finding the same theme recurring in the Fourth Gospel.

Can we make any clear decision as to what scripture passages exactly lie behind this astonishing hymn? We may certainly conclude that by the time of our author Jewish exegetical specula-tion had been active over both Genesis 1:1 and Proverbs 8:22f. If we turn to the version of Genesis 1:1 given in the Palestinian Targum we find that it runs as follows:

> From the beginning (the Word) of Yahweh, together with Wisdom, created and completed (*acheva*) the heavens and the earth.

This is my translation of Le Déaut's French rendering; Le Déaut believes the missing word is *memra* (= Word). He comments that the author of the Targum presents us with a double translation of *berē'šīt;* he understands it as both 'beginning' and 'wisdom'. Le Déaut adds that the original paraphrase must have been 'in wisdom', but that 'with' had been substituted so as to exclude a personification of wisdom. Next we may accept Aletti's conclusion that the New Testament writers generally refashioned the wisdom tradition for their own use (p. 166), and perhaps also his dictum (p. 187) that 'Colossians 1:15 uses the wisdom category in order to say how Christ differs radically from all beings, without this difference constituting in fact a separation'. We cannot possibly deny that the author of Colossians has utilized contemporary exegetical tradition about both Genesis 1:1 and Proverbs 8:22–30 in order to express his highly exalted Christology. As for more detailed conclusions, the author of Colossians certainly harks back to Genesis 1:26 by his use of *eikōn* in 1:15; the word *prōtotokos* ('firstborn') in verses 15 and 18 recalls Psalm 89:27; *archē* ('the beginning') in verse 18 consciously recalls *rē'šīt* in Genesis 1:1; and it is probable that verse 19 is based on Psalm 132:14. In other words, the author of Colossians, though he never quotes scripture, is dependent on scripture for most of his significant christological terms.

Our second passage is Colossians 2:3:

in whom are hid all the treasures of wisdom and knowledge.

This seems to be based on Isaiah 45:3:

I will give you the treasures of darkness,
and the hoards in secret places.

The LXX renders 'treasures' with *thēsaurous,* the same word as we have in Colossians 2:3, and it translates 'secret hoards' with *apokruphous aoratous.* The first of these words is the same as that translated 'hid' in Colossians 2:3. The original meaning of the Isaianic passage was that the conqueror Cyrus would be permitted by God to plunder the treasuries of the kingdoms he conquered, perhaps with special reference to his conquest of the wealthy kingdom of Lydia. But speculation had been at work on this passage for 500 years. We have already noted on p. 22 above that some rabbis objected to the idea that Cyrus should be called 'the anointed one', as occurs only two verses earlier. Only about fifty years after the time when Colossians was written we find an early Christian writer blithely accepting a Christian reading of the Greek of Isaiah 45:1, so as to get the sense: 'The Lord said to my Lord Christ.' See Ep. Barnabas 12:11, where the author has read *kuriō/i* for *kurō/i* ('to Lord' for 'to Cyrus'). We cannot be confident that the author of Colossians had this reading in his Greek text, though it is by no means impossible. But in any case he would see Isaiah 45:1f. as an address by God to his servant the Messiah, whom Christians identify with Jesus Christ. The second half of Isaiah 45:3 runs thus in the LXX:

That you may know that I am the Lord God
who calls your name, the God of Israel.

This may be echoed in Colossians 2:2c: 'the knowledge of God's mystery, of Christ'. The words 'the knowledge' render *eis epignōsin* in Greek, which is cognate with the verb the LXX uses, 'that you may know', in Isaiah 45:3b. The hidden name is now revealed as 'Jesus Christ'. Gnilka well remarks of this passage: 'Christ, as the mystery, not the mystery that is Christ.' Lohmeyer denies any reference to Isaiah 45, but he adds that the treasures being hid means that they are open only to faith. Lohse, who allows a reference to Isaiah, says that the secret is penetrated by the aid of the Holy Spirit.

We now turn to a passage where nobody has suspected a reference to scripture. But when it is disclosed, as it seems to me, it throws considerable light on one of the most obscure corners of the Epistle. This is 2:14–15:

having cancelled the bond which stood against us with
its legal demands; this he set aside, nailing it to the cross.
v. 15   He disarmed the principalities and powers and made a
public example of them, triumphing over them in him.

This passage is full of obscurities: the RSV translation treats God
as the subject throughout, hence its rendering 'in him (Christ)'
not 'in it (the cross)'. But it is very difficult to believe that the
disarming of the powers is to be attributed to God not Christ. If
we take Christ as the subject of verse 15, however, we must accept
that C. F. D. Moule calls 'an illogical transition from one (subject)
to another in the course of this sentence'.

Behind these verses, I maintain, lies a passage in Numbers
25:1–5. This is the account of the way in which the Israelites were
enticed into idolatry by the people of Moab. God's anger is
kindled by this, and he says to Moses: 'Take all the chiefs of the
people, and hang them in the sun before the Lord, that the fierce
anger of the Lord may turn away from Israel.' There follows the
story of Phinehas' act of vindication, when he pierced through
with his spear an Israelite who was mating with a Midianite
woman. Now in the LXX version of these events the word used
for 'hang them up' is *paradeigmatison*. This word, a translation of
the Hebrew verb *HQ*^c, is cognate with the word used in Colossians
2:15 for how Christ treated the powers: *edeigmatisen*, 'he made a
public example of them'. It is also used in Hebrews 6:6 for the
action of apostates: they 'crucify the Son of God on their own
account and *hold him up to contempt*'. It is worth noticing also
that both the people slain by Phinehas, Zimri and Cozbi, were
connected with the rulers of Israel and Midian respectively. Thus
by God's command the sinful rulers are hung up, or pierced
through (see Num. 25:6–15).

Now we turn to rabbinic tradition for further light on this
passage. The *Targum of Palestine*, which contains some ancient
material predating the Jewish–Christian division, paraphrases
Numbers 25:1–5 thus:

And the people of the house of Israel joined themselves to
Baala-Peor, like the nail in the wood, which is not separated
but by breaking up the wood. And the anger of the Lord was
kindled against Israel. And the Lord said to Moses, Take all
the chiefs of the people . . . and let them give judgement against
the people who have gone astray after Peor, and hang them
before the word of the Lord upon the wood over against the
morning sun, and at the departure of the sun take them down
and bury them, and turn away the strong anger of the Lord
against Israel.

Le Déaut gives a translation of the neofiti manuscript of the *Targum of Palestine,* not available in Etheridge's day, in which the reference to crucifixion is explicit:

> Take all the chiefs of the people and constitute them as a Sanhedrin before Yahweh, so that they should be judges. Whoever has merited to be put to death, him they will crucify on the cross. (My trans. of Le Déaut on Numbers 25:4.)

This interpretation of Numbers 25:1–5 has moved the narrative nearer to Colossians 2:14–15 in two respects: it makes reference to a nail in the wood, which reminds us of Colossians 2:14 where 'the bond that was against us' is described as 'nailed to the cross'; and secondly it brings in a reference to Deuteronomy 21:23, the verse quoted in Galatians 3:13 in connection with Jesus' crucifixion. It may even be that the author of Colossians knew the tradition lying behind this targum, and that it is from there that he draws the detail of nailing the bond to the cross.

When we read on in the targums, we find other remarkable connections with our passage in Colossians. The *Targum of Pseudo-Jonathan* (ms. Add. 27031 in the British Library) embellishes the scriptural narrative with *haggada.* Phinehas pierces his two victims with a lance and bears them aloft:

> When he bore them aloft, the lintel was uplifted for him until he had gone forth. He carried them through the whole camp, six miles, without fatigue. He held them up by his right arm, in sight of their kindred, who had no power to hurt him. The lance was made strong, so as not to be broken with the load. The iron transpierced them, but was not withdrawn. An angel came and made bare their corpses in the sight of the people.

(For references and further details see my *Studies in Paul's Technique,* etc. pp. 1–12. Etheridge has bowdlerized the original, which is fuller and coarser; see Le Déaut on Numbers 25:1f.)

It does not seem unreasonable to conclude therefore that the author of Colossians is in this difficult passage, 2:14–15, giving us a typological treatment of Numbers 25: the hanging up of the culprits at Baal Peor and the piercing of Zimri and Cozbi are regarded as constituting a type of the cross. First Moses and then Phinehas represents Christ, and the guilty idolaters as well as the two victims of Phinehas' zeal represent the hostile and sinful 'powers' or 'rulers' (see v. 15) whom Christ overcame on the cross. The great difference between type and fulfilment is of course that whereas under the old dispensation the guilty were punished by being hung up or pierced through by the righteous, under the new it was the guiltless Christ who suffered the hanging up and the piercing. But this is after all the whole point of the crucifixion, the astonishing new element in God's strategy that not the clearest type of the old dispensation could adequately predict. The author of Colossians has shown himself to be a master of this particular method of scriptural interpretation. He is well acquainted with traditional exegesis and does not hesitate to use it in his expression of the significance of the cross.

The last reference can be disposed of briefly. In 2:22 we have the phrase: 'according to human precepts and doctrines'. The Greek very definitely echoes the LXX of Isaiah 29:13c, which in the Hebrew means 'and thus fear of me is a commandment of men learned by rote', but in the Greek is literally

> In vain do they worship me, teaching the commandments and teachings of men.

We have met this text already in connection with Mark 7:6–7 (par. Matt. 15:8–9), where it was used to confirm Jesus' rejection of the scribal *halaka* (see above, p. 34). This can hardly be its exact purpose here, since we have no reason to think that the author of Colossians was faced with the opposition of Pharisaic Judaism. It seems very likely, however, that the form of divergent teaching which he was opposing had an element of Jewish dietary regulations in it, and the tag from Isaiah would be very appropriate in such a context. Houlden's comment is just: 'Both passages (Mark 7:6–7 and Col. 2:22) use Isaiah 29:13 to give scriptural support to a liberal approach to the Jewish law.' Gnilka remarks with considerable insight that the author in using this citation distances himself from Paul but draws nearer to the teaching of Jesus.

Ephesians

There is no shortage of overt scriptural allusions in this Epistle. Indeed, in trying to select the most significant we may seem to suffer from an *embarras de richesses*. We will be content to look at eight passages:

> 1:6: to the praise of his glorious grace which he freely bestowed
>   on us in the Beloved.

That phrase 'the beloved' occurs in a significant context in Deuteronomy 33:5, 26. In both places it translates the Hebrew *yᵉšurūn*, a sort of pet word which Yahweh uses for Israel. Deuteronomy 33:5 runs thus in the LXX:

> And there shall be a ruler in the beloved
>   when the rulers of the peoples have been gathered together,
>   together with the tribes of Israel.

This renders the Hebrew adequately enough, except that it is 'people' not 'peoples' in the MT. The *Targum of Onkelos* represents Moses as 'the beloved', but the *Targum of Palestine*, representing probably an earlier tradition, takes it messianically: 'And a king shall rise from the house of Jacob.' (See Etheridge p. 674; Le Déaut, *Nombres* 33:5.) The author of Ephesians lays great stress on the exaltation of Christ over all the *aiōns*, and might well see in Deuteronomy 33:5 a prophecy of Christ's resurrection–ascension. He would find Deuteronomy 33:26 equally appropriate. Once more I translate the LXX rendering:

> There is none like the God of the beloved,
>   him who rides on the heaven as thy helper,
>   and the magnificent one of the firmament.

The *Targum of Palestine* expands the passage thus (Etheridge p. 681):

> There is none like the God of Israel, whose glorious Shekinah dwelleth in the heavens, and his magnificence in the high expanse. In his abode hath the Shekinah dwelt before they were, and under his power he bringeth the world.

Here not the Messiah but the Shekinah, God's presence in some sense hypostatized, is identified with 'the beloved', and we note with surprise that its distinct pre-existence to the heavens is asserted. If we may suggest that the author of Ephesians knew the tradition behind this targum, he would find in it both an exalted Christology and the inspiration for his doctrine of 'recapitulation' which he sets forth in subsequent verses. I have no doubt myself that a study of these passages in Deuteronomy has been one of the sources of the thought of Ephesians.

> 2:17: And he came and preached peace to you who were far off and to those who were near.

This seems to be a composite quotation (so Armitage Robinson; Dibelius–Greeven only allow a reference to Isaiah 57:19). The two passages echoed here are Isaiah 52:7; 57:19. The first runs:

> How beautiful upon the mountains are the feet of him who brings good tidings, who publishes peace, who brings good tidings of good.

And the second:

> Peace, peace, to the far and to the near, says the Lord.

The first passage leads on to the last great servant song, so much quoted by early Christians; but the context of the second passage would also seem very significant to an early Christian. Once more we quote the LXX, assuming that this is more likely to be the form in which our author read it (Isa. 57:16–18):

> For a spirit will go out from me, and I have created all breath. Because of sin for a short time I grieved him and struck him and turned my face away from him. . . I have seen his ways and I healed him and comforted him and gave him eternal comfort.

Then follows the quotation already given. An early Christian would certainly see in this a prophecy of the sending of the Holy Spirit, of the vicarious death of Christ on behalf of sinners, and of Christ's resurrection. The author of Ephesians uses the words of verse 19 about those near and those far off to apply to Jews and Gentiles, so we may add that he also finds in this passage a prophecy of the accession of the Gentiles. Of course the mistranslation of the LXX has helped him. In the Hebrew the reference to the spirit means only that God created man's spirit. But this is neither the first time nor the last that the LXX has succeeded quite unintentionally in giving a Christian accent to scripture.

2:20: Jesus Christ himself being the cornerstone.

This is of course a reference to Isaiah 28:16, a favourite text with early Christians. There the LXX uses the same word, *akrogōniaios,* for the cornerstone as we have here. This word also occurs in the LXX translation of Psalm 118:22:

> The stone which the builders rejected
>   has become the head of the corner.

In each passage it translates the Hebrew *pinnah,* which can mean a cornerstone. The word *akrogōniaios* is only found in biblical Greek. Moulton and Milligan suggest that the translators of the LXX coined it. The Targum on Isaiah 28:16 drops all 'stone' language and interprets the verse in directly messianic terms: 'Therefore I will appoint in Zion a king, a strong king, powerful and terrible.' Strack–Billerbeck point out that the Targum on Psalm 118:22 also interprets the stone as referring to the King-Messiah. Hence our 'cornerstone' in Ephesians 2:20 has a wide-ranging scriptural background. It makes one wonder whether those scholars may not be right who interpret the 'prophets' in this verse as the canonical prophets, not the prophets of the early Christian church. For an able treatment of the 'stone' theme in the early church, see R. J. McKelvey's book *The New Temple.*

4:7–10: Here is an absolutely explicit citation of Psalm 68:18. Indeed the whole passage can quite properly be called a midrash on Psalm 68. The point that strikes us at once is that the author has apparently altered the psalm in order to accommodate it to the meaning he wishes to extract from it. The original was this: (Ps. 68:18 abc, MT 68:19; LXX 67:19):

> Thou didst ascend the high mount,
>   leading captives in thy train,
>   and receiving gifts among men.

The LXX renders this with some difference:

> Thou hast ascended on high,
>   thou hast led captivity captive,
>   thou hast received gifts in a man.

We can see at once that the version in Ephesians agrees exactly with neither the MT nor the LXX. In the first place it has the main verb in the third person with a participle agreeing with it, whereas the Hebrew and the Greek have two verbs in the past tense, both in the second person singular. Secondly, it reproduces the meaning of the Hebrew, though not the literal sense, in translating 'men', not 'man'. On the other hand it has altered 'among men' to 'to men'. (The rendering 'thou hast led captivity captive' is not significant; the LXX has merely translated the Hebrew literally.) Most important of all, Ephesians has departed from both the Hebrew and the Greek in translating 'thou hast given gifts to men' instead of 'thou hast received gifts from men'. The other differences can be put down to the author of Ephesians' desire to adapt his citation to his context, but not this one. However, it is now clear that the reason why he has altered 'received' into 'given' is because he is following the tradition of the Targum. The *Targum on the Psalms* wishes to adapt this verse to the incident of Moses going up Mount Sinai to receive the Torah, then coming down with the Torah as God's gift to man. Hence the MT *lāqaḥta* ('thou hast received') was changed to *ḥālaqta* ('thou hast inherited' – hence 'bestowed'). This alteration also necessitated translating *beʾādām* (literally 'in a man') as 'to men'.

But another question has to be answered: what was the intention of the author of Ephesians in making this midrash on Psalm 68? The obvious solution would seem to be that he was following the targumist tradition. The Targum sees it as a description of Moses ascending Mount Sinai and bringing down the Torah. The author of Ephesians sees it as a type of Christ's descent from heaven, death and descent into the underworld, and his victorious resurrection–ascension whereby he gave to men the gifts of the Spirit and the Church. In fact the psalm passage does not provide any reference to a descent into the underworld, so the writer has to infer it. This is what he is doing in verses 9–10. It is true that a group of scholars maintain that there is no reference to the descent into the underworld, the *descensus ad inferos*, here. All that the author is doing here, they suggest, is referring to the incarnation: our sublunary sphere is described as 'the lower parts of the earth'. The powers which Christ overcame are thought of as existing 'in the heavenly places', not under the earth. But the parallel with Romans 10:5–9 (already referred to on p. 37 above) is against this. So is the LXX usage of the Greek phrase rendered 'the lower parts of the earth', which nearly always refers to Sheol. We shall be examining another passage in Ephesians presently which will prove, we believe, also to contain a reference to the *descensus ad inferos*. In the phrase 'he led a host of captives' our author would certainly see a reference to Christ's conquest of the powers, which cannot be dissociated from his cross, death (and hence *descensus*) and resurrection. There is rabbinic evidence to show that Jewish tradition associated Moses' receiving of the Torah from God in heaven with fierce opposition by the angels, which he had to overcome. We may finally observe that rabbinic tradition also saw a reference to the resurrection of the dead in verse 9 of this psalm:

> Rain in abundance, O God, thou didst shed abroad,
>   thou didst restore thy heritage as it languished.

(For a fuller exposition of this passage in Ephesians see *The New Testament Interpretation of Scripture*, pp. 136–41.) We may perhaps pause to note Abbott's explanation of why Paul (as he believed the author to be) used the psalm quotation in this way: 'An expression of Scripture occurs to him which strikes him as being *le mot de la situation*' – a classic example of old-fashioned misunderstanding of how New Testament writers use scripture!

> 4:25–6: Let everyone speak the truth with his neighbour, for we are members one of another. Be angry, but do not sin.

In these verses are included two echoes of scripture: Zechariah 8:16b has 'Speak the truth to one another', and Psalm 4:4 runs: 'Be angry but sin not.' One could suggest a context for these citations in salvation history. The words in Zechariah come after a section describing the felicity of the coming messianic era; and the previous line in the LXX version of Psalm 4 has 'and know that the Lord has made his holy one marvellous'. But it is more likely that we have here examples of the use of scripture in early Christian ethical teaching, as Dibelius–Greeven suggest. It is interesting to observe that our author, for all his undoubted ability in scriptural exegesis of a typological nature, can use it in a perfectly straightforward manner for ethical paraenesis. Indeed we may have here a glimpse into early Christian catechesis.

> 4:30: And do not grieve the Holy Spirit of God, in whom you were sealed for the day of redemption.

The theme of grieving God's Spirit is found in Isaiah 63:10:

> But they rebelled,
>   and grieved his holy Spirit.

The LXX does not use the same verb for 'grieve' as we find in Ephesians 4:30. It uses *paroxunan*, whereas we have *lupeite* in Ephesians. But the Hebrew word which *paroxunan* translates, *ᶜātab*, is rendered occasionally with *lupein* by the LXX translators in other contexts. (See Gen. 45:5; 2 Sam. 19:3.) The parallel is not exact, since *lupein* is used in the sense of 'grieve, mourn' (intr.) and translates the Niph'al of *ᶜātab*. But there does not seem to be any reason why someone rendering Isaiah 63:10 into Greek should not use *lupein* as an adequate translation. The context in Isaiah 63 is quite appropriate for the citation in Ephesians. The previous verse, as mistranslated by the LXX, emphasizes that it was God himself, not an angel or a delegate, who saved Israel. It runs thus in the LXX version:

> No elder, nor angel, but the Lord himself saved them, because he loved them and spared them. He himself redeemed them.

The word for 'redeemed' is *elutrōsato*, the same root as we meet in Ephesians 4:30: 'the day of *redemption' (apolutrōsis)*. And in the subsequent verse to that echoed in Ephesians 4:30 we have in the LXX the phrase 'he who exalted from the earth the shepherd of the sheep'. In the Hebrew this is a reference to God's leading Moses at the head of his people out of Egypt, but to an early Christian it would certainly be taken as a reference to the resurrection–ascension of Jesus Christ, a leading theme in Ephesians. It looks as if we have here the handling of a scriptural passage so as to make it apply to the new people of God, redeemed through the exalted Christ.

> 5:14: Therefore it is said,
>   'Awake, O sleeper, and arise from the dead, and Christ shall give you light.'

It is generally agreed that this is not a conscious citation of scripture, but a quotation from an early Christian hymn. The question has been raised, however, as to whether some passage from scripture lies behind the hymn. There is no obvious parallel in the LXX at least. Most scholars are content to quote Isaiah 60:1 as the nearest parallel:

Arise, shine, for your light has come,
and the glory of the Lord has risen upon you.

But there are no verbal links in the Greek. I prefer a suggestion originally made by my brother, R. P. C. Hanson (*Allegory and Event*, p. 177n.) that this quotation echoes Jonah 1:6. Jonah is asleep in the hold, and when the storm bursts the captain of the ship says to Jonah: 'What do you mean, you sleeper? Arise, call upon your god!' The LXX word for 'arise' here is *anasta*, the same word as we have in Ephesians 5:14. Moreover, the LXX translation of the Hebrew phrase describing Jonah's sleep in Jonah 1:5 is *ekatheuden kai erenken*. The second verb means literally 'he was snoring' and the LXX translates 'you sleeper' in the next verse with the same verb, literally 'Why do you snore?' This verb would hardly pass in a liturgical context such as we have in Ephesians 5:14, so it is not surprising that *katheudein* is used instead.

It is possible that the cry of 'Arise from sleep' in the Jonah story has already been used in a Christian context in Matthew's Gospel. In the story of the wise and foolish virgins in Matthew 25:5, all the bridesmaids, wise and foolish alike, are described in the phrase 'they all slumbered and slept', a phrase which would be an excellent rendering of Jonah 1:5: 'And had lain down, and was fast asleep.' Perhaps in Matthew's parable the virgins represent the dead generally; the wise virgins are those who have received the oil of baptism, i.e. Christians, who are prepared to meet their Lord at the parousia. If so, this phrase about sleeping was already associated with the resurrection. In Ephesians 5:14, quite conformably with the theology of the rest of the Epistle, it is associated with the resurrection to new life which membership of the Christian church can give. We can add to this the consideration that in rabbinic tradition Jonah became quite a saviour figure. His journey, in the course of which he was swallowed by the fish, was regarded as having been undertaken for the sake of Israel. On the basis of Jonah 2, the psalm in which Jonah claims to have gone down to Sheol (2:2; and see 2:6), he was believed to have been given the rare privilege of visiting the place of the dead, and returning again to earth. For evidence about all this, see *The New Testament Interpretation of Scripture*, pp. 142–50. It is therefore by no means unreasonable to claim that behind the words of this Christian hymn in Ephesians 5:14 there lies a typological treatment of the story of Jonah.

6:13–17: we have a whole series of phrases to describe the Christian's spiritual armour, mostly taken from the words of scripture:

Therefore take the whole armour of God. . . Stand therefore,

having girded your loins with truth . . . and having shod your
feet with the equipment of the gospel of peace. . . And take
the helmet of salvation, and the sword of the Spirit, which is
the word of God.

The phrase 'the whole armour' is *panoplia* (literally 'panoply') in
Greek. The word occurs in Wisdom 5:17, where it is part of the
description of God's offensive armament when he punishes the
ungodly. It speaks also of the breastplate of righteousness, and
mentions a shield, a sword and fiery darts, all part of God's
armoury. But *panoplia* is also used in Aquila's translation of
Psalm 91 (90):4c. The RSV runs: 'His faithfulness is a shield and
buckler.' The exhortation to gird one's loins with truth comes
undoubtedly from Isaiah 11:5, where it is part of the description
of the coming king, who would of course be identified by Christians with Christ. The Targum on this passage accepts the subject
of the description as being the Messiah and renders: 'And the
righteous shall be round about him, and the faithful shall be
brought near unto him.' This is an interesting step towards the
Christian conception of the faithful being 'in Christ'. The faithful
actually correspond to the Messiah's armour. A similar transposition occurs at Isaiah 59:17:

He put on righteousness as a breastplate,
    and a helmet of salvation upon his head.

The Targum offers: 'Strength and salvation shall he bring with his
Memra for them that fear him to do them.' In other words, the
spiritual armour of God is interpreted in terms of the faithful,
who are associated with the Messiah. This is at least halfway
towards the Christian image in Ephesians 6:13f., where the breastplate and the salvation are part of the Christian's armour in Christ.
The 'equipment of the gospel of peace' is an echo of Isaiah 52:7
(par. Nahum 1:15). This is a famous 'evangelistic' passage, and
would probably be in the author's mind as a general background
to the preaching of the gospel. 'The sword of the Spirit' seems to
be a conflation of Isaiah 11:4, where the coming king will 'smite
the earth with the rod of his mouth' and Isaiah 49:2, where it is
written of the servant: 'He has made my mouth like a sharp
sword.' In the first of these passages the LXX translation has:

He shall smite the earth with the word of his mouth,
    and in a spirit through his lips he shall slay the ungodly,

which is nearer Ephesians 6:17b.

Strack–Billerbeck quote various passages in which the Torah
is compared to a sword. Von Soden's comment is just: 'The
Spirit himself acts as a sword.' Dibelius–Greeven think that the

reference to the Spirit comes from Isaiah 11:4. We may conclude therefore about this passage that the author of Ephesians is not explicitly quoting scripture but he is the heir to a tradition in which many of these references to spiritual armament have been applied to the Messiah and to the faithful in the days of the Messiah, and he has therefore no difficulty in applying them to the spiritual armour of the Christian in Christ. The technique can legitimately be described as an illustrative use of scripture, but it is a usage based on a knowledge of traditional exegesis.

The author of Ephesians has thus shown himself to be a master of the theological use of scripture. Without at all obtruding his scriptural learning, he has used it in a wide variety of ways: conscious quotation, typological interpretation, illustrative allusion. He is as much a master of the use of scripture as was Paul. He has shown himself well able to use and develop Paul's technique and adapt it to the needs of his own day. Though he does not have the same obligation as Paul had to use scripture for polemical ends, he can use it very effectively in both an explicit and an implicit manner. As a writer in the Pauline tradition he proves a worthy successor to his master.

The Use of Scripture in Hebrews

Whereas it would be possible for a superficial student of the Fourth Gospel, for instance, to ignore its use of scripture, no one with the slightest acquaintance with the Epistle to the Hebrews would try to understand it without considering its use of scripture. Explicit quotations from scripture litter the pages of the Epistle; many of the points the author makes are backed up by scriptural quotations; a whole chapter (the eleventh) consists of an extended review of scriptural characters (but see below, p. 112). As one might expect, therefore, the author of Hebrews has a method of using scripture which is peculiar to himself. The obvious person with whom to compare him is Paul. Michel actually suggests (comm. p. 83) that the author has consciously improved on Paul's technique. He differs from Paul, however, in several striking ways: in the first place, he does not distinguish the various authors of scripture as Paul does, Moses, David, Isaiah. Sometimes (e.g. 2:6: 'It has been testified somewhere') he gives us the impression that he does not know the exact context in scripture from which his citation is taken. Again, Paul's citations of scripture are distributed unevenly throughout his writings. Romans 1—12 is full of them. Philippians has comparatively few. The author of Hebrews uses scripture constantly throughout his thirteen chapters. Above all he differs from Paul in his attitude to the Torah. For Paul the Torah is both obsolete and relevant, obsolete as a God-given means of daily living, still relevant as a 'dyke against sin', a means of showing up sin, and a sketch of the sort of moral and religious character whom God approves. Hebrews finds a different value in the Torah.

The Torah is for the author of Hebrews only significant as far as concerns its ritual and liturgical requirements, and even within this area most especially the ordinances connected with the Day of Atonement. This is not to say that he is not interested in the rest of scripture; he sees the whole of scripture as capable of providing prophecy and exhortation concerning the new Christian dispensation, but within scripture the ritual ordinances of the Torah have a special function. Michel, in his masterly exposition of Hebrews' use of the Torah, says that the Torah for the author of Hebrews consists not of the decalogue but of the writings containing the priestly and cultic rules concerning ritual purity (comm. p. 182). The relation between this part of the Torah and the Christian dispensation, he says, can be summed up under three headings: correspondence; superiority; fulfilment (ibid., p. 183). Spicq describes the author's method of scripture interpretation as consisting in an attempt 'to unveil the messianic meaning of the Old Testament, to decode *(déchiffrer)* the ultimate significance which God has inserted into scripture' (p. 333). Paul, he says (p. 342), emphasizes rather the abolition of the law, but the author of Hebrews views the law as a preliminary sketch *(ébauche)*. He adds that 'the relation of the two dispensations is that of the temporal to the spiritual' (p. 345), which is true enough. But we must take issue with him when he concludes (p. 346): 'One must therefore conceive of the entire New Testament as figurative.' This is not completely accurate, as we shall be seeing presently. Both Spicq (p. 339) and Kuss (p. 60) point out that the author of Hebrews must have regarded the LXX as inspired, as Philo certainly did, since our author draws important arguments from the details of the Greek text. There is no sign that he knew any Hebrew or that he had access to the Hebrew text, as Paul must have had, and as the author of the Fourth Gospel probably had.

The author uses typology extensively, though he uses the word *tupos* only once, where it means not the imperfect prefigurement, but the true model laid up in heaven (Heb. 8:5). His words for 'type' are *antitupos* (9:24), *skia* (literally 'shadow'), see 8:5, 10:1; and *parabolē* (9:9, 11:19). Sowers (p. 104) acutely suggests that by *skia* the author meant both the foreshadowing of what was to come and an imperfect image of the perfect reality which was in heaven. Sowers also claims (pp. 78–80) that one can trace a regular schema in the author's references in scripture. We have first a citation of scripture, then a rejection of the Jewish interpretation, and finally an exposition of the christological meaning. This may be true for many of his citations of scripture, but does not apply to all of them. For example, in 10:5–9, which, as we shall be seeing, is a citation of central importance to the author, I can find no trace of the rejection of the Jewish interpretation of this passage. However, Sowers is quite correct when he writes: 'Basic to Hebrews' understanding of scripture is *Heilsgeschichte*.' Typology only makes sense in the context of an ongoing history of God's saving acts. We may illustrate our author's view of the law by an example from 9:8, where he cites certain details of the ritual prescribed for the Day of Atonement, and comments:

> By this the Holy Spirit indicates that the way into the sanctuary is not yet opened as long as the outer tent is still standing (which is symbolic (Greek *parabolē*) for the present age).

The Holy Spirit, by prescribing the details of ritual and of the equipment of the sanctuary, was indicating that the perfect sacrifice had not yet come. We may conclude therefore that the ordinances prescribed in scripture were not mistaken attempts at worshipping God correctly, nor yet ciphers awaiting allegorical interpretation, but seriously intended directions whose purpose was to prepare the worshippers for the coming perfect dispensation.

The author certainly believed in the pre-existence of him who appeared on earth as Jesus Christ. The first four verses of the Epistle are sufficient to demonstrate this. It is not, however, clear exactly what name he would have given to the pre-existent being. He calls him *apaugasma* ('reflection') and *charaktēr* ('facsimile') in 1:3, but these are functional epithets rather than names. It does not seem likely that he thought of him as Son, since the most likely meaning of 1:2a is 'in these last days he has spoken to us in the mode of Son', thereby suggesting that Christ only began to be a Son at the incarnation. In 1:6 he calls him 'the first-begotten', but he does not use this name elsewhere for the pre-existent being, and he does use it in 12:23 for the elect in heaven. Perhaps he would have used the name *kurios*, 'Lord', or even, conceivably, in view of 1:8, *theos*, 'God' (but see below). Michel (p. 82) agrees that the author had a 'pre-existence Christology'.

But we can go further than this: we can produce evidence which strongly suggests that the author, like Paul, thought of the pre-existent being (whom we will call Christ for convenience) as present and active in Israel's history. We will confine ourselves to two instances. First we take 11:24–7. Here the author is pursuing the career of Moses; he describes him as 'choosing rather to share ill-treatment with the people of God than to enjoy the fleeting pleasures of sin'. The words 'share ill-treatment' render the Greek *sunkakoucheisthai.* He goes on to say that Moses 'considered abuse suffered for the Christ greater wealth than the treasures of Egypt'. The phrase 'abuse suffered for the Christ' is *ton oneidismon tou christou*, which is a quotation from Psalm 89:50-1 (LXX 88:51-2). One may well ask how ill-treatment suffered hundreds of years before the birth of Jesus can be described as 'the abuse of the Messiah' (which is what the phrase means in Greek). The answer is surely that the author thought of the appearance to Moses at the burning bush as an appearance of the pre-existent Christ. In the LXX of Exodus 3:7-8 the apparition in the burning bush says to Moses: 'I have indeed seen the ill-treatment (*kakōsis*) of my people . . . and I have come down to rescue them out of the hand of the Egyptians.' Now, if the author regarded these as the words of the pre-existent Christ, we can see how appropriate it is that Moses, in returning to Egypt after the epiphany, should be described as sharing 'the abuse of the Messiah'; the pre-existent Christ had told him that he was coming down to intervene in his people's sufferings. This will also give a new and remarkable significance to 11:27b: 'For he (Moses) endured as seeing him who is invisible.' In the appearance in the burning bush he had seen the pre-existent being who represented the visibility of the invisible God.

Our second piece of evidence is drawn from the author's references to Melchisedech. We must bear in mind that in chapter 1 the author has strongly emphasized Christ's absolute superiority to all angels. Then in 7:3 he describes Melchisedech thus:

> He is without father or mother or genealogy, and has neither beginning of days nor end of life, but resembling the Son of God he continues a priest for ever.

Now someone who is ungenerate and eternal is either a rival to Christ, which the author cannot allow, or Christ himself. The author, it seems, is intimating that Melchisedech is an appearance of the pre-existent Christ. It is to be noted that he never applies any word suggesting a type to Melchisedech, neither *antitupos* nor *skia* nor *parabolē*. Commentators have often said that in Hebrews Melchisedech is a type of Christ (e.g. Spicq p. 341), but he has none of the characteristics of the type in Hebrews; he is not an imperfect sketch; he belongs to the world of perfection and reality. He 'resembles the Son of God', i.e. the incarnate Christ, because he is the pre-existent Christ. It may be objected that if this is what the author meant he could have said so plainly, but we may point out that the author complains in 5:11-14 that his readers are 'dull of hearing', though he has 'much to say which is hard to explain' about Melchisedech. In other words, the author believed that Melchisedech was a christophany, but did not quite have the nerve to say so directly. We may therefore qualify Spicq's claim, referred to above, that for the author everything was figurative: history was real, and the appearance of the pre-existent Christ in Israel's history was real.

As a very good specimen of the author's scriptural exposition we may turn to 10:5–10. As we have indicated above (p. 106), this is the very centre of his argument. He wants to show the nature of the offering that Christ has made, and it is most significant that in order to do so he chooses to expound a passage of scripture, Psalm 40:6–8 (MT 40:7–9; LXX 39:7–9). This is a psalm of great penitence, in which the writer declares that the sacrificial cultus is not what God requires but, rather, obedience to his will. This at least is the meaning of the MT as it stands, and equally of the LXX. If you read the psalm in the New English Bible you gain quite a different impression, but that cannot concern us here. Our author is quite content to take the LXX version as the inspired word of God. In 10:5 he puts the psalm in what he regards as its right context: it is addressed by Christ to the Father at the moment of the incarnation: 'When Christ came into the world, he said . . .' Our author then benefits from a mistranslation of the LXX, which runs:

> Sacrifices and offerings thou hast not desired,
>   but a body thou hast prepared for me.

A most happy prophecy of the incarnation! The original Hebrew is obscure. The RSV has 'but thou hast given me an open ear'. This may not be correct, but it is certain that the LXX is equally far from the sense, though scholars are not agreed as to how the LXX translators arrived at their rendering. Certainly it serves our author's turn most conveniently. He then continues to quote the psalm, and is able to use it most effectively to show not only that God requires obedience rather than animal sacrifices, but also that this obedience of Christ was foretold in scripture:

> as it is written of me in the roll of the book.

Scholars are puzzled about this reference to a book; one school of thought, represented by the NEB translators, would omit it as a gloss. But our author has no doubts. The psalm citation is exactly what he needs. It proves to perfection that Christ had come to abrogate the sacrificial cult, and that the essence of his offering was his perfect obedience to the Father – and that all this was foretold in scripture. The very next verse to that which he quotes runs:

> I delight to do thy will, O my God;
>   thy law is within my heart.

Our author certainly had this verse in mind even though he does not quote it, for in 8:7–12 he quotes an extensive passage from Jeremiah 31:31–4 in which a new covenant is promised whereby God's law would be written in the hearts of the Israelites; and again, just after the passage we have been studying, in 10:16–17 he cites Jeremiah 31:33 again, including the reference to the law being written in the hearts of God's people.

This is therefore a superb example of our author's use of scripture. He employs it in order to drive home the very central point of his argument, the nature of Christ's offering. And it must be admitted that, once grant the legitimacy of his appeal to the LXX text, scripture serves him very well, since it not only provides him with an explicit reference to the incarnation, but also certifies that the incarnation and offering of Christ is in accordance with scripture itself. Psalm 40 must have seemed to the author of Hebrews very much what John 17 is to Christians who live after the emergence of the canon of the New Testament, a brief and classic description of the purpose of the incarnation.

We have observed that in Psalm 40 our author thinks that Christ is addressing the Father. This discovery of dialogue between what we would call the first two members of the Trinity is a characteristic of Pauline interpretation of scripture (cf. Rom. 15:3), and a marked feature of Hebrews. (Compare 1:5, 8f., 10f.; 2:12–13; 5:5–6.) If we follow the argument of 1:8–9 literally we must conclude that according to our author God the Father addresses Christ as 'God'. Citing Psalm 45:6–7 (MT 45:7–8 LXX 44:7–8), he writes: 'Thy throne, O God, is for ever and ever', etc. This may well be what our author intends, but several scholars interpret the passage otherwise. Thus Thomas (p. 305) paraphrases it thus: 'Thy (the Son's) throne is God (the Father) for ever and ever and the sceptre of uprightness (the Son's) is the sceptre of his (the Father's) kingdom.' Our author, he claims, has actually altered the LXX 'a sceptre of uprightness is the sceptre of thy kingdom' to 'and the sceptre of uprightness is a sceptre of his kingdom'. Similarly, in 10:16 (referred to above) our author has transposed two phrases in the LXX of Jeremiah 31:33. The LXX has 'on their mind . . . on their heart'. Our author quotes it as 'on their heart . . . on their mind' in order to bring 'heart' into closer connection with 'laws' (Thomas p. 311). These are probably examples of simple midrash: the author has altered or paraphrased the words of scripture in order to bring out more clearly what he believes is their meaning. He did not have our apparatus of inverted commas, italics, square brackets, and so on.

Several scholars state very emphatically that our author does not use allegory in dealing with scripture (see Bruce p. 1; Sowers pp. 90f., 137; Williamson p. 532). This is true in the sense that he has nothing like Philo's deliberate employment of allegory. But, just as when Paul presses his typology beyond a certain point it begins to develop into allegory, so with Hebrews. We can point to various passages where allegory is not far off. One is 7:2, where the author sees a special significance in Melchisedech's name and title. Williamson recognizes this (ibid.) but claims that these etymologies were probably a commonplace as they are found in Philo. Another such passage is 10:20, where the curtain that lay over the entrance to the holy of holies is equated with Jesus' flesh. A third is 13:12: here the fact that the bodies of the two animals sacrificed in the temple on the Day of Atonement were to be burned outside the camp is seen as a foreshadowing of the fact that Jesus was crucified outside the gate of Jerusalem. Admittedly the 'outsideness' is in common between type and fulfilment, but it would have been a more convincing type if the animals had been slaughtered outside the camp. One feels that the author here has reached the limit of his ingenuity. One more step and he would be launched into a fully Philonic sort of allegory.

Scholars have earnestly debated the question of our author's relation to Philo. Opinions have varied between Spicq's belief that he was a converted Philonist and Williamson's contention that there is no evidence for the direct influence of Philo. Sowers certainly provides plenty of evidence that the author was acquainted with the background of Alexandrian Judaism (pp. 66–72). Philo calls his Logos an *apaugasma* of God (cf. Heb. 1:3). Philo says that man's spirit is stamped by the *charaktēr* of God (cf. ibid.). It was through his Logos that God made the world (Heb. 1:2). Philo can write of 'the Word who cuts in two' (*Logos tomeus*; cf. Heb. 4:12). In Philo also significance is seen in the fact that God swears by himself because there is none greater he can swear by (cf. Heb. 6:13). Philo calls the land which Abraham sought, a city (see Heb. 11:10, 16). On the other hand Williamson is fully justified in pointing to the marked differences between Philo and our author. Philo's direct exegesis of scripture is almost confined to Genesis (p. 499). There is no typology and no messianism in Philo (p. 530), nor is Philo interested in eschatology (p. 535). Hebrews lacks any suggestion of the prophetic ecstasy in which Philo believed (p. 536). Williamson admits that the quotation of Exodus 25:40 in Hebrews 8:5 looks very Philonic: 'See that you make everything according to the pattern which was shown to you on the mountain' (p. 537). This is a text that would have a strong appeal to Philo, since it seems to suggest a vein of Platonism in the Pentateuch. The fact that our author quotes it shows that he had been influenced by the Platonic element in Alexandrian Judaism. There is also the remarkable fact that Philo and the author of Hebrews give an apparent citation from scripture in a form which does not exactly correspond with any one passage in scripture, though Deuteronomy 31:8 seems the nearest (p. 570). (But cf. Josh. 1:5.) See Hebrews 13:5b: 'I will never fail you nor forsake you.' Williamson points out that our author applies it quite differently from the way in which Philo does. He suggests that Philo and our author must have got it from a common Alexandrian source. Perhaps James Moffatt's conclusion (p. lxi) is the best we can hope for on this question: 'The more he (the author of Hebrews) differs from Philo in his speculative interpretation of religion, the more I feel, after a prolonged study of Philo, that our author had probably read some of his works.'

Last of all we may ask how far our author was conversant with contemporary Jewish exegesis of scripture. Sowers (p. 128) points out that the author makes extensive use of one technique of scriptural interpretation recognized by Hillel, the *a fortiori* argument, *qal waḥomer* in Hebrew. He sometimes introduces it by a phrase such as 'how much more . . .?' (9:14), 'much less . . .' (12:25), 'how much worse . . .' (10:29). The same technique without a distinctive phrase occurs in 2:2–3. Sowers also points out that Esau's licentiousness, referred to in 12:16, is not implied in scripture but was part of the traditional view of him among Jewish exegetes. It is also found in Philo (he refers to *De Virtute* 208 as an example). Another example pointed out by Sowers is 11:24–36 (p. 136). Moses is described as repudiating his status as a son of Pharaoh's daughter. Scripture says nothing about this, it was part of *haggada*. But once again Philo is also acquainted with this tradition. Indeed, if one examined that eleventh chapter in detail one would learn much about our author's understanding of scripture. One suspects, for instance, that he sees some christological significance in the apparently unimportant detail that the dying Jacob, after blessing his descendants, was 'bowing in worship over the head of his staff' (11:21). The LXX has turned the 'bed' of Hebrew into a staff. Perhaps our author saw here a type of the cross. Some of the fathers took the staff to mean 'the stem of Jesse', the coming Messiah (see Westcott in loc.). In verse 27 we are told that Moses was not afraid of the anger of the king. This directly contradicts Exodus 2:14, which relates that Moses was afraid when he realized that his killing of the Egyptian was known. But long before the first Christian century Jewish tradition had turned Moses into a hero who must not be allowed any human weaknesses, and our author of course inherited this traditional view. One could also point to the conception of the heavenly temple, where a non-material sacrifice was offered. We have plenty of evidence from later rabbinic tradition for this belief. The fact that it occurs in Hebrews shows that it existed already in the first century. Thomas (p. 315) points out that in quoting

Deuteronomy 32:35 in the form 'Vengeance is mine, I will repay', the author is following the version of Paul and of the *Targum of Onkelos*, and not of the LXX (see Rom. 12:19). This suggests an acquaintance with midrashic tradition on the part of both these New Testament writers; but it does not follow that our author understood Hebrew, as Howard claims (p. 213). It is most unlikely that he knew any more Hebrew than Philo did, and Philo's knowledge of Hebrew was absolutely minimal (see my article 'Philo's Etymologies' in *JTS*, vol. 18, part 1 (1967), pp. 128–39). Zarb (p. 117) draws attention to the fact that in 11:34–5 the author refers to the story of the martyrdom of the sons of Eleazar which is found in 2 Maccabees 6:18—7:42. He concludes that our author accepted 2 Maccabees as part of scripture. But this does not follow. In verse 37 there is an undoubted reference to the story that Isaiah was sawn asunder, a tradition which is only found in apocryphal books that our author could not possibly have regarded as canonical. In chapter 11 our author is reviewing the heroes of Israel's history, not a gallery of exclusively scriptural heroes.

It does not seem very likely, therefore, that the author of Hebrews had the wide knowledge of traditional exegesis possessed by Paul or by the author of the Fourth Gospel. But he certainly had as much as was available to educated Jews of the Alexandrian school who read their bibles in Greek, not Hebrew. As we survey our author's technique of scriptural exegesis, however, we cannot surely withhold our admiration for the confidence, virtuosity and consistency with which he uses scripture in the exposition of his lofty theme of Christ as the great and ultimate high priest. Indeed, that theme itself is provided by scripture and would be quite meaningless without a scriptural background. No one else in the New Testament attempts so original an enterprise: we might almost call it 'the liturgical interpretation of Jesus'; and no one else in one relatively brief work manages to include so much deeply Christian interpretation of scripture. In relative brevity and in intensity of references, the only rival is the Book of Revelation. But, as we shall be seeing, the technique used by John the Divine is completely different from that of Hebrews. The achievement of the author of Hebrews remains unique. I suspect that scholars have not yet fully explored the implications of his approach to scripture.

6

JOHN'S USE OF SCRIPTURE

In studying the Fourth Gospel we are dealing with a book the material of which has probably been more profoundly thought out than that which we find in any other part of the New Testament. This is not because the actual structure of the Gospel is a carefully finished product. On the contrary, there are signs that the material it contains may have been subject to dislocation, and it seems very probable that the last chapter is an addition written by an editor who lived after the death of the original author. It is rather that the material itself has been subjected to a long process of employment as homily or exhortation and has been written by someone who has spent long years studying scripture. He incorporates his conclusions into his Gospel material and frequently attributes them to Jesus when they are in fact the product of his own meditation and study. We will call him John without prejudice to the question of any connection with John the apostle.

As we might expect in these circumstances, the allusions to scripture do not always lie on the surface. Specific citations of scripture are not very common. There is nothing like Matthew's frequent claim that such and such an event happened in order to fulfil what had been written by the prophet. A superficial reader of the Gospel might carry away the impression that John was not greatly interested in scripture, but he would be completely wrong. In fact the Fourth Gospel is full of allusions to scripture. The author was soaked in scripture. Through his Gospel runs an unobtrusive but very important strain of belief in predestination. All the events connected with Jesus were part of God's plan, and, therefore, nothing that happened to him was not foreknown by God – and foretold. And of course scripture is the place where it was foretold. When John represents Jesus as telling the Jews that they search scripture in vain (5:39–40, 46–7), he does not mean that any searching of the scriptures was in vain. In 10:35, when Jesus is represented as saying that 'scripture cannot be broken', he is not, as Bultmann suggests, simply playing the Pharisees at their own game of text-slinging. He believes as firmly as any Pharisee ever did that the scripture cannot be broken. But his principle of scripture interpretation is different to theirs: for him

Christ is the key to scripture, and in a variety of subtle ways he demonstrates in his Gospel how this key is to be used.

I propose in this chapter to follow the outline which I found useful in chapter 6 of my book *The New Testament Interpretation of Scripture*. But I will of course adapt it to our purpose in this work. I distinguished five various ways in which John uses scripture. As we shall see, they are not mutually exclusive ways, and the same passage of scripture can be used in more than one way. But I think it is helpful to distinguish them:

1 *Traditional citations from scripture:* John, in common with all the evangelists, reproduces a number of citations from scripture that were part of his written tradition. They come originally from the very earliest Christian community, and they constitute an integral element in any Gospel. A clear example is Isaiah 40:3 quoted in John 1:23: 'I am the voice of one crying in the wilderness, "Make straight the way of the Lord".' This is cited by the other three evangelists and belongs to the tradition concerning John the Baptist. Other examples are the two quotations which he applies to Jesus' entry into Jerusalem in 12:13–15. These are Psalm 118:25–6 and Zechariah 9:9. The first of these is quoted by the other three evangelists in one form or another, and the second by Matthew (Matt. 21:5). The citation from Psalm 118 here also falls into another category, as we shall be seeing later. Another example of what we might call traditional citations occurs in 12:40, where the verse about God having blinded the eyes of the Jews is cited from Isaiah 6:10. It is cited by both Matthew and Mark, and is one of the most frequently quoted passages from scripture in the New Testament. John does not, however, use it in any conventional or purely formal way, since he sees in it a proof that Isaiah saw the pre-existent Word (see below, p. 122). Then we can point to one or two places where John has made explicit scripture references that were certainly implicit in the other Gospels. Thus in the account of the Last Supper John quotes Psalm 41:9 (MT 41:10; LXX 40:10) of Judas' betrayal at 13:18. This reference is very near the surface at Mark 14:18 and implicit at Matthew 26:23; Luke 22:21. It is interesting to observe that this passage is also used by the author of the *Hodayoth* of Qumran (see 1 QH 5:23–4). This particular hymn may well have been written by the original Teacher of Righteousness himself, since there is evidence that a section of his followers deserted him. Similar is the citation of Psalm 22:18 at 19:24:

> They parted my garments among them,
>   and for my clothing they cast lots.

The phrase is repeated in all the other Gospels without an explicit quotation.

John believes of course all these quotations to be examples of how Jesus fulfilled scripture throughout his career; he is often idiosyncratic in the form in which he quotes them and even in the context in which he places them; but he did not discover them for himself and on the whole he does not see in them any more than what the other evangelists saw.

2   *Scripture is cited with an introductory formula:* this category overlaps with the previous one, since two of the citations that fall into the first category are introduced by the formula 'that the scripture may be fulfilled' or 'this was to fulfil the scripture' (see 13:18, 19:24). But it is worth while putting citations that are formally marked in a class by themselves, since John obviously regards them as having some peculiar importance. There are seven such citations. Two we have already dealt with (Ps. 41:9 and Ps. 22:18). The other five are 12:38–40; 15:25; 17:12; 19:28–9; and 19:36–7. The first of these we have already alluded to, because here John combines two citations from Isaiah, Isaiah 53:1 and Isaiah 6:10. Both are favourite quotations in the New Testament, though John's combining of them in this way is unique. It is worth noting that John does not attach these two citations very specifically to any one incident in Jesus' ministry. They occur at a point where John seems to be giving his readers a summary of the full significance of the Lord's ministry and teaching. These two quotations from Isaiah are given as prophetic testimony to Israel's blindness. The double quotation tells us much about how John viewed the operation of prophecy. The prophet knew a great deal about the future, and, as we shall be seeing, had been granted a vision of the pre-existent Word. At 15:25 we have a 'formula quotation' of Psalm 69:4: 'They hated me without a cause.' The same phrase occurs in Psalm 35:19, but we know that John regarded Psalm 69 as messianic, since he quotes it in 2:17 and 19:28, so it is very likely that he has it in mind here. He has altered the original (whether in the MT, Psalm 69:5 or the LXX, 68:5) from the present participle to an aorist indicative. But that is no doubt merely part of his technique of quotation. Then at 17:12 in the course of the 'high-priestly' prayer Jesus is represented as saying:

> None of them is lost, except the son of perdition, that the scripture may be fulfilled.

What scripture does John have in mind? It is unlikely in the extreme that he means 'scripture in general'. As J. H. Bernard well points out, '*hē graphē* ("the scripture") always refers to a definite passage in the Old Testament'. We are in fact reduced to two (we do not have to choose between them): Psalm 41:9, already referred to above, and Psalm 109:8. Psalm 109:8b is quoted of

Judas in Acts 1:20b. All scholars whom I have consulted prefer Psalm 41:9 as the reference there, on the basis of its having been quoted in 13:18 (with the exception of Bultmann, who does not discuss the question at all). But in our consideration of the scripture citations in Acts 1:20 we were able to trace a connection between Psalm 109:6 and Satan's entering into Judas as narrated in John 13:27: see above, pp. 83–4. What is needed is a scripture which foretells the 'perdition' of Judas. Psalm 109:8 fulfils this function better than does Psalm 41:9, which merely refers to Judas' betrayal. Though we need not rule out the influence of Psalm 41:9, it seems more in accordance with John's theology to conclude that the passage he had in mind was Psalm 109:8 (LXX, 108:8). The LXX version is:

> May his days be few;
> may another take his office.

This citation is part of the special tradition which John shared with Luke. It is not common to all the evangelists.

In 19:28–9 we are told that Jesus said 'I thirst . . . to fulfil the scripture', and that he was given a sponge full of vinegar. This is another example of a citation that is implicit in the Synoptics being made explicit in John. The incident is mentioned in all the Gospels. Only John refers to Psalm 69:21b: 'For my thirst they gave me vinegar to drink.' He underlines it by representing Jesus as saying 'I thirst'. Finally, two citations peculiar to John are introduced by the formula 'For these things took place that the scripture might be fulfilled', in 19:36. The first citation comes from Exodus 12:46 (it also occurs in Numbers 9:12); it is part of the instructions as to what is to be done with the passover lamb. Since there is no other citation of this verse in the New Testament and since it occurs in a passage of detailed instructions about ritual very unlikely to attract the attention of an early Christian, it seems probable that this is John's own discovery. He represents Jesus as having been crucified at the time when the passover lambs were to be slaughtered, and this is his way of underlining the typology. Since it would be quite pointless if he had deliberately altered the time of Jesus' death so as to agree with this prophecy (it would not in that case be prophecy actually fulfilled), we must conclude that in John's historical tradition Jesus was actually crucified on the day of preparation and not the passover day proper. Some scholars have claimed that John is here quoting not a passage from the Pentateuch, but a verse from a psalm. Psalm 34:20 runs: 'He [God] keeps all his bones; not one of them is broken.' It is true that Psalm 34 is quoted quite frequently in the New Testament, and may even be referred to in John 9:30; but it is most unlikely that it is quoted here. The context is of God's providential

care for the material well-being of the righteous. To apply it to
the corpse of Jesus, who had been executed with the utmost
cruelty, would be hopelessly inappropriate. For a discussion of
this question see B. H. Grigsby, pp. 58, 73. The other citation
which he gives us here is from Zechariah 12:10b: 'They shall look
on him whom they have pierced' (19:37). This is also echoed in
Revelation 1:7, together with the first half of the verse. This latter
(12:10a) is also quoted in Matthew 24:30. It is therefore plainly a
favourite text with early Christians. The verse is echoed as well
in Hebrews 10:29. The pattern of quotation is therefore as follows:

    12:10a echoed in Hebrews 10:29;
    12:10b quoted in John 19:37 and Revelation 1:7;
    12:10c echoed in Revelation 1:7; Matthew 24:30.

The MT is slightly corrupt, and the LXX has a completely
different rendering of 12:10b to what we have in the New Testament: literally 'they shall look towards me because of their dancing
in triumph'. The translator has probably misread the Hebrew verb
dāqar ('pierce through') as *rāqad* ('dance' – *resh* and *daleth* in
Hebrew are easily confused), and did his best with the resultant
nonsense. The New Testament writers translated direct from the
Hebrew, which both John and the author of Revelation were well
able to do. Or else there was a Greek translation current in the
first century AD which rendered the Hebrew correctly. Aquila uses
the same verb for 'to pierce' as we find in the New Testament
citations. John has thus given us here a well-known christological
citation.

So far, then, we have confined ourselves to those quotations
which John regarded as 'public' or 'traditional' in the sense that
any early Christian, on having his attention drawn to them, would
readily admit that these are clear examples of the way in which
Jesus fulfilled scripture. It is significant that all in these two
categories without exception deal with the ministry, reception,
betrayal, suffering and death of Jesus. That is, they are all
prophecies of what everyone knew actually happened to him.
Even the one citation which we have suggested John found for
himself (Exod. 12:46 quoted in 19:36) is quite straightforward
once we have accepted that the passover lamb is a type of Christ.
This is not a belief peculiar to John, as the reference to it in 1
Corinthians 5:7 proves. The other three classes of citation are all
less public, less obvious, more peculiar to John, and more subtle.
Indeed, as we go through these five categories we are in fact
penetrating deeper and deeper into the thought behind the
Gospel.

    3 *Scripture is explicitly cited, but without any introductory
formula.* The absence of the formula is in my opinion an indication

that we are here dealing with quotations which John had discovered for himself. But he wishes to share them with his readers. I find six examples of this usage in the Fourth Gospel. We will take them in order:

1   Psalm 69:9a is quoted in 2:17: John tells us that after the resurrection Jesus' disciples realized that the words of the psalm applied to Jesus' cleansing of the temple: 'Zeal for thy house will consume me.' As we have already seen, Psalm 69 was a favourite with early Christians. Paul quotes the second half of the verse in Romans 15:3 of Jesus:

> The reproaches of those who reproached thee fell on me.

John means to indicate that the cleansing of the temple was at least one reason why Jesus incurred the enmity of the rulers and hence was put to death. This is an example of something we have already met in Paul and Hebrews: a New Testament writer recognizes a dialogue between the Son and the Father in scripture. The psalms are the most likely areas from which such quotations can be drawn. It is significant that when we see this citation in its context in the Fourth Gospel, we find that it is part of the argument to the effect that the eternal Word is now the true temple for all true worshippers of God. Thus we are already led on towards the next category of citations which are all christological. For a full treatment of this passage see *The New Testament Interpretation of Scripture*, pp. 114–17.

2   Numbers 21:8–9 is referred to in John 3:14. This is the episode in the wilderness story in which the people were attacked by serpents, but were saved by a bronze serpent set on a pole by Moses. Whoever looked at the serpent recovered from the snakebite. This element in Israel's tradition caused embarrassment in later times, whatever its original significance was. Hezekiah had the ensign destroyed on iconoclastic grounds (2 Kings 18:4). Much later, probably not much more than a hundred years before the Fourth Gospel was written, the author of the Book of Wisdom goes out of his way to avoid all suggestion of idol worship that this incident might convey. He writes (Wisd. 16:6–7):

> They were troubled for a while, as a warning,
>   and received a token of deliverance to remind them of thy law's command.
> For he who turned towards it was saved, not by what he saw,
>   but by thee, the Saviour of all.

It is interesting that he refers to the pole with the serpent on it as a 'token' (*sumbolon*). The LXX at Numbers 21:8–9 translates the Hebrew word for pole with *sēmeion*, literally 'a sign'. It seems very likely that both the LXX 'sign' and the author of Wisdom's 'token' indicate a desire to avoid the obvious implications of the text. By the standards of Deuteronomy, for example, it was very shocking that God should actually have commanded Moses to make the image of a serpent and set it on a pole to be gazed at. It looked very like licensed idolatry, and had become idolatry by Hezekiah's time. John therefore inherits a tradition of interpreting the incident in a non-literal manner. For him this is easy: the incident of the bronze serpent was a type of Christ's crucifixion. The fact that John uses that word *sēmeion* to indicate Jesus' mighty works is very significant. It suggests very strongly that he regarded the cross as the last and greatest sign.

3   In 6:31 the people, arguing with Jesus about the miracle of the loaves, quote Psalm 78:24: 'He gave them bread from heaven to eat.' Just because this is quoted by the Jews, who are always in the wrong when arguing with Jesus in the Fourth Gospel, we must not conclude that John means us to understand that this quotation does not apply to Jesus. It does apply to him, perhaps in a double sense. It certainly means that Jesus is the true bread, the spiritual food sent from above by God. It probably also bears a eucharistic reference. Jesus gives them himself in the bread of the Eucharist. P. Borgen has suggested with great probability that John is here using homiletic material based on a sermon on the giving of the manna interpreted as a foreshadowing of the true bread from heaven, Christ. There are parallels, as he demonstrates, with Philo's treatment of Moses as the dispenser of wisdom (see Borgen pp. 1–20). It is even possible that there is a third meaning latent here: it was not Moses but the pre-existent Christ who gave the manna to Israel of old (cf. 1 Cor. 10:3).

4   In 6:45 John cites Isaiah 54:13: 'And they shall all be taught by God.' The MT is literally: 'And all thy sons shall be disciples of Yahweh.' The LXX has rendered this accurately enough, except that it has translated the divine name with *theos*, 'God'. John seems to be basing his citation on the LXX. The point is that, though the Jews do not recognize it, it is God himself in the person of the Son who is teaching them. It is quite likely that John was attracted to this passage by a mistranslation in the LXX two verses later. The LXX translator has understood the Hebrew *gōr yāgōr*, which means 'he shall stir up strife', as if it came from *gēr*, 'a proselyte' and hence renders it 'behold proselytes shall come to you'. Freed (pp. 18–20) suggests that John has omitted the reference to sons because he wished to show that the quotation applies to Gentiles as well. In the LXX rendering of Isaiah 54:15 he would have found confirmation of this interpretation: in the

last days God himself, in the person of the Word, would teach all men, Jews and Gentiles alike.

5   In 7:37–8 we read:

> On the last day of the feast, the great day, Jesus stood up and proclaimed, 'If any thirst, let him come to me and drink. He who believes in me, as the scripture has said, "Out of his heart shall flow rivers of living water".'

This is a problem passage, because it is quite certain that the alleged quotation from scripture does not appear in any recognizable form in any writing that John could possibly have regarded as scripture. We can, as in the case of 17:12 (see p. 115 above), rule out the suggestion that there is a general reference to water in scripture. John has some passage or passages in mind. Two passages in particular stand out, though neither gives us anything like a verbal echo of verse 38b. The first is the often used 'stone' passage from Isaiah 28:16. Jesus is identified with the 'foundation' or 'tested stone' of that passage. But there is no sign of water there, so we must add to it a second reference. This is to the water-giving rock in the wilderness. We have already seen how Paul has identified the pre-existent Christ with this rock in 1 Corinthians 10:4, and in John 6:31 Christ pre-existent has already been associated with the giving of the manna. But two other passages should be mentioned: there is probably an echo also of Zechariah 14:8:

> On that day living waters shall flow out from Jerusalem.

Jerusalem was regarded as the 'navel' of the earth, i.e. its centre point. This certainly gives us the notion of flowing waters, and perhaps of the Greek word translated 'heart', which is *koilia,* literally, 'belly'. This citation is in fact closest to John 7:38b, though still not very close. Finally, we might mention Psalm 40:8. The LXX (39:9) has:

> I have wished, my God, to do thy will,
>   even thy law in the midst of my heart (*koilias*).

This does give us the word used in verse 38b. There are echoes of Psalm 40 in an earlier part of chapter 7 (vv. 17–24). Instead of the Torah in his heart, Jesus has God's will. If I am right in suggesting that no less than four passages of scripture lie behind this one reference, we can well appreciate how long a process of study and meditation lies behind John's Gospel.

6   In 10:34–6 Jesus, in argument with the Jews, says: 'Is it not written in your law, I said, "you are gods". If he called them gods to whom the word of God came (and scripture cannot be broken)

do you say of him whom the Father consecrated and sent into the world "You are blaspheming" because I said "I am the Son of God"?' John is certainly using an argument drawn from scripture here; the question is, for what purpose is he using it? The scripture quoted is Psalm 82. But we cannot understand the citation unless we read the whole of the psalm. In the psalm God begins by arraigning beings called 'gods' or 'sons of the Most High' in the divine council. He accuses them of corrupt administration of justice, and commands them to protect 'the weak and needy'. He then condemns the judges for their blindness and prophesies that they will all 'die like men'. The psalm ends with a plea to God:

> Arise, O God, judge the earth;
> for to thee belong all the nations!

Whatever this psalm meant in its original setting, it was regarded in rabbinic tradition as an address by God to Israel, or to the rulers of Israel. The stronger tradition took it to be God's speech to Israel just after the giving of the Torah on Sinai: reception of the Torah had promoted them to a quasi-divine rank, but the episode of the golden calf would soon reduce them to the level of men again. The Qumran sectaries understood the psalm as addressed by Melchisedech (whom they took to be a superior angel) to the subordinate angels (some of them fallen) who rule the world. John uses the psalm (and we must realize that he is referring to the whole psalm, not only the verse he quotes) in order to provide a proof that it is legitimate for Jesus to claim to be the Son of God. He is probably closer to the rabbinic interpretation here than to that of Qumran, for he would have no sympathy with the identification of Melchisedech with an angel. But he very significantly describes the recipients of the psalm's message as those 'to whom the word of God came'. Perhaps we should point it 'Word of God'. It seems probable, therefore, that John viewed Psalm 82 as an address by the pre-existent Word of God to the Jews as a whole representing unbelieving Israel through the ages. He recognizes their privileges, but prophesies their downfall because of their unbelief. The last verse will then be regarded as a prophecy of the resurrection of Christ ('Arise, O God') and the accession of the Gentiles. It proves the point that John wishes to prove by an *a fortiori* argument: those whom the Word of God addressed could be called gods. How much more the pre-existent and incarnate Word! So elaborate a piece of scripture exegesis must be John's own composition. It is in the highest degree improbable that it goes back to Jesus. (For a detailed exposition of this account of John 10:34f. see two articles by me in *NTS* 11 (1965), pp. 158–62 and 13 (1966), pp. 363–7.)

    4 *Scripture can be traced as providing the basis of John's*

Christology. In all the categories of usage which we have mentioned so far, John has been explicitly quoting scripture. He draws the attention of his readers to it. But in our last two categories this is not so. His use of scripture is implicit. The reader is not necessarily expected to recognize the allusion, though no doubt John hoped that those who belonged to his school would recognize it. What we are doing, therefore, in the case of category 4 at any rate, is explaining the springs of John's christological thought. In all four cases we are claiming that John had a doctrine of the pre-existent Word active in Israel's history such as we have already traced in Paul and in Hebrews. Indeed we have already referred to this doctrine in connection with John 12:37–41 (see p. 114 above). We shall give four examples of this christological use of scripture, and then refer to two others suggested by other scholars:

1   John 1:14: 'And the Word became flesh and dwelt among us, full of grace and truth; we have beheld his glory, glory as of the only Son from the Father.' In this verse John is actually reproducing the words of Exodus 34:6, where God describes himself as 'abounding in steadfast love and faithfulness'. John's phrase 'full of grace and truth' is a literal rendering of the Hebrew. The Hebrew word translated by the RSV with 'love' is *ḥesed*, which John renders with *charis*, 'grace'. This is an unusual rendering of *ḥesed*, very rare indeed in the LXX, but found in some of the alternative Greek translations of the Hebrew scriptures. The word 'faithfulness' is how the RSV renders the Hebrew *'emet*, which John translates with *alētheia*, by no means an uncommon translation for the word in the LXX. The LXX rendering of this phrase in Exodus 34:6e is quite different. We may therefore conclude with great probability that John has translated direct from the Hebrew. When we look at the context of Exodus 34:6, we realize how very significant John's reference is. The verse itself occurs in the narrative of a theophany: God has undertaken to show himself partially to Moses, who is hidden in a cleft of the rock. When he does manifest himself, he proclaims his name and nature in this very verse. If we read back as far as 33:12, we shall see that Moses has asked for a vision of God's glory, which in this context means his true nature. John has therefore taken this supremely significant phrase from what was regarded as the narrative of the normative self-revelation of God in scripture, and has applied it to Jesus Christ. Very important indeed in this connection is John 1:18: 'No one has ever seen God; the only Son [or, a more likely reading in my opinion, 'the Only-begotten'], who is in the bosom of the Father, he has made him known.' In other words, John is actually claiming that he whom Moses saw revealed on Sinai was the pre-existent Word and that this Word has now been fully revealed in

Jesus Christ. For a full exposition of this argument see *The New Testament Interpretation of Scripture*, pp. 97–109.

2   In 1:51 Jesus is represented as making the startling claim: 'You will see the heaven opened, and the angels of God ascending and descending upon the Son of Man.' Practically all commentators agree that we have a reference here to Genesis 28 in which Jacob at Bethel has his famous vision of the ladder set up from earth to heaven and the angels ascending and descending on it. Nor can this be merely a literary allusion. On the contrary, only when we examine both what precedes this verse and the context of Jacob's vision in Genesis 28 can we understand what John is trying to convey by means of this scriptural allusion. Jacob, who had deceived his father in order to gain the blessing, receives the vision of God at Bethel; but he only recognizes that it is God whom he has seen when he wakes up; he exclaims: 'Surely the Lord is in this place; and I did not know it' (Gen. 28:16). In a similar way in John 1:31 (cf. also v. 33) John the Baptist is represented as saying: 'I myself did not know him', alluding to Christ. He goes on: 'But for this I came baptizing with water, that he might be revealed to Israel.' But the Bethel vision was a revelation of the Lord to Jacob–Israel. Moreover, when Nathanael first sees Jesus, Jesus exclaims: 'Behold, an Israelite indeed, in whom is no guile', and Nathanael responds by recognizing Jesus as the Son of God and the King of Israel (John 1:47, 49). Thus John the Baptist corresponds to the historical Jacob, who deceived his brother and did not recognize the Lord at first encounter; and Nathanael corresponds to ideal or true Israel ('an Israelite indeed') because in him is no guile and because he recognizes Jesus as Son of God at his first encounter with him. It follows therefore that in this elaborate piece of scriptural exegesis Jesus corresponds not to Jacob–Israel, as has often been asserted, but to the Lord who in Jacob's vision stood at the top of the ladder. On the other hand, the phrase 'Son of man' is normally employed by John to refer to the Word incarnate, so we are to understand that in the encounter with Jesus which is given to Nathanael the Lord is not content to remain in heaven as in Jacob's vision, but has descended to earth while still remaining the heavenly Son. We may also suggest that John knew the rabbinic tradition that the Bethel vision was an anticipation of the temple; he is therefore implying, as he does later in 4:22–4, that the incarnate Son is the true dwelling place of God where he is to be worshipped. For a full explication of this interpretation, with references to the views of commentators, see *The New Testament Interpretation of Scripture*, pp. 110–14. This is of course another passage in which an appearance of the pre-existent Word in scriptural history is

indicated. It is not at all surprising to find that some fifty years later Justin Martyr makes precisely the same claim about Jacob's vision at Bethel (see *Dialogue with Trypho* 58:15; 86:17).

3   In 5:35 we have another piece of christological interpretation of scripture. Jesus is represented as saying of the Baptist:

> He was a burning and shining lamp and you were willing to rejoice for a while in his light.

There is a slight but significant mistranslation of the Greek by the RSV here. It should be rendered: 'He was *the* burning and shining lamp.' What lamp? Why is the Baptist described in these terms, and why does John use the verb *agalliathēnai* for 'to rejoice' here, a word which strictly refers to festal joy? The answer is to be found by referring to two passages in scripture. The first is Exodus 27:20–1, where Moses is commanded to place a lamp (*luchnos* in the LXX, the same word as that used in John 5:35) 'in the tent of meeting, outside the veil which is before the testimony' and that it is to be kept burning continually (the same word is used in the LXX for 'burning' as is used in 5:35). Thus the lamp is to illuminate the way into the holy of holies where God's presence was believed to reside. The second passage is Psalm 132:16–17. This psalm is about God's choice of Zion as the place where he will dwell. In verse 14 we are told:

> This is my resting place for ever;
>   here will I dwell, for I have desired it. . .
> Her priests I will clothe with salvation,
>   and her saints will shout for joy.
> There I will make a horn to sprout for David;
>   I have prepared a lamp for my anointed.

(Ps. 132:14, 16–17; LXX 131:14, 16–17). The LXX translation of 'shout for joy' is *agalliasontai*, the same verb as we find in John 5:35; and in verse 17 the 'lamp' is *luchnos*, and of course '*my anointed*' is '*christos*'. An early Christian reading Psalm 131:17b in the LXX would have no difficulty in finding a prophecy of Christ here. This is what John has done. John the Baptist is the burning lamp which shows the way into the holy of holies, that is to Christ, who is the place where God dwells. The Baptist is a lamp for Christ, as David prophesied hundreds of years after Moses. The joy of the 'saints' is reflected in the joy with which the Baptist's mission was at first received, though no doubt the author of the Fourth Gospel would claim that the lasting joy belongs to Christians who recognize not only the lamp that shows the way to Christ but also Christ himself.

We should observe that here John has overstepped the bounds

of typology and lapsed into allegory. John the Baptist is not compared to a person in scripture, but to a thing. There is no integral connection between the Baptist and a lamp. We need hardly add that, as in the case of all the references to scripture which come under this category, there can be no question of this piece of scriptural interpretation going back to Jesus himself. John has no reservation about attributing to the historical Jesus interpretations of scripture which he has composed himself.

4 In John 8:39–40 Jesus is engaged in acrimonious dialogue with the Jews. He says to them:

> If you were Abraham's children, you would do what Abraham did, but now you seek to kill me, a man who has told you the truth which I heard from God; this is not what Abraham did.

We may legitimately draw the conclusion from this that Abraham did what the Jews do not do, that is, he believed the words of one who had come from God. Now in Genesis 18:1–15 this is precisely what Abraham is represented as doing. He is visited by three men, who tell him that he is to have a son by Sarah. He receives them with courtesy and addresses one of them as 'My Lord' (18:3). They prove in the event to be angels of God. It is not Abraham but Sarah who shows herself incredulous in 18:11–15. We read on in the Johannine narrative and we find that in 8:56 Jesus is represented as saying: 'Your father Abraham rejoiced that he was to see my day; he saw it and was glad.' There was a strong rabbinic tradition that on the occasion described in Genesis 18 Abraham was granted a vision of the whole future history of his descendants. But John says more than that: he says that Abraham saw Jesus' day. This is the way the Jews understand it, for they exclaim in 8:57: 'Have you seen Abraham?' (the alternative reading, 'Has Abraham seen you?' makes no difference to the argument). Jesus does not deny this, but goes on to make the astounding claim: 'Before Abraham was, I am' (8:58). When we put together the verses from chapter 8 which I have quoted here, we must surely draw the conclusion that, according to John, he whom Abraham saw at the oaks of Mamre was none other than the pre-existent Word. John no doubt believed that the angel whom Abraham addressed as 'My Lord' was the pre-existent Word. Perhaps he would have identified the other two figures as angels, though traditional Eastern Orthodox iconography loves to represent this scene as a visit to Abraham by the Holy Trinity. Perhaps nowhere does John's belief in the activity of the pre-existent Word in scriptural history come nearer to the surface of the Gospel than at this point. But we must conclude that here we are not in touch with Jesus' own interpretation, but with John's. The historical Jesus did not claim to remember the events of a pre-incarnate period.

Before we turn to the fifth and last of our categories, we should give some attention to two other examples of John's handling of scripture suggested by scholars. In John 11:52 John says of Jesus that he was destined to die in order 'to gather into one the children of God who are scattered abroad'. And in 17:21 Jesus is represented as saying 'that they all may be one', meaning all the present and future members of the Church. Dr Bruce Chilton (p. 292) suggests with much probability that this is a reference to Zechariah 14:9 where we are told that at the end time

> the Lord will become king over all the earth; on that day that Lord will be one and his name one.

The Targum, Chilton says, refers this prophecy to the Kingdom. So John has found one more christological prophecy in those chapters of Zechariah which were so popular with early Christians, and even (as we have suggested above, pp. 30, 35) with Jesus himself.

The other passage is the famous parable of the vine in John 15:1–6. Zarb (p. 117) claims that this is an actual citation of Ben Sira 24:17, where wisdom says of herself:

> Like a vine I caused loveliness to bud,
>   and my blossoms became glorious and abundant fruit.

We need not pause to consider Zarb's claim that this proves the canonical character of Ben Sira's work in John's eyes, because in fact we can find vine language in canonical scripture itself. We think of the song of the vineyard in Isaiah 5:1–7, and of Psalm 80:8: 'Thou didst bring a vine out of Egypt.' In such passages as these it is Israel who is the vine. But in John 15:1f. Jesus could well be presented as Israel, the true vine. His father is the vine-dresser, as 5:1f. and Psalm 80. The most that can be said for the passage from Ben Sira is that it may have made it easier for John to identify the pre-existent Word with the Father's vine. At any rate we certainly have vine typology here, though the way in which vine, vinedresser and branches are all carefully identified in the parable suggests that John is verging towards allegory. Jesus himself could compare his message to new wine. It was left to John much later to work out the analogy in christological detail.

5   We now turn to the last and most subtle of John's categories of scriptural interpretation: in certain places *the words of scripture can be shown to have influenced his narrative*. This is a form of scripture usage which is very unusual and is almost confined to the Fourth Gospel. In the sixth chapter of *The New Testament*

Interpretation of Scripture I give five examples, but I will confine myself here to three:

1 In 10:24, 11:41 and 12:13 John refers to or quotes Psalm 118. In 10:24-5 we learn that 'the Jews gathered round Jesus'. They challenge him to tell them plainly if he is the Christ, and he replies: 'The works that I do in my Father's name, they bear witness to me.' Now this seems to be reflecting Psalm 118:10 (LXX 117:11):

> All nations surrounded me;
> in the name of the Lord I cut them off.

The word for 'surrounded' is translated by the same verb in the LXX (*ekuklōsan*) as John in 10:24. Repelling one's opponents in the name of the Lord is also common to the two passages. Then at 11:41, when Jesus is about to raise Lazarus from the grave, he makes his prayer in the following words:

> Father, I thank thee that thou hast heard me.

This is a quotation of Psalm 118:21: 'I thank thee that thou hast answered me.' John does not exactly reproduce the LXX, but his rendering is just as faithful to the Hebrew. Thirdly, we have already observed John's use of Psalm 118:25-6 at 12:13, the triumphal entry (see above, p. 114). Why does John make this use of Psalm 118? The first two examples at any rate are extremely unobtrusive, for they have eluded the notice of commentators until today. It seems probable that he found in Psalm 118, a favourite psalm with early Christians, what he believed to be a sort of timetable for the passion narrative: it describes how the destined Messiah repels his opponents in the name of the Lord; how he called upon God in prayer and was answered; how he was for a brief moment recognized by the people. John incorporates these quotations into his narrative by way of showing in an unobtrusive way that all Jesus' career, and notably his passion, had been foretold in scripture.

2 In 11:11-13 a remarkable example of this technique is to be found. John echoes the LXX of Job 14:12-15. We can understand perhaps why John should have been attracted by this passage, because Job 14 discusses the possibility of God granting man life after death, though it dismisses such a possibility as a pipe-dream. However, the LXX translator has misunderstood the Hebrew and consequently produces a version which could give, to an early Christian at least, the impression that there is hope of a resurrection. Here is a translation of the LXX of Job 14:12-15a; as we read it we must bear in mind that the first two lines cited could be taken as a question, not a denial:

A man when he falls asleep will never arise . . .
   and they will not be wakened from their sleep.
I wish you would guard me in Hades,
   you would hide me until your wrath has ceased,
   and appoint me a time when you will remember me,
For if a man die he shall live
   having completed the days of his life;
   I will wait until I am born again.
Then you will call and I will obey you.

What this passage has in common with John 11:11–14 is the use
of the significant words *koimasthai*, meaning 'fall asleep', an early
Christian euphemism for death; and *exhupnizen*, meaning 'to
awaken'. John would regard this passage in Job as being a
prophecy both of the raising of Lazarus and of the Christian's
own resurrection. Indeed, the Lazarus story itself is used by him
partly as a pointer to the Christian's hope of life after death. The
penultimate line in the LXX refers to being born again, a form
of Christian language which John himself uses in 3:3f. The references to being hidden in Hades and then called would also fit in
well with the Lazarus narrative. For a more detailed exposition
of this passage see my article 'The Old Testament Background to
the Raising of Lazarus'.

3   A third example may probably be found in the remark of the
Pharisees recorded in 12:19 and Jesus' subsequent comment in
12:32. I suggest that this is influenced by Job 21:32–3. In 12:19
the Pharisees complain: 'Look, the world has gone after him' and
in 12:32 Jesus claims that

   I, when I am lifted up from the earth, will draw all men to
   myself.

The Job passage in its original context is a description of the
magnificent funeral which the rich man receives, but, as in Job
14, the LXX has misunderstood and mistranslated the Hebrew
and gives the following sense to 21:32b and 33b:

   And he lay awake on the bier. . .
   and every man shall go off after him.

This last line is very like John 12:19b. We must bear in mind that
the raising of Lazarus is mentioned in 12:9–10 in connection with
the number of people who believed in Jesus; and immediately
after the Pharisees' remark comes the passage in which the Greeks
seek to see Jesus. This in turn leads on to Jesus' declaration in
12:32 that by his crucifixion–resurrection he will draw all men to
him. John might therefore see in this Job passage a prophecy of
Jesus' death and resurrection and the accession of the Gentiles.

It is interesting that the correct translation of the Hebrew of Job 21:33b is 'he will draw all men after him', almost exactly what Jesus says in John 12:32. Could it be that John is taking advantage of both the Greek and the Hebrew versions of this line from Job? The Greek version expresses the matter from the point of view of unbelievers: all men, because of the raising of Lazarus, are going after Jesus. The Hebrew expresses the full truth as understood in John's day: the death and resurrection of Jesus are attracting all men into the church. But this is perhaps too speculative.

This fifth category is the most mysterious of all the ways in which John uses scripture. We can easily appreciate the fourth category. John may not expect all his readers to recognize his christological understanding of scripture, but once it is revealed we can follow his reasoning well enough. This fifth usage is different. Could John have expected anyone to have appreciated this usage? It seems unlikely. I think we must conclude that John employed this method primarily for his own satisfaction. He believed that scripture was full of inspired prophecies and types of Christ, some obvious, some deeply hidden. When he finds, as he sees it, some very subtle reference he does not go out of his way to underline it, but unobtrusively introduces it into his narrative, as if the use of the very words of scripture somehow confirms and illuminates what he has to say, even if the source of the illumination is largely hidden. This technique is almost unique in the New Testament though we can sometimes perhaps trace a similar practice in Paul (see *The New Testament Interpretation of Scripture*, p. 171). Can we find an analogy in Dante's use of Virgilian phraseology in the *Inferno*? Dante does not quote the *Aeneid* explicitly, but one can find frequent echoes. Both John and Dante are steeped in their respective authorities and both use the language of their authorities to strengthen and illuminate their own.

Before we attempt to sum up John's use of scripture, we ought to ask two more questions; the first is: does John use the typology of the * caqēdah*? The *caqēdah* is the name which the rabbis gave to the sacrifice of Isaac narrated in Genesis 22, literally 'the binding'. There is evidence that, at least in the period after the fall of Jerusalem in AD 70, the sacrifice of Isaac was accorded great atoning value in Jewish thought, and scholars have often suggested that the *caqēdah* has influenced the account which New Testament writers give of the value of Christ's atoning death. As far as John is concerned, the nearest he gets to any such suggestion is 3:16: 'For God so loved the world that he gave his only Son.' There may be a remote echo of Genesis 22 here, though the word for 'only-begotten' is not the same as that which the LXX uses in Genesis 22. But on the whole it seems unlikely that John uses the typology of the sacrifice of Isaac. Indeed, it must be confessed that the evidence for the influence of the *ca*qēdah in the New Testament as a whole is not very impressive. There seems indeed to be an echo of Genesis 22:16 in Romans 8:32, but it is not more than an echo. Generally Paul seems to avoid using the *ca*qēdah as a type. In Galatians 4:28–31 he uses the incident of the expulsion of Hagar which immediately precedes the story of the *ca*qēdah, and which was closely connected with it by the rabbis. But he does not go on to use it. The truth is that the *ca*qēdah would have spoiled his typological scheme. He wanted to use Abraham as the type of the Christian believer; to use him at the same time as the type of God the Father would have introduced intolerable confusion.

Even the two places in the New Testament where the *ca*qēdah is explicitly referred to are disappointing from the point of view of one who would argue for its influence on New Testament thought. In Hebrews 11:17–19 the *ca*qēdah is treated more as a type of the resurrection of Christ than of his atoning work and nothing is said about the value of the sacrifice. And James 2:21 uses it as an example of Abraham being justified by works rather than making any use of it in order to illuminate the quality of Jesus' death. We may very well conclude therefore that the *ca*qēdah, whether or not it played a big part in Jewish thought during the first century of our era, has not left very much impression upon the New Testament.

The second question concerns John's ability in Hebrew. Was he able, as Paul certainly was, to consult the Hebrew text if he wished to? It seems very probable indeed. I have already suggested (see p. 122 above) that he translated Exodus 34:6d for himself directly from the Hebrew, and have even hinted that he may have consulted the Hebrew of Job 21:33b. Waard (pp. 65–7) believes that John in 13:18 has translated Psalm 41:10b directly from the Hebrew. Certainly his version: 'He who ate my bread has lifted his heel against me' is much closer to the Hebrew than is the LXX (Ps. 40:10b): 'He who eats my loaves has increased his deceit against me.' We may therefore reasonably conclude that John did know Hebrew and did consult the Hebrew text of scripture on occasion. This is the third New Testament writer who has proved himself able to do this (Paul and the author of the First Gospel are the other two). There is one more still to come.

As we review John's technique in using scripture, we must concede that he is as much a master as is Paul, and perhaps more of a master than Matthew. As well as the generally accepted scripture texts, he can find his own and expound them with great conviction. He is well versed in traditional Jewish exegesis; but he can also search the scriptures for himself. Above all we must admire his christological use of scripture. His use of the great revelation to Moses narrated in Exodus 34, his handling of Jacob's vision in Genesis 28, his application of the visit of the three angels to Abraham at the oaks of Mamre in Genesis 18, all show that he was deeply versed in the most thoroughgoing New Testament interpretation of the great turning points of scripture in terms of Christ; that he stood squarely in that interpretation of the pre-existent Christ as active in Israel's history which he shared with Hebrews and Paul; and that he saw all this not in any exclusively messianic sense, but in terms of God's revelation of himself to mankind. Indeed, one might almost say that John, coming at the end of the christological development of the first century, had outgrown the purely messianic understanding of Jesus. By his use of scripture, he presents Jesus as God's decisive revelation of himself to the world. He has taken Jesus out of Judaism and he would like to take the Jewish scriptures out of Judaism also, and make them over to the Christian church.

At the same time one cannot suppress certain doubts and mis-givings about John's use of scripture. In a sense he is too subtle, too ready to find Christ anywhere and everywhere in scripture. If a christological reference can be found in Exodus 27:20–21 and in Job 21:33, it can be found anywhere. We have already noted that John is tending to turn typology into allegory. Both Paul and Hebrews were somewhat tentative in putting forward their doctrine of the pre-existent Christ active in Israel's history. Not so John. He is ready to find the pre-existent Christ everywhere. This prepared the way for the grossly exaggerated christological exegesis of the Jewish scriptures which we find in Justin's *Dialogue with Trypho*, and to the indiscriminate allegorizing of what was by that time regarded as the Old Testament by the later fathers. But there is another danger also: in John the Word seems to be the visibility of the Father. Not only so but his audibility also (see 5:37), and indeed his apprehensibility. Pushed to an extreme, this doctrine of revelation could end in the concept of an utterly transcendent, unknowable Father mediated by a Word or Son who is adapted to sublunary conditions – and who is therefore by nature different from the Father and ontologically inferior to him. Not that John ever reached this point. On the contrary, he is constantly aware of the need to emphasize that the Father really is revealed by means of the Son; cf. 1:18; 14:6–10. But in other hands the doctrine, probably held by John, that the Son is the apprehensibility of the Father, could lead to strongly subordina-tionist conclusions. It did so lead in Arianism, and it is significant that the Arians ardently embraced the notion of the pre-existent activity of the Word in Israel's history. The Word, they said, had been visible, audible, tangible within our sensible world, and hence must be ontologically inferior to the suprasensible Father. This enthusiasm on the part of the Arians explains why the post-Nicene orthodox fathers make so little use of the doctrine of christophanies in what they regarded as the Old Testament.

Hence we may well conclude that the Fourth Gospel has gone far enough in exploiting the possibilities of the traditional early Christian interpretation of scripture. Magnificent though John's grasp of scripture is, however impressive be his deeply christocentric approach to the great central themes of the bible, his interpretation as a whole perhaps strikes us as over-ripe; he is verging just a little too close to Philo in his methods. We may well be grateful that John represents the *ne plus ultra* of the New Testament interpretation of scripture.

The brief letters called 2 John and 3 John, like Paul's letter to Philemon, are too personal and too limited in scope to afford any room for scriptural exegesis. 1 John is also strangely bare of scriptural references. If Raymond Brown is right in his hypothesis that the Johannine Epistles are written by a successor to the author of the Fourth Gospel, but a member of the same school, then he did not share his master's deep interest in scripture. One or two references, however, can be traced. In *Studies in the Pastoral Epistles* (pp. 91–6) I suggested that parts of 1 John 1:7—2:9 were based on Psalm 130. And Le Déaut believes that he has found a treatment of a traditional theme in scripture which the author of 1 John has inherited from his master. Le Déaut points out that in John 8:44 the devil is called 'a murderer from the beginning' and that this theme is elaborated in 1 John 3:8–12 which contains the sentence: 'We should love one another and not be like Cain who was of the evil one and murdered his brother.' This probably reflects the traditional belief, to be found in some parts of the intertestamental literature, that Cain was not the son of Adam, but was born of a union between the serpent (i.e. Satan) and Eve. See R. Le Déaut, *The Message of the New Testament and the Aramaic Bible*, pp. 41–2.

7

THE USE OF SCRIPTURE IN THE PASTORAL EPISTLES AND THE CATHOLIC EPISTLES

In this chapter we shall be dealing with a rather miscellaneous collection of documents. What they all have in common is that they seem to have been written towards the end of the New Testament period. It is true that there are still to be found reputable scholars who defend the Pauline authorship of the Pastoral Epistles, and also those who believe that the Epistle of James is a very primitive Christian document, not to mention those who believe that St Peter wrote the First Epistle of Peter. But they are definitely the minority among informed students of the New Testament. The decision to group all these writings together as belonging to the latter half of the first century AD has not been taken merely by way of bowing to a majority view, but because I am convinced that they were actually composed during that period. The order in which I discuss them in this chapter is not to be taken as strictly chronological. It may be, for instance, that James was written before the Pastoral Epistles. Having once grouped them as among the later writings, I am content to deal with them according to my own convenience.

The Pastoral Epistles

In my commentary on the Pastoral Epistles (New Century Bible 1982) I have explained in full why I do not regard these three documents as being authentically Pauline at all. Certainly if one rejects the Pauline authorship of most of Colossians and of all of Ephesians, one would be in a peculiar position if one then accepted the Pauline authorship of the Pastorals, for they are much more unlike the authentic Paul than is either Colossians or Ephesians. I take them to have been written in Asia Minor very early in the second century (before the letters of Ignatius of Antioch) by an admirer of Paul who had access to some genuine historical tradition about Paul and who knew most of the authentic Pauline letters, but who had no other direct connection with Pauline teaching. The question of the historical tradition does not affect our estimate of the author's use of scripture. In my exposition I am following the lines of an article of mine that was published in *Irish Biblical Studies*, autumn 1981.

The composition of the Pastorals is quite unlike what we meet in an authentic Pauline Epistle. In the latter we have one work written by one person, using scripture consciously for his own purposes. Paul may quote liturgical material from his church tradition (e.g. Phil. 2:6–11 and cf. Col. 1:15–20) but he does so deliberately, with full knowledge of what the quotation contains. The author of the Pastorals, on the other hand, is much more a compiler than an original author. He draws his materials from many different sources; we can find in his three 'letters' extracts from liturgical prayers, references to church rules, perhaps scraps of homilies, certainly fragments of Christian hymns, some quotations from credal formulae. He was not a creative theologian like Paul, but rather a church leader who wished to use all the material at his disposal in order to attain his great aim, the instruction of contemporary church leaders in how to deal with the false teaching (probably incipent Gnosticism) with which they were faced. We must always ask, therefore, when we find a scriptural reference in the Pastorals, whether it is made directly by the author himself from scripture, or whether it is part of material which he has taken from some other source; and if the latter be the case, whether he was aware that he was using scriptural material.

For purposes of convenience in exposition we will divide scriptural references in the Pastorals into four categories:

1   *Unconscious quotations:* these are passages where the author is using a source which contains scriptural references of which he is not apparently aware. I shall give two instances of these. The first occurs in 1 Timothy 2:5:

> For there is one God, and there is one mediator between God and men, the man Christ Jesus.

This is in all probability a credal formula, in use perhaps in the author's church. I have argued in *Studies in the Pastoral Epistles*, pp. 56–64 that this passage was originally based on Job 9:32–3 in the LXX. This is my rendering of the LXX of this passage:

> For thou art not a man like me to whom I might reply,
>   that we might come together to judgement.
> I wish there were our mediator and reprover
> And one to hear the case between us both.

The Job passage is the famous one in which Job wishes that there might be an umpire between himself and God, for he is confident that an impartial umpire must decide in his favour. But the LXX, as we have so often noticed before, gives the Hebrew a distinctly

Christian flavour by using the word *mesitēs* ('mediator'), and calling him 'our mediator', as if Job were speaking on behalf of mankind. What the LXX passage has in common with 1 Timothy 2:5 is the use of the very significant word *mesitēs* and the statement that God is not a man, with the implication perhaps for an early Christian that the mediator would be a man. I do not suggest that the author of the Pastorals was aware of the scriptural origin of his quotation; but I believe that the credal formula is based on the LXX of this passage from Job.

The second passage comes from 1 Timothy 3:15, where 'the church of the living God' is described as 'the pillar and bulwark of the truth'. I believe in fact that we have a mistranslation here, and that the word rendered 'bulwark' (*hedraiōma*) should be translated 'foundation'. It is an unusual word. This is its first appearance in extant Greek literature. But a cognate word, *hedrasma*, occurs in some manuscripts of the LXX of 1 Kings 8:13 (in the LXX it appears as 3 Kingdoms 8:53a). The passage in 1 Kings 8 describes the dedication of the temple by Solomon; verse 13 runs in the RSV:

> I have built thee an exalted house, a place for thee to dwell in for ever.

In some manuscripts of the LXX 'the place' is translated by *hedrasma*. We must conclude therefore that the correct translation of 1 Timothy 3:15c is 'the pillar and foundation of the truth'. But verse 15a has just described the church as 'the household of God'. We have therefore in this passage references to the church as 'house of God', 'pillar of the truth' and 'foundation of truth'. All these figures can be found in the description of the consecration of the temple in 1 Kings 8: Solomon says he has built a *house* for God, it is described (in some Greek manuscripts at any rate) as a 'foundation', and in 8:10–11 we learn that at the dedication 'a cloud filled the house . . . so that the priests could not stand to minister because of the cloud; for the glory of the Lord filled the house of the Lord'. This was the sign of God's presence, which elsewhere in scripture is described as the *pillar* of cloud. In the context in 1 Timothy 3:15 all these references must have originally be intended to mean that under the Christian dispensation the place of God's dwelling, where his presence was to be found, was no longer a building but a community, the community of the Messiah. We have met this doctrine already in the Fourth Gospel (see above, pp. 123–4). It is also interesting to observe that a similar idea occurs in the Qumran documents, where the community is described as 'a foundation of truth', precisely the same phrase as we have here (1 QS 5:5f.).

Now it is not to be supposed that our author was aware of the

scriptural background to the words he is using. He has taken them
no doubt from some source accessible to him, probably liturgical,
and has incorporated them into his 'letter' in order to add dignity
and solemnity, much as he has included the Christian hymn which
immediately follows. It is most instructive, however, to unravel
these phrases and to learn from them of how early Christians could
interpret even 'the former prophets' in a christological sense.

2   *Deliberate citations of scripture:* our author is quite capable of
quoting scripture on his own initiative. Here is an example from
1 Timothy 5:18–19:

> For the scripture says, 'You shall not muzzle an ox when it is
> treading out the grain', and 'The labourer deserves his wages'.
> Never admit any charge against an elder except on the evidence
> of two or three witnesses.

In the first verse we have a citation of Deuteronomy 25:4. But by
the time of our author this had become a standard text for justi-
fying the remuneration of the clergy. Paul uses it in 1 Corinthians
9:9 (see p. 51 above). It is technically allegory, for there is no
integral connection between a clergyman and an ox; but no doubt
the text had become so well worn that nobody stopped to ask
whether it was allegory or not. The same might well be said of
the third text quoted here, the one about the need for more than
one witness. It comes from Deuteronomy 17:6; 19:15, and is often
referred to in the New Testament; cf. Matthew 18:16; John 8:17;
2 Corinthians 13:1; Hebrews 10:28. What is surprising is the citation of a dominical precept between two scriptural references (see
Luke 10:7; Matt. 10:10). It shows that some collections of sayings
of Jesus, even perhaps some of our Gospels, were already beginning to be regarded as scripture.

   For the other two explicit citations we must turn to 2 Timothy
2:19:

> But God's firm foundation stands, bearing this seal: The Lord
> knows those who are his', and, 'Let everyone who names the
> name of the Lord depart from iniquity'.

We should notice the context in which this double citation occurs:
the author has been writing about the teachers of erroneous
doctrine. He is particularly troubled by the fact that they have
arisen from the very bosom of the church; they are apparently
baptized Christians in good standing. Moreover, by way of adding
authority to the way he handles this theme, he is modelling himself
on a passage in Romans 9, in which Paul discusses an analogous
question: why have the majority of Jews, who are God's people,
failed to recognize Jesus as Christ? Paul uses the figure of a potter

who makes various vessels for various purposes, and our author
adopts the same figure, though he does not use it exactly as Paul
does. He wishes to say *both* that God alone knows who will remain
faithful and attain salvation *and* that it is always possible for
someone who has erred to reform himself and return to the fold.
In order to do this he employs two sentences from scripture. The
first is clear enough: it comes from Numbers 16:5, which forms
part of the story of the revolt of Dathan and Abiram against the
authority of Moses and Aaron. In the Hebrew the sense is that
the Lord will show who are his, by ruthlessly destroying the rebels.
Our author follows the LXX, which merely indicates that God
knows who are his. We can see how appropriate this quotation
would be to our author's purpose: it would associate the teachers
of error with the rebels who perished miserably by God's miraculous intervention.

The second citation is more doubtful: it seems to be a conflation
of Isaiah 52:11 and an echo of Leviticus 24:16. The Isaiah passage
runs:

> Depart, depart, go out thence,
>   touch no unclean thing,
> Go out from the midst of her, purify yourselves,
>   you who bear the vessels of the Lord.

There are several verbal echoes of the LXX of this verse in the
passage from 2 Timothy 2. The reference to naming the name of
the Lord may be an echo of Leviticus 24:16, which runs in the
LXX: 'He who names the name of the Lord shall be put to death.'
Admittedly this is just the opposite of what our author means,
but the quotation may originally have been intended to contrast
the old dispensation, under which uttering the sacred name was
a capital offence, with the new epoch, in which Christians, far
from concealing the name of the Lord, are publicly associated
with it in baptism. I say 'originally' because I do not think that
our author found these quotations for himself in scripture. It
seems more likely that he received them as part of material originally used in a baptismal context. They would fit well into this:
the citation of Numbers 16:5 would point to the objective side of
baptism, what God does for us. The other two citations would
underline the effort that must be made by the person baptized
and the privilege involved.

3   *Use of haggada:* our author can use *haggada* in a fairly conventional way. One instance occurs in 1 Timothy 2:12–15:

> I permit no woman to teach or to have authority over men; she
> is to keep silent. For Adam was formed first, then Eve; and
> Adam was not deceived, but the woman was deceived and

became a transgressor. Yet women will be saved through bearing children.

Our author is using the same piece of *haggada* as we have already noted in Paul (see above, p. 45). The legend was that the serpent actually seduced Eve. But there is a marked difference in the way in which the two New Testament writers use the same tradition. Paul merely uses it as an illustration and makes no theological capital out of it. Our author on the other hand draws from this piece of unscriptural embroidery important conclusions about women's status in the church, and even introduces the most unPauline idea that women can attain salvation by means of childbearing.

The other example of the use of *haggada* is found in 2 Timothy 3:8:

As Jannes and Jambres opposed Moses, so these men also oppose the truth.

Jannes and Jambres are legendary figures, not found in scripture, who were among the magicians of Egypt. It will be remembered that when Moses began to alarm Pharaoh by means of a succession of miraculous plagues, the magicians are represented as attempting to rival him in miracle-mongering. The earliest reference to them by name comes in the Qumran documents (CD 5:19), where there is a mention of 'Jannes and his brother'. It looks as if the brother had not yet acquired a name at that stage. In fact his name is probably an assimilation of the Hebrew *mamrey*, which means 'the opposer', originally an epithet of Jannes. The brother was no doubt needed as a second 'baddy' to correspond to Aaron. In later rabbinic tradition the legend was greatly elaborated. Our author employs them as useful figures of evil with which to associate the false teachers, implying that they are opposing divinely authorized church leadership. The reference is interesting evidence that he had access to Jewish exegetical tradition independently of his model, Paul.

4   *The use of scripture to provide a structure for narrative:* several examples of this could be quoted, but we will confine ourselves to two: *2 Timothy 4:16–18* and *Psalm 22:* Lock, followed by Spicq, has claimed that in his account of Paul's trial the author has been influenced by the wording of Psalm 22. If we put the words from 2 Timothy parallel with the LXX version of Psalm 22 (where it is numbered as Psalm 21), we can see the resemblance:

2 Timothy 4:16–18	*Psalm 22*
All left me, but the Lord stood by me.	Why did you leave me? Do not depart from me.

And all the nations will hear.	All the tribes of the earth will worship before you.
I was delivered from the lion's mouth.	Save me from the lion's mouth.
The Lord will deliver me from every evil work.	A group of evil-doers surrounded me.

It seems probable therefore that the author regarded the words of Psalm 22 as suitable for describing Paul's ordeals. If so, he has departed from his master's rule: Paul would have regarded Psalm 22 as applicable primarily to Christ, and only to Christ's servants in as far as they were 'in Christ'.

1 Timothy 2:3–5 and Isaiah 45:21–2
We have already cited the passage from 1 Timothy 2 and described it as containing a credal formula. But we will reproduce it again in order to make this point clear:

This is good, and it is acceptable in the sight of God our Saviour, who desires all men to be saved and to come to the knowledge of the truth. For there is one God, and there is one mediator between God and men, the man Christ Jesus.

The passage in Isaiah by which these lines may be inspired runs thus, translated literally from the LXX (Isa. 45:22b–23):

I am God, and there is none other apart from me; there is none righteous and a saviour except me. Turn to me and be saved, you are from the end of the earth; I am God, and there is none other.

These two passages have in common the description of God as Saviour, the emphasis on the universality of God's salvation, and a proclamation of the unity of God. If scholars are right in assuming that 1 Timothy 2:5 is a credal formula taken by the author from his tradition, then verses 3–4 will be the author's own composition, inspired by the passage from Isaiah 45 which in its turn may originally have interested him because of its link with the credal formula beginning 'there is one God'. If this reconstruction is correct, we see our author here using scripture quite effectively, very much in the way in which Paul used it on occasion.

One could spend more time on the author of the Pastorals. It would, for example, be interesting to explore how far he lives up to his own standards of scripture study as he sets them out in 2 Timothy 3:16, where he says that scripture is 'profitable for reproof, for correction and for training in righteousness'. But we cannot spare space in this work for such an investigation. We must be content with the verdict that the author of the Pastorals, though not nearly as profound as Paul in his handling of scripture, is by no means a novice. He can go direct to scripture for his theology and exposition; he resists the temptation to hold up scripture characters as models for Christian behaviour, as Clement of Rome all too frequently does. Among his contemporaries in the very beginning of the second century he must be rated as a competent handler of scripture.

The First Epistle of Peter

In this brief writing, scripture is constantly referred to. For the author, scripture was the source of much of his theology. As Goppelt says (p. 55), it is by the help of scripture that he understands the Christian message. Besides explicit citation of scripture, which is very frequent, he has echoes and allusions. He nearly always quotes scripture from the LXX and shows no knowledge of the Hebrew. He is almost unique among New Testament writers in one respect: he speculates as to how the prophets of old came to utter their prophecies. See 1:10–12:

> The prophets who prophesied of the grace that was to be yours searched and inquired about this salvation; they inquired what person or time was indicated by the Spirit of Christ within them, when predicting the sufferings of Christ and the subsequent glory. It was revealed to them that they were serving not themselves but you.

We have already noted rabbinic speculation about the extent to which the prophets knew about the fulfilment of their own prophecies (see p. 24 above), and the Qumran sectaries show a similar interest (referred to at p. 16 above). We may dismiss at once E. G. Selwyn's claim that the prophets spoken of here are Christian prophets. He published his commentary on 1 Peter in 1946, too early for him to have known the Qumran Commentary on Habakkuk in which the reference to prophetic inspiration occurs. But Selwyn did have the insight to give a cross-reference to Hababbuk 2:1–4, the passage which inspired the Qumran comment. It runs like this in the LXX:

> I shall stand on my watch and mount a crag and keep on looking out to see what he will speak in me and what I shall answer to my accusation. And the Lord answered me and said: 'Write the vision and (write it) clearly on a tablet, in order that he who reads it may overtake [Heb. 'that he may run who reads it']. Because the vision is yet for a season, and it will rise to a conclusion, and it will not be in vain. If it delays, wait for it, for a Coming One will come and will not tarry. If he draws back, my soul will have no pleasure in him. But the Righteous One shall live by my faith.

Here the prophet is behaving very much as the prophets are described as behaving in 1 Peter 1:10–12: he is searching and seeking for an answer, and when the answer comes it tells him that he must wait for the fulfilment of his prophecies until the Coming One, who is of course understood as the Messiah, shall arrive. The prophet is commanded to write his message down, and in the LXX, rendering the Hebrew literally, he is represented as expecting God to speak in him. The Habakkuk passage is quoted elsewhere in the New Testament; see Galatians 3:11; Romans 1:17; Hebrews 10:38.

We may safely conclude therefore that when the author of 1 Peter writes of the Spirit of Christ as speaking within the prophets of old in order to indicate beforehand the crucial events of Christ's career, he means that the pre-existent Christ inspired them to utter these things. It is true that in the whole of the rest of the New Testament, as in contemporary Jewish literature, it is the Holy Spirit who speaks by the prophets, but our author would not necessarily distinguish between the Spirit of Christ and the Holy Spirit, least of all during the period before the incarnation. So we have here an interesting account of the rationale of inspired prophecy. This is the nearest the author of 1 Peter comes to constructing for himself a midrash on scripture. It is in line with what Paul believed, though perhaps Paul would have contended that the greatest of the prophets, among whom he would number Moses and Isaiah, had an even clearer vision of the future than that which they are allowed in 1 Peter.

Next we should observe that our author lays great stress on Jesus as the fulfilment of the fourth servant song in Isaiah 52:13—53:12. We first meet an echo of the song in 1:19, where there is a reference to 'the precious blood of Christ, like that of a lamb without blemish or spot'. This in itself might refer to the daily offering of a lamb in the temple, or even to the passover lamb. But the ensuing citation in 2:22–5 makes it clear that he has the servant of Isaiah 53 in mind, who is compared in 53:7 to a lamb that is led to the slaughter. In 2:22–5 our author recalls in quick succession Isaiah 53:9 (Jesus' innocence), 53:4–5 (his vicarious sufferings), and 53:6 (we had gone astray like sheep). For so short a writing, the emphasis on Jesus' fulfilment of the prophecy in Isaiah 52—3 is remarkable. Indeed, it provides him with his theology of the atonement.

The author also makes use of some of the other traditional christological texts; thus in 2:6–8 he quotes Isaiah 28:16, the well-known text about the precious foundation stone; Psalm 118:22, the text of the rejected stone becoming the head of the corner; and Isaiah 8:14 about the stone of stumbling. It looks as if our author had access to a catena of 'stone' texts. We might also add

Hosea 2:23, which he quotes in 2:10. This is also quoted by Paul in Romans 9:25–7. It concerns the calling into the people of God of those who formerly were not the people of God.

This last is a citation about the church, and this brings us to another notable feature of 1 Peter: the author unhesitatingly applies to the Christian church scriptural phrases which in the original were used of Israel. This is all to be found within the brief passage which we have been referring to, 2:1–10, where we can find a whole theology of the church drawn from scripture. He begins in verses 4–5 with an extension of the 'rejected stone' theme from Psalm 118:22; Christians also are to be stones built up into a spiritual house for the use of a holy priesthood. This concept of all Israel being priests is found in Exodus 19:6: 'You shall be to me a kingdom of priests, a holy nation', and also in Isaiah 61:6: 'You shall be called the priests of the Lord.' The author of 1 Peter clearly indicates what we are to do as priests; we are to offer 'spiritual sacrifices acceptable to God through Jesus Christ'. In other words, our priestly offering consists of ourselves, very much in line with Romans 12:1, where Paul urges the Christians in Rome to 'present your bodies as a living sacrifice, holy and acceptable to God, which is your spiritual worship'.

But our author is not content with this one allusion. In 2:9 he returns to his theme with a glittering cascade of phrases lifted from scripture (where they refer to Israel) and applied direct to the Christian church. Christians are 'a chosen race'. This comes from Isaiah 43:20, where God describes in those terms the exiles who are to be miraculously led back to Jerusalem. Christians are next called 'a royal priesthood'. This phrase is the LXX rendering of the Hebrew original, which means 'a kingdom of priests'. It does not imply that the Israelites themselves were kings, and it is unlikely that this is what is meant in 1 Peter. In Revelation 1:6, 5:10, similar language is used, but there it is 'a kingdom, and priests'. In Revelation 20:6, however, those who have part in the first resurrection are promised that they will be priests and will reign with Christ for a thousand years. Probably we are to understand that we are now a kingdom of priests, but our reigning is only to be expected at the parousia. Then comes the phrase 'a holy nation', which brings us back again to Exodus 19:6: 'You shall be to me a kingdom of priests and a holy nation.' This is followed by the words 'God's own people' (the RSV mg is more accurate with 'a people for his possession'), 'that you may declare the wonderful deeds of him who called you out of darkness'. This is another citation from Isaiah 43:21, continuing the quotation with which this catena began: 'The people whom I formed for myself that they might declare my praise.' This accurately renders the Hebrew, but the LXX, which our author follows here, has 'my people whom I won for myself in order to recount my mighty deeds'. This suits our author's intention very well, since he means that Christians ought to proclaim the mighty deeds of God's salvation brought about in Christ. Indeed, one is tempted to read into this a eucharistic reference: the kernel of the spoken part of the early Christian Eucharist was the thanksgiving prayer, in which the celebrant recounted with thanksgiving all God's mighty acts in Christ, from the creation of the world by the agency of the Word, right through to the giving of the Spirit and the calling into being of the church. Thus our author in these densely packed ten verses has clothed the Christian church in all the attributes and responsibilities of Israel of old, and has extended salvation history to cover not only the history of Israel but also God's culminating action for salvation in Jesus Christ. This is surely a brilliantly successful use of scripture in a christological sense.

Our author can also use scriptural typology. Goppelt (p. 55) claims that there is an Exodus typology implicit in 1:13, 'gird up your minds', presumably on the analogy of the Israelites celebrating the Passover, who were to have their loins girt ready for a journey. Similarly in 2:11 Christians are described as 'aliens and exiles' in the world, reminiscent perhaps of Israel's status in Egypt. But these are faint indications compared with the very specific typology which we meet in 3:20–21. The author makes a mysterious reference to 'the spirits in prison', by which he seems to mean those, whether men or angels, who lived and died before the coming of Jesus Christ, and he describes them as those 'who formerly did not obey, when God's patience waited in the days of Noah, during the building of the ark, in which a few, that is, eight persons, were saved through water. Baptism, which corresponds to this, now saves you. . .' The RSV has had to make a choice among various possible translations of the Greek, which is literally: 'which also as an antitype now saves you, baptism'. As Selwyn points out, antitype could refer to either the type or its fulfilment. One could translate either '. . . saved through water, which as type now saves us in the (fulfilled) form of baptism'. Or 'water, which now saves us in the form of a fulfilled type, baptism'. The word *antitupos* is used as an adjective in Hebrews 9:24 applied to the furniture of the tabernacle which is regarded as foreshadowing the true sanctuary into which Christ as high priest has entered. On the whole it seems more likely that the RSV rendering is correct, and that our author is describing baptism as the antitype (i.e. fulfilling event) of the flood, which is regarded as a type. In any case we have a clear case of typology here: as Noah and his family attained (temporal) salvation by passing through the waters of the flood in the ark, so Christians may attain eternal salvation by means of the water of baptism.

But in fact a more complicated use of scripture seems to be behind this passage. The phrase in 1 Peter 4:1, 'whoever has suffered in the flesh has ceased from sin', has often been compared with a similar phrase in Romans 6:7, 'he who died is freed from sin'. This passage in Romans has much in common with 1 Peter 3:18—4:6: both are concerned with baptism, and with a death to sin; both associate the rite and the experience with Christ's death and resurrection. It has also been suggested that both passages are inspired by a number of verses in Psalm 88, where the psalmist describes himself as 'free among the dead', compares his enemies to waters engulfing him, and expresses hope in God's power to save. The conception of Christ visiting the dead during the triduum between the death on the cross and the resurrection may have been partly inspired by a christological interpretation of Psalm 88. The whole matter is discussed in detail in my *New Testament Interpretation of Scripture*, pp. 122–35. At any rate it seems likely that the author of 1 Peter is here reproducing a piece of early Christian tradition about the *descensus ad inferos*, which was itself originally based on a christological interpretation of scripture.

Our author does not show any marked acquaintance with Jewish *haggada*. He refers in 3:5–6 to the wives of the patriarchs as examples to be followed by Christian wives:

So once the holy women who hoped in God used to adorn themselves and were submissive to their husbands, as Sarah obeyed Abraham, calling him Lord.

Strictly speaking, this is not very true to the scriptural narratives. There is no particular suggestion in scripture that the wives of the patriarchs dressed modestly, and Sarah's addressing Abraham as 'my lord' was only conventional practice. But our author needs to find an example of good wifely behaviour in scripture and is therefore severely restricted in his scope. By his time, as we have seen, both the patriarchs and their wives had become stained-glass window figures (see above, p. 44). An excellent example of this occurs in Wisdom 10:10. Jacob, who had just disgracefully cheated his brother out of his father's blessing is described thus:

When a righteous man fled from his brother's wrath,
  she (wisdom) guided him on straight paths.

(See above, p. 48.) The Book of Wisdom was written many centuries after the events alleged to have taken place in Genesis 28; in the intervening period the patriarchs had become holy figures who could do no wrong. We do not need to conclude that the author of 1 Peter is relying on any haggadic tradition in 3:5–6. He is simply following out the consequences of looking for examples of Christian behaviour in a pre-Christian bible.

Finally we must remark that the author of 1 Peter, proportionally far more than Paul, uses scripture for simple illustration. Perhaps we should not use that word 'simple', for, as we shall see, his usage is not absolutely straightforward. We take four examples:

1 In 1:24 he quotes Isaiah 40:6–8. He compares the eternity of the word of God with the ephemeral nature of human life. This is essentially illustrative, but we may note two ways in which our author's use of this quotation differs from what we find in rabbinic exegesis. First, the *Targum on Isaiah* renders it 'all the wicked are as grass'. This is the meaning neither of the original author of Isaiah 40:6–8 nor of the author of 1 Peter, who has rightly divined that all humanity is contrasted with the eternity of God's word. Second, Jewish commentators are uncertain as to what exactly is the word of God. In the midrash on Psalm 119:25 (Braude (2) p. 259) the word is identified with the promise to Abraham in Genesis 28:14: 'Thy seed shall be as the dust of the earth', but at Psalm 119:89 (Braude (2) p. 271) it is interpreted as referring generally to God's decrees about human history. The author of 1 Peter, writing from a Christian point of view, has no doubts: the word is the gospel message concerning Jesus Christ.

2 In 3:10–12 our author gives a long citation from Psalm 34:13–16. It seems to have no particularly Christian significance at all: if we try to live a good life we shall be rewarded by prosperity. When the rabbis deal with this passage they identify 'doing good' (Ps. 34:14) with observing the Torah, as we would expect. See *Abodah Zarah* 19b. No doubt our author interpreted 'life' in Psalm 34:12 as eternal life, but then so did the rabbis. See *Midrash on Psalms*, 39:32, where 'life' is identified with life in the world-to-come (Braude (1) p. 431).

3 In 4:18 he quotes Proverbs 11:31:

> If the righteous man is scarcely saved,
>   where will the impious and sinner appear?

Our author here according to his custom quotes the LXX. The Hebrew does not give this sense, but is thus translated in the RSV:

> If the righteous is requited on earth,
>   how much more the wicked and the sinner!

It is relevant to note that the Hebrew text in the first line is suspect. Some scholars wish to emend it so as to give the sense of the LXX. At any rate it is the LXX sense that our author requires: the Hebrew as it stands would not agree with his sentiment at all, for it claims that both righteous and unrighteous receive their deserts in this life, whereas he has the parousia in mind. In this respect we might well say that our author gives a Christian, or at least an eschatological, interpretation to this text from scripture. His easy assumption that the Christian believer can be identified with 'the righteous' as contrasted with 'the wicked' is most unPauline.

4   In 5:5 he quotes Proverbs 3:34:

God opposes the proud, but gives grace to the humble.

This is a purely illustrative usage, though it is in accord with the general Christian emphasis on humility, which itself stems from the humility of God manifested in Jesus Christ. The LXX, as so often happens, helps the Christian sense. The second half of the verse in Hebrew is rightly rendered by the RSV:

but to the humble he shows favour.

The LXX has translated the Hebrew *hen* with *charis*, the very general word used in the New Testament for the grace of God manifested in Christ. The same verse is quoted in James 4:6, to which we shall pay attention presently. As we review these four purely illustrative uses of scripture in 1 Peter, we may well endorse Beare's penetrating remark that our author's knowledge of scripture is literary rather than rabbinic (p. 27).

The author of 1 Peter, then, is a bold and creative handler of scripture. He has not got the profundity or insight of Paul, perhaps, but he can employ it to a very effective christological purpose; he is well acquainted with the standard christological texts and even when he uses it in a purely illustrative way, he shows that he uses it as a Christian rather than as someone who only calls on the Jewish tradition of exegesis.

Scripture in the Epistle of James

The Epistle of James is a mysterious work: it has been judged by some to be very early, by others to be comparatively late, in the New Testament period. It is written in relatively sophisticated Greek, but seems to have a very elementary Christology. The great problem is: why are there so few explicitly Christian features? However, for our purpose it is most profitable, since there is extensive use of scripture throughout the Epistle.

Nobody as far as I know has devoted an entire work to the use of scripture in James, and the following remarks are largely the result of my own rather sporadic researches. It will be seen that there is no shortage of material. I will restrict myself to eight passages in the letter:

1   1:25: 'He who looks into the perfect law, the law of liberty'. This appears to be an echo of Psalm 19:7: 'The law of the Lord is perfect, reviving the soul.' It is true that the LXX (where it is Ps. 18:8) does not have the word for 'perfect' which James uses, *teleios*. But this translation is found in Aquila's version, which, as we have seen, was based on a version current in New Testament times. Moreover, rabbinic comment suggests that James is here dealing with traditional material. The *Pesikta de Rab Kahana*, commenting on Psalm 19:8 (as it is numbered in the MT), has a piece of *haggada* to the effect that at the exodus God wanted to give the Torah to Israel, but the Torah is perfect and some in Israel were crippled, blind or deaf. He was unwilling to wait until the next generation grew up, so at Sinai he healed them all temporarily. He is represented as saying: 'As I make you new again, I show you a kind of earnest of the world to come' (Piska 12:19, 242). This reminds us of James 1:18, only a few verses earlier: 'Of his own will he brought us forth by the word of truth, that we might be a kind of first-fruits of his creatures.' The 'word of truth' here takes the place of the Torah, which appears by name, though modified in a Christian direction, in verse 25. It is a Christianizing of the midrash.

2   2:1–8 seems to offer a sort of commentary on Leviticus 19:12–18. We can draw up a table of parallels thus:

Leviticus	James
19:12: You shall not swear by my name falsely and so profane the name of your God.	2:7: Is it not they who blaspheme that honourable name by which you are called?
19:15: You shall do no injustice in judgement: you shall not be partial to the poor or defer to the great.	2:4: . . . have you not made distinctions among yourselves, and become judges with evil thoughts?
19:18: You shall love your neighbour as yourself.	2:8: You shall love your neighbour as yourself.

In James 2:9 we have 'But if you show partiality', where the verb is *prosōpolēmpteite*, an amalgamated form of the phrase used in the LXX of Leviticus 19:15 for 'be partial', *lēmpsei/ prosōpon*. James 2:8 of course explicitly quotes Leviticus 19:18.

3   2:21–5: the examples of the two scriptural characters are cited,

Abraham and Rahab. Abraham is of course well used as a significant figure from scripture by New Testament writers: we think of
Paul, Hebrews and John. It is usually assumed that James is here
indulging in covert polemic against Paul's citation of Abraham as
an example of faith in contrast to works, or at least with a later
misunderstanding of the Pauline teaching about Abraham. But it
is worth considering whether he may not have the Epistle to the
Hebrews in mind rather than Galatians or Romans. After all,
Hebrews quotes Abraham as an example of faith in 11:8–12, and
cites the example of Rahab, whom Paul ignores (see Heb. 11:31).
James's mention of Rahab is very interesting because she became,
in the intertestamental period and later, a subject of extensive
haggada. Josephus, who was probably an exact contemporary of
the author of James, says that Rahab knew about the coming
Israelite victory because she had been 'instructed by signs from
God' (*Ant.* v:2, 8). After the destruction of Jericho, she is
rewarded by lands from Joshua (7:30). In view of the later development of the legend, it seems likely that Josephus regarded
Rahab as a prophetess, gifted with a technique for discovering
the future. Rahab is referred to in Matthew's genealogy of Jesus
(Matt. 1:5) along with four other women, all of whom come as
exceptions in an otherwise all-male genealogy. The others are
Tamar, Ruth, Bathsheba and Mary the mother of Jesus. Probably
Matthew meant to imply that all of them have some special
circumstance that makes them significant. He makes Rahab the
mother of Boaz, who married Ruth and became the great-grand-
father of David. In Hebrews 11:31 it is Rahab's faith that is
emphasized; the author of Hebrews is probably claiming her as a
Christian by anticipation, as were all the other characters whom
he names in his roll-call of the heroes of the faith.

Immediately after James's time we have a reference in 1
Clement that shows a wide acquaintance with *haggada* about
Rahab. In 1 Clement 21:1 and 7–8 we learn that Rahab was saved
by her faith and her hospitality. The red cord which was given as
a sign indicated that there would be 'redemption by the blood of
the Lord for all who believed and put their hope in God', and he
describes Rahab as an example of prophecy as well as of faith.
Since he refers to her as a harlot, he probably regards her also as
an example of Christian penitence and conversion. It may well be
that he is aiming at reconciling the accounts of both Hebrews and
James, since he refers to her faith as well as to her works. In the
Talmud Rahab is presented as a remarkable character: she was
more profligate than any woman before her; she was converted
to belief in Israel's God; she married Joshua and became the
ancestress of various characters in later Israelite history, such as
Jeremiah and Ezekiel. She had herself the gift of prophecy.

James's reference to Rahab is quite modest compared with all the others which we have cited. He probably regarded her as an example of faith as well as works. How much of the *haggada* about her he knew we have no means of telling, but it is most unlikely that he knew nothing more than the narrative in Joshua chapters 2 and 6. A fuller account of the legend of Rahab, with references, will be found in my article 'Rahab the Harlot in Early Christian Tradition'.

4   In 3:6–8 James seems to be using traditional material about the dangers attending the use of the tongue: 'The tongue is a fire, the tongue is an unrighteous world among our members . . . no human being can tame the tongue – a restless evil, full of deadly poison.' We can find parallels in intertestamental and in rabbinic literature for much of this. In *The Books of Adam and Eve,* an intertestamental work already referred to (see above, p. 45), Eve is relating the story of her temptation by the serpent: 'And when he (the serpent) had received the oath from me, he went and poured upon the fruit the poison of his wickedness which is lust.' Here is a serpent with a tongue which deceives, and pours his deadly poison into others (see R. H. Charles, *Apocrypha and Pseudepigrapha of the Old Testament,* vol. ii). Again, in the *Midrash on Psalms,* 120:3 (Braude (2) pp. 290–91) God addresses the evil tongue and says: 'As a serpent thou spokest evil to Adam.' Even closer to James is a comment in the same passage attributed to Rabbi Jose ben Zimra. The tongue, he says, though imprisoned within the mouth, can do great damage: 'Yet no man can withstand it.' Both these phrases seem to be very similar to what we find in James. The RSV translation of 3:6b is perhaps misleading. A literal rendering would be: 'And the tongue is a fire, the world of iniquity, the tongue is established among our members.' Is this a hint of the rabbinic observation that though the tongue is fixed and hemmed in, it can do more damage than any other member of the body? And certainly Rabbi Jose's comment, 'No man can withstand it', is very like James's phrase, 'No human being can tame the tongue.' And James's 'a restless evil, full of deadly poison' would apply very well to Satan's activity in the temptation of Eve. We may therefore confidently conclude that James is using traditional Jewish paraenesis here. It is very remarkable that there seems to be no specifically Christian element in it at all.

5   In 3:18 James is offering us a midrash on Isaiah 32:15–17. The Isaiah passage runs:

> . . . until the Spirit is poured out upon us from on high,
>   and the wilderness becomes a fruitful field,
>   and the fruitful field is deemed a forest.

Then justice will dwell in the wilderness,
  and righteousness abide in the fruitful field.
And the effect of righteousness will be peace,
  and the result of righteousness quietness and trust for ever.

James might well take this as a prophecy of the end time. The
Spirit is to come from above (incidentally, this is an interesting
example of the identification of the Spirit with the divine wisdom,
for in 3:17 James writes of 'the wisdom from above'). The
Targum's rendering of the opening words of the Isaiah passage
emphasizes the connection between the Spirit and the Shᵉkinah:
'Until there come for us a Spirit from before him whose Shᵉkinah
is in the highest heavens.' It seems likely that the author of
Hebrews knew of this midrash also, for in Hebrews 12:11 we read:

> For the moment all discipline seems painful rather than plea-
> sant; later it yields the peaceful fruit of righteousness to those
> who have been trained by it.

Hebrews introduces two other themes into this midrash, holiness
and seeing God; see 12:14:

> Strive for peace with all men, and for the holiness without which
> no one will see the Lord.

James has this element of holiness, for in 3:17 he describes the
'wisdom from above' as 'pure'. The word is *hagnē*, which has the
connotation of separation and therefore holiness.
  Possibly a secondary scriptural source is Psalm 34:13–14:

> Keep your tongue from evil,
>   and your lips from speaking deceit.
> Depart from evil and do good,
>   seek peace and pursue it.

This psalm, as we have seen, is extensively quoted in 1 Peter
3:10–12. We have in James 3 first a passage on the importance of
controlling the tongue, and then a reference to peace. But when
we have these four passages before us, Isaiah 32:15–17; Psalm
34:13–14; Hebrews 12:7–14 and James 3:6–18, we can bring in a
fifth, Matthew 5:8–9:

> Blessed are the pure in heart, for they shall see God.
> Blessed are the peacemakers, for they shall be called the sons
>   of God.

This contains several of the elements we have noted in the other
passages, holiness, seeing God, making peace. The new feature,
'sons of God', is in fact present in the Hebrews passage: Hebrews
12:5–9 is all about Christians as sons of God and therefore being

obliged to accept God's fatherly discipline. We could draw up a
table of relationship between these five passages:

Isaiah 32:15–18
The Spirit from on high
peace and righteousness
agricultural reference

Hebrews 12:5–14
Father of Spirits,
  sonship
peace and righteousness
  seeing God
  holiness
agricultural metaphor

Matthew 5:8–9
  peace
  holiness
  seeing God
  sons of God
(v. 6: hungering and
  thirsting for
  righteousness)

James 3:6–18
divine wisdom from above
  it is holy
peace and righteousness
restraining tongue
agricultural metaphor

Psalm 34:13–14
(v. 11: Come, O sons, and listen to me)
  restraining the tongue
  peace

We may add that in rabbinic exegesis Isaiah 32:15–20 is freely
allegorized. See *Baba Bathra* 9a; *Aboth* (Mishna 7); *Baba Kamma*
17a; *Sifre zu Numeri* (ed. K. G. Kuhn as vol. 3 in *Tannaitische
Midraschim)*, 136. The New Testament treatment of the Isaiah
text implies that it had already been fairly thoroughly allegorized.

We must not draw unjustifiably dogmatic conclusions from this
evidence, but it is safe to say that James is giving us the elements
of an extensive midrash on Isaiah 32:15–20, supported perhaps by
Psalm 34:11–14. It was a midrash known to the author of Hebrews
and also to the author of the First Gospel. This in turn presents
us with the possibility that Jesus himself knew of the midrash and
indeed originated its use in the Christian church. If so, this would
not be the only place in which James seems to be using dominical
material without overt acknowledgement.

6   4:5–6: this has caused much trouble to scholars, since James
makes an explicit reference to scripture:

> Or do you suppose it is in vain that the scripture says 'He yearns
> jealously over the spirit which he has made to dwell in us'?

The difficulty is that this alleged quotation cannot be found in
scripture. We are not, however, reduced to Dibelius–Greeven's
conclusion that James is quoting from an unknown apocryphal

work, a device which is the bankruptcy of scholarship. It seems better to suppose that James is offering a loose paraphrase of Genesis 6:3–7; Genesis 6:3 runs: 'My spirit shall not abide in man for ever, for he is flesh.' The targums on this passage offer us various versions which more or less approximate to James's words. Thus the *Targum of Pseudo-Jonathan* has 'Have I not put in them my spirit of holiness, in order that they should accomplish good works? But behold, their works are evil' (see Le Déaut, translating Add. 27031, which is one of the major manuscripts of the *Targum of Pseudo-Jonathan*). Both this Targum and the *Targum of Palestine* emphasize that God does not intend to treat the generations after the flood with the same severity, and that Noah obtained grace from God not because he merited it, but as a special favour. The neofiti manuscript of the *Targum of Palestine* has 'But Noah, because there was no righteous man in (this) generation, found grace and mercy before Yahweh' (Le Déaut in loc.). What James has done to the text is to take the argument one step beyond what the Targum offers: the Targum says God has given his Spirit to men, but they have done evil deeds. James makes it say that God has given his Spirit to dwell in men, but in them it has turned into a spirit of jealousy. We must therefore ignore the RSV translation of James 4:5b and render it some such way as this:

The Spirit which dwells in us gives way to bitter jealousy.

This means, it is true, that James uses 'spirit' both of God's Spirit and of man's spirit, but we can find a partial parallel for this in the Qumran documents. P. Wernberg-Møller, in his edition of the *Manual of Discipline*, says of 1 QS 3:14f. (p. 67): 'There is no doubt that *RWH* ('spirit') in this essay is used in both a metaphysical and a psychological way, designating at the same time the principle of either good or evil *and* the individual spirit of every man.' Assuming that Genesis 6:5–8 does lie behind this passage, then James is using typology here: the crisis of the flood is a type of the crisis caused by the coming of Jesus Christ. In both situations God has mercy on those who turn to him.

If this is correct, then the ensuing citation of Proverbs 3:34 fits in very well. In the targumic account of Genesis 6:5–8 we had first a protest that man had corrupted the spirit that God gave him, then the example of Noah as one who received God's unmerited grace. The Proverbs quotation, as presented in the LXX version quoted by James, speaks of God giving grace to the humble. Indeed, James himself emphasizes this with his sentence in 3:6a: 'But he gives more grace.' This Proverbs passage is a favourite one with the early church: it is quoted, as we have seen in 1 Peter 5:5, and it also occurs in 1 Clement 30:2 and Ignatius

Eph. 5:3. James's has in common with 1 Peter an eschatological context, a warning against pride and a reference to the constant need to guard against the devil (cf. James 4:7 with 1 Peter 5:8). Both also exhort their readers to humble themselves before God. Clement also has a reference to the need to draw near to God, and to hold up to God hands unstained by sin. This is exactly the content of James 4:8. Ignatius, besides quoting Proverbs 3:34, merely urges his readers to be obedient to God (and not to resist the bishop!). Dibelius–Greeven comment: 'Evidently there is an underlying paraenetic schema of loosely connected admonitions which makes use of Proverbs 3:34' (my trans.).

Rabbinic comment on Proverbs 3:34 throws light on this midrash: in *Shabbath* 104a the verse is interpreted to mean that God will not prevent the wicked from going their own way, but will positively help those who try to resist evil. In James 4:8 we have annexed to the Proverbs citation an echo of Zechariah 1:3: 'Return to me, says the Lord of hosts, and I will return to you.' In *Pesikta Rabbati* this is explained thus: 'Consider the parable of a prince who was far away from his father – a hundred days journey away. His friends said to him: "Return to your father." He replied: "I cannot: I have not the strength." Thereupon the father sent word, saying to him: "Come back as far as you can according to your strength, and I will go the rest of the way to meet you." So the Holy One, blessed be he, says to Israel, *Return to me, and I will return to you*' (Piska 44:9; Braude (2) p. 779). We seem to have strayed into the orbit of the parable of the prodigal son. The Piska interprets the Zechariah passage in very much the same way as the passage in Proverbs was taken in the Talmud. It looks as if the two texts may have already been associated in a midrash when James used them. At any rate we may be sure that here once again we are encountering a midrash well known among early Christian writers, which James has reproduced, though we are only justified in attributing the reference to Genesis 6:5–8 to James himself.

7   Our last two passages are much more straightforward: in 5:11 James refers to Job:

> You have heard of the steadfastness of Job, and you have seen the purpose of the Lord, how the Lord is compassionate and merciful.

The word translated 'purpose' is *telos,* which probably means 'outcome' here: because Job bore his sufferings with steadfastness, he was eventually restored by God. In fact of course Job showed himself very far from steadfast, but James is commenting on the traditional picture of Job. His words 'the Lord is compassionate

and merciful' recall Exodus 34:6, where the famous theophany to
Moses on the rock is described. But James does not reproduce
the words of Exodus 34:6 exactly and certainly does not follow
the LXX. Is he perhaps comparing the theophany on the rock
with the theophany to Job in the whirlwind? If so, he is perhaps
suggesting that the revelation to Job must be interpreted in the
light of the normative revelation. This would be a profound implication, but we cannot be at all sure that it is intended. It is baffling
that, when he is looking for an example of suffering, patience and
steadfastness, he does not take that of Jesus as does the author
of 1 Peter.

8   In 5:16–18 James writes:

> The prayer of a righteous man has great power in its effects.
> Elijah was a man of like nature with ourselves, and he prayed
> fervently that it might not rain, and for three years and six
> months it did not rain on the earth. Then he prayed again, and
> the heaven gave rain, and the earth brought forth its fruit.

At first sight it looks as if this was a perfectly simple reference
with no extra-biblical embroidery implied. But in fact there is
haggada behind this reference. In the first place, the narrative of
1 Kings 17–18 does not say that Elijah prayed that there should
be a drought. It merely represents Elijah as declaring that 'there
shall be neither dew nor rain these years except by my word' (1
Kings 17:1). This probably means that Elijah in virtue of his
prophetic power knew when rain would come. It is true that
Ahab assumes that Elijah is responsible for the drought since he
addresses him as 'You troubler of Israel'. But Elijah responds by
accusing him of having troubled Israel, i.e. the drought is caused
by God's anger at the infidelities of Ahab and his family (1 Kings
18:17–18). So Elijah is not represented as having prayed for
drought. Similarly, it is not quite certain that he prayed for rain
either: he goes to the top of Carmel and engages in a mysterious
action of putting his face between his knees. In an earlier version
of the story this may well have been rainmaking magic; but in the
narrative in 1 Kings 18:42–6 he appears to be in a prophetic
ecstasy and to be rather foreseeing the rain than praying for it.
When the land had been cleansed by the slaughter of the prophets
of Baal the rain could once more fall. So James is following
haggada in describing Elijah as praying for both drought and rain.
   Secondly, the period of the drought specified by James, three
and a half years, is not mentioned in scripture. This too is the
product of *haggada* also found, incidentally, in Jesus' sermon in
the synagogue at Nazareth in Luke 4:25. Three and a half is
perhaps the traditional period for the prevalence of evil: during

the period of the Antiochean persecution three and a half years elapsed between the desecration of the temple by Epiphanes and its re-dedication by Judas Maccabaeus. Three and a half is half of the perfect number, seven.

Finally, Bottini suggests (p. 168) that James's whole account of intercessory prayer, which he is recommending to his readers, is inspired by the description of Solomon's prayer at the consecration of the temple in 1 Kings 8:35–6. He seems to have made out a good case for this theory.

James has shown himself very well versed in the scriptures and thoroughly in touch with the contemporary tradition of Jewish exegesis. On the whole he seems to regard scripture as useful chiefly for purposes of paraenesis and illustration. But he is not simply a Jewish commentator with Christian trimmings: his paraenesis is inspired by his belief in Christ for the most part and he does seem to be capable of elaborating typology. It is very probable that further research would unveil more scriptural and midrashic material in James. Perhaps this brief treatment may inspire someone else to give the subject the treatment it deserves.

The Use of Scripture in Jude and 2 Peter

We begin with two assumptions about these two writings, assumptions which we have not space to prove but which would be accepted by the majority of scholars: 2 Peter has made use of Jude and not vice versa. Secondly, both these writings are late; 2 Peter is probably the latest book in the New Testament to be written. It is surely not necessary in this day and age to labour the point that 2 Peter cannot possibly have been written by the apostle Peter.

Jude for all its brevity holds some surprises for us: he is the only writer in the New Testament explicitly to quote one non-canonical book and to refer to another. In verse 9 he appears to quote a book which in the form in which it has survived belongs to the second century after Christ, the *Assumption of Moses*. He mentions an episode, apparently narrated in it, in which Satan claims the body of Moses after his death, but he is withstood by the archangel Michael. We cannot be certain that this is a verbatim citation because this particular episode is missing from the version of the *Assumption of Moses* that we have, but it looks very like it. He also refers to a passage in the Book of Enoch, Enoch 1:9 (see Jude 14–15). The *Epistle of Barnabas*, which may well be contemporary with Jude, quotes the Book of Enoch and seems to regard it as scripture. Kelly points out that Jude has introduced 'the Lord' as the subject of the action in verse 14, which is not in the original, thereby giving the citation a messianic interpretation.

It is interesting that he uses only warning examples from scripture, thereby resembling the author of the Pastoral Epistles.

There is another surprising feature about Jude: he quite unostentatiously betrays a belief in the activity of the pre-existent Christ in Israel's history. In verse 5b the RSV offers:

He who saved a people out of the land of Egypt, afterwards destroyed those who did not believe.

It is perplexing that the RSV translators should give such a rendering, since they have chosen a reading that does not occur in any manuscript of the Greek New Testament. It is in fact what Westcott and Hort in their edition of the Greek text concluded must have been the original reading. Far more satisfactory is the reading given here in the Bible Societies' version: *Iēsous*. Jesus as the subject of the sentence is read by Codex Alexandrinus and Vaticanus, as well as by two other Greek uncials, some manuscripts of the Old Latin, by the Vulgate, the Ethiopic version and by Jerome. Other alternative readings give the same sense, e.g. *ho kurios*, 'the Lord', which must refer to Christ (a great many Greek uncials and some fathers). There is one most bizarre reading: *theos Christos*, 'God Christ' (which is verging on ditheism) is read by papyrus 72, a third- or fourth-century fragmentary papyrus. One hand in Claromontanus reads 'God', and Sinaiticus and an eighth–ninth-century codex from Mount Athos read *kurios*, 'Lord', which would indicate God rather than Christ. But by any normal canon of textual criticism we must prefer the reading 'Jesus', and only a sense of embarrassment at the strange theological consequences of this reading could have induced any scholar to prefer any other. Jude not only attributes to Jesus the deliverance from Egypt and the slaughter of those Israelites who disobeyed Moses, but also the (purely apocryphal) imprisonment of the rebellious angels. Nowhere else in the New Testament, fortunately, do we find this belief so crudely expressed.

The author of 2 Peter, though he bases his work on the Epistle of Jude, deliberately omits Jude's quotations of apocryphal literature. However, he also manifests a distinct tendency to regard Paul's letters as canonical scripture (see 2 Peter 3:15–16), and may even be quoting one or more of the Synoptic Gospels in his reference to the Transfiguration in 1:17. In three places he makes use of *haggada*, all three copied from Jude: in 2:4 he refers to the imprisonment of the rebellious angels; in 2:11 he makes an oblique reference to the incident explicitly mentioned in Jude. This is the legend of Satan claiming Moses' body and being resisted by Michael. The third piece of *haggada* is the presentation of Balaam as an example of extreme wickedness: see 2:15–16. In the pages of scripture Balaam is not actually condemned, but in Jewish exegetical tradition he had acquired a shocking reputation, chiefly because of his association with the incident of Baal-Peor in Numbers. The text of scripture does not bring him into this narrative, but, since it comes immediately after the Balaam narratives in Numbers 22–4, Jewish commentators assumed that Balaam must have encouraged the Moabites/Midianites to tempt Israel to indulge in idol worship. Another piece of *haggada* taken for granted by the author of 2 Peter is the virtuous character of both Noah and Lot. In 2:5 Noah is described as 'a herald of righteousness' and we have a moving description of the moral agonies suffered by 'righteous Lot' in the midst of the profligate citizens of Sodom and Gomorrah (see 2:7–8).

But 2 Peter has a very definite theory about the inspiration of scripture, which he is able to illustrate from scripture itself. It seems that in his church community some Christians were claiming to interpret scripture for themselves, in a sense contrary to that held by most of the church. He therefore writes in 1:20–21:

> No prophecy of scripture is a matter of one's own interpretation, because no prophecy ever came by the impulse of men, but man moved by the Holy Spirit spoke from God.

The author has here committed himself to the theory of inspiration which we find most clearly expressed by Philo. It was essentially the Hellenistic or 'oracular' theory of inspiration: the writers of scripture had no mind of their own, but were possessed by the Holy Spirit. It is not the same as Paul's understanding of inspiration, or even that of the author of 1 Peter, who allows the prophets more understanding of what they were saying. However, the author of 2 Peter has the courage of his convictions, for at 2:16 he refers to the incident of Balaam's ass rebuking her master (Num. 22:21–35). The rebuke was just; it is recorded in scripture; an ass therefore spoke with the voice of inspiration.

It seems likely that our author followed Jewish tradition not only in regarding Balaam as a bad character, but also in believing nevertheless in his plenary inspiration. In 1:19 he refers to 'the prophetic word'. In view of his mention of 'the morning star' in the previous verse, it is probable that he is referring to the famous words in Balaam's utterance in Numbers 24:17, 'a star shall come forth out of Jacob', which was taken by both Jews and Christians to be a messianic prophecy. The rabbis, we know, were sometimes perplexed by the phenomenon of Balaam: 'Seeing that he did not know the mind of his ass' one of them asks, 'could he know the mind of the Most High?' (*Sanhedrin* ii, 717ff.). Our author seems to have no such misgivings. The whole topic of the attitude of the New Testament writers towards the inspiration of scripture is further discussed in chapter 4 of *Studies in the Pastoral Epistles*, pp. 42–55.

There may be a feeble sort of typology of the flood in 2 Peter 2:5, but it is not made clear, as it is in 1 Peter 3:20–21. He quotes Proverbs 26:11 in a purely illustrative manner, in parallel with a secular proverb in 2:22. At 3:13 he seems to be echoing the vision of a new heaven and a new earth which we find in Isaiah 65:17; and in 3:8, in answer to those who ask when the parousia is to be, he paraphrases Psalm 90:4. These are not brilliant examples of the use of scripture, but we may surely reject Fornberg's judgement (p. 138): 'The Old Testament is not important in 2 Peter, apart from the passage common to Jude.' On the contrary, 2 Peter shows a lively interest in scripture.

When, however, we review the use of scripture in what are probably the two latest books in the New Testament, we may well conclude that their understanding of scripture is feeble and their method of exposition second-rate. Jude shows as much interest in non-canonical books as he does in the bible of the Jews; and 2 Peter has a crude and literalistic approach to the inspiration of scripture. As in their theological and literary qualities, so also in their use of scripture, Jude and 2 Peter represent a low-water mark in the New Testament.

8

SCRIPTURE IN THE BOOK OF REVELATION

Commentators have often pointed out that, though there are no explicit citations of scripture in the Book of Revelation, the author (whom we shall call John the Divine without prejudice to any theories of authorship) uses scripture more extensively and more effectively than any other writer of the New Testament. Moreover, his method of using scripture is very different indeed from that of all other New Testament writers. Unique in the New Testament he certainly is, though as we shall be seeing, he is not quite unique in ancient literature. Partial parallels to the way in which he employs scripture can be found. Nevertheless, so remarkable is the technique, and so integral to the purpose of his book, that he merits a chapter to himself.

What is remarkable about John the Divine is that, instead of quoting scripture, either explicitly or implicitly, as having been fulfilled in the events concerning Jesus Christ, he uses the language and images of scripture and applies them to Christ, to Christians and to the church as a whole. Also, he never argues or expounds as other New Testament writers do, using scripture as their source of proof. He is not concerned to prove anything. His is much more a prophetic, one might almost say a descriptive, work: he is setting forth the significance of contemporary history. Since he believes that the long-term plan of God, partially disclosed in the older dispensation, is being revealed in contemporary events, he simply narrates them in terms of scripture. A great deal of his narrative is set forth in symbolic terms: we meet bizarre symbols at every turn; a figure with a sword proceeding from his mouth (1:16), four living creatures with six wings each (4:8), horses with heads like lions and tails like serpents (9:17–19), a harlot seated on a scarlet, seven-headed beast (17:3–4), gates each made up of a single pearl (21:21). But these symbols are nearly all taken from scripture. Indeed, it is John the Divine's method to convey his message much more by means of presenting us with a series of striking symbols than by setting out an ordered discourse. If we did not have scripture available, his message would be totally incomprehensible to us, as it has been, it must be confessed, to many Christians down the ages.

A few examples of his technique will illustrate this. In Revelation 2:8 the risen Christ, addressing the church in Smyrna, is described thus:

The words of the first and the last, who died and came to life.

The first half of this sentence is an echo of Isaiah 44:6:

I am the first and the last;
  besides me there is no god.

John the Divine does not claim that the prophecy of Isaiah 44:6 is fulfilled in Jesus Christ: he simply claims for Jesus Christ what is said of God in Isaiah 44:6. Again, in 13:1–8 we have a description of a beast rising from the sea with ten horns and seven heads, and having various characteristics of a leopard, a bear and a lion. Nearly all these features are taken from Daniel 7:1–7, where they belong to a succession of beasts, each more terrible than the last. In Daniel they refer to the successive empires that have enslaved Israel, culminating in the régime of the Seleucid king Antiochus IV. Now John the Divine, in applying these characteristics to his beast, does not say: 'The various beasts described in Daniel 7 all find their fulfilment in this beast.' It is not even quite clear that this is what John the Divine meant. After all, he probably shared the view of all educated Jews that the prophet Daniel was describing the historical conquerors of Israel. He simply uses the scriptural beast imagery in order to describe the adversary, Satan, whom in all probability he sees as instigating the persecuting activity of the Roman Empire of his day. What he is doing, then, is to use a scriptural image, with all its historical associations, in order to convey the full significance of the events of his day. It is no doubt a form of typology.

Another example could be found in 19:11–16: here we have a brilliant vision of a man seated on a white horse: he is clad in a 'robe dipped in blood', and 'in righteousness he judges and makes war'. The main inspiration for this vision comes from Isaiah 63:1–6, a grim picture of God returning from making war against Israel's enemy Edom, his garments stained with the blood of those whom he has slain. The figure in Revelation 19:11–16 is undoubtedly that of the risen and victorious Christ. The blood on his garments is therefore his own blood shed on the cross. He seems to be followed by the army of martyrs, for they are clad in white linen. John the Divine is not here saying anything as simple as 'that prophecy in Isaiah 63 is fulfilled in Christ' because Christ's victory has been achieved by methods absolutely opposite to those which the prophet believed God had used against Edom. If we want to express his message in terms of rational discourse we would have to say something like this: 'God, who in the description given by the prophet of old seemed to overcome Israel's enemies by means of human warfare, has now manifested in the career of Jesus Christ that he overcomes the power of evil by means of suffering voluntarily undertaken by his servants.' But how much we would lose by reducing it to this! It would be like describing Shelley's *Ode to a Skylark* as a poem in which Shelley said that the skylark was a very remarkable bird.

A last example can be taken from the two visions in chapters 4 and 5. Most of the details of the vision of God described in chapter 4 can be found in Isaiah 6 and Ezekiel 1: the throne, the winged creatures and the angelic hymn (the trishagion) come from Isaiah 6. The lamps of fire, the lightning, the crystal sea, the rainbow colours, the diverse characteristics of the living creatures come from Ezekiel's vision. Thus John the Divine has taken the two most celebrated prophetic visions of God in scripture and has combined them in order to depict the God and Father of Jesus Christ. We should observe that he does not do what the author of the Fourth Gospel does: he does not identify the figure of Isaiah's vision with the pre-existent Christ. See John 12:41, where Isaiah is said to have seen Christ in his vision in the temple. What John the Divine does is to follow the vision of chapter 4 with another vision in which the slain lamb appears between God's throne and the angelic host. He takes the book, which represents God's plan of salvation, and then receives the worship of heaven. The detail of the lamb slain is probably taken from Isaiah 53 and certainly indicates Jesus' sacrificial death; his taking and opening the book means that he has carried out God's plan. The worship of heaven signalizes his divine status. He has already in verse 5 been called 'the Lion of the tribe of Judah, the Root of David', both messianic titles. So John uses this vivid symbolism, every detail of it taken from scripture, in order to place the career of Jesus Christ in the very centre of God's design of salvation and to associate him as closely as possible with God's being and action.

This is the most thoroughly Christianized interpretation of scripture which we meet in the entire New Testament. It is not *pesher,* 'this means that'; it is much more subtle. It has close links with typology, but it is not exactly the typology which we meet, for example, in Paul. Paul claims that certain events in Israel's history are types of events and things in the Christian dispensation. John the Divine does not need to say that in so many words: he takes scriptural language and images for granted and weaves them into his prophetic narrative in such a way that they carry with them all that is important in their scriptural context, and yet thereby he shows that God has made all things new. Scripture can be used for interpreting the events of the Christian era, but in being used, it is transformed.

W. Bousset quite correctly wrote of the Revelation, 'in apocalyptic the symbol (*Bild*) takes first place' (p. 3). The symbol is in
fact John the Divine's primary tool in expressing his prophecy.
But when Bousset goes on to say (p. 12) 'allegory is also the first
and most important medium of the apocalyptic writer', we must
ask whether he is completely accurate. We have defined allegory
as an *arbitrary* association of something in the old dispensation
with something in the new: there is no natural connection between
John the Baptist and a lantern (see above, pp. 123f.); there is no
natural connection between the threshing ox being free from a
muzzle and clergy being paid (see p. 51 above). But the symbols
of John the Divine are not arbitrary: a scroll being opened (Rev.
5:1–7) is a natural symbol for the unfolding of a plan. A terrible
beast is a natural symbol for a tyrannical and destructive empire.
Only when John the Divine deals in cryptic numbers are we
justified in accusing him of dealing in allegory, as he does in
13:17–18 and 17:9–12. Charles (p. cviii) claims that the seven seals
in chapter 6 and seven bowls in chapter 16 are allegories. Strictly
speaking they are, but there is a reasonably natural connection
between seals being opened and striking events following and the
figure of the bowl of God's wrath being poured out is, as we shall
see below, well attested in scripture. A better expression of how
John the Divine handles scripture is to be found in Lohmeyer; he
writes: 'The Old Testament is indeed for the Seer holy scripture,
but it is also for him the material of his proclamation, the atmosphere which creates, as he is "conditioned (bestimmt) by it" ' (p.
196). Less satisfactory is F. Jenkins's opinion that the allusions to
scripture are not intended to indicate the fulfilment of prophecy,
though they are to some extent intended to serve as literary
adornment. Nor are they proof-texts. He concludes that John the
Divine uses scriptural allusions primarily because the genre of
apocalyptic writing demanded it (pp. 27–8). This seems to be
doing less than justice to the author of Revelation: his scriptural
allusions are very far from being the mere trappings of apocalyptic. They are the material with which he works, the medium
through which he expresses himself. Jenkins is nearer the mark
when he says (p. 47) that the book is 'a reinterpretation of
prophecy'. Best of all is John Sweet; John the Divine, he writes,
'had an astonishing grasp of the Jewish scriptures, which he used
with creative freedom' (pp. 39–40). He adds: 'In fact Revelation
can be seen as a Christian re-reading of the whole Jewish scriptural
heritage, from the stories of the Beginning to the visions of the
End.' The implications of this admirable conclusion we must
consider later on.

   Whence did John the Divine derive this method? It is not
enough to reply, 'from the apocalyptic tradition', for not all apoca-

lyptic works use scripture as he does, and in any case the fact that
he is a Christian apocalyptist puts him in a special category. He
was not, for example, like the various authors of the Book of
Enoch, who were attempting to interpret contemporary Jewish
history in the light of what they knew of scripture. John the
Divine is interpreting contemporary history in the light of scripture
understood as finding its full significance in Jesus Christ. The
parallels which we will cite can at best only be partial, and the
Christian parallels are very partial indeed. As a Christian apocalyptist John the Divine is very nearly unique in his handling of
scripture.

Our first parallel is found in the *Psalms of Solomon*. These are
a series of psalms, preserved in full only in Greek but originally
composed in Hebrew, which belong to the second half of the first
century before Christ. They refer to Pompey's desecration of the
temple in 63 BC and also to his death in Egypt in 48 BC (see
2:26–7), cf. Charles (2), pp. 265f. Here we certainly find the use
of scriptural imagery without explicit quotation. Thus in 2:25 we
read (my trans.):

> Do not delay, O God, to repay them upon their heads,
> in order to proclaim with dishonour the arrogance of the
> dragon.

Pompey is here the dragon, and the dragon comes originally from
Jeremiah 51:34:

> Nebuchadrezzar the king of Babylon has devoured me . . .
> he has swallowed me like a monster.

The LXX (28:34) has translated the Hebrew *tannin* with *drakōn*,
a dragon. John the Divine uses this symbol also; see Revelation
12:3f.

We encounter another scriptural symbol in 8:14 (my trans.):

> Therefore God mixed for them a spirit of error,
> he made them drink a cup of undiluted wine that they might
> become drunk.

This is taken from Isaiah 51:17f., where the figure of the intoxica-
ting cup which God forces on men is used to describe the destiny
of suffering inherited by Israel because of her infidelity. The
author of the *Psalms of Solomon* uses it here to characterize the
sufferings of the Jews when Pompey besieged and took Jerusalem
in 63 BC. He regards these sufferings as God's punishment for
Israel's reckless behaviour. John the Divine uses the same image;
see Revelation 14:19–20; 19:15. Again in 14:3b–4a we have a very
interesting use of paradise imagery (my trans.):

The garden of the Lord, the trees of life, are his holy ones, their plant is rooted for ever.

The author is referring to the faithful in Israel, the elect community; he identifies them with the trees in God's garden. The symbol comes originally of course from the Eden story in Genesis 2—3: but there are passages in scripture where the faithful are called trees of God's planting, e.g. Isaiah 61:3. John the Divine promises that the faithful will eat of the tree of life; see Revelation 2:7; 22:2, 14. Compare also Enoch 25:4–5, where the fruit of the tree of life is to be food for the elect.

There can be no doubt then that we find the same technique in the *Psalms of Solomon* as we find in Revelation: scriptural images are taken over and applied to the events of the author's day. In what way, therefore, do the *Psalms of Solomon* differ from Revelation? We may reply that Revelation differs in inspiration. I do not mean that the Book of Revelation has a special aura of inspiration belonging to it, but that the inspiration of John the Divine is different. The author of the *Psalms of Solomon* could only look forward to the complete vindication of Israel, which he believed had partially taken place with the death of Pompey, in history or at the end of history. John the Divine believes that God has acted supremely in the Messiah and by means so unexpected that most of Israel has failed to recognize him. This gives him a much more specific, arresting and satisfying theme to convey by means of scriptural images.

This technique of using scriptural images without claiming specific fulfilment of scripture is also found in the *Hodayoth*, the Hymns of Thanksgiving of the Qumran Community. In 1 QH 3:8–12 we have an elaborate figure of a pregnant woman labouring to be delivered of her child. This is an image widely used in scripture: in Numbers 11:12 Moses protests bitterly to God that he did not bring forth Israel:

Did I conceive all this people? Did I bring them forth, that thou shouldest say to me: 'Carry them in your bosom, as a nurse carries the sucking child!'

In Isaiah 42:14 God is compared to a woman in labour: a long period of gestation ends in a sharp climax of labour; so God, who appears to have done nothing for Israel for a long time, is about to act energetically and decisively for her redemption. And in Jeremiah 4:31 and 13:21 the birth-pangs of a mother are used as a symbol for the sudden onset of disaster. In the *Hodayoth* the pregnant woman represents the messianic community, and is, of course, identified with the Qumran sect itself. John the Divine uses the same image in Revelation 12:1f.; there the woman in labour represents the messianic community, i.e. the Christian church. But she actually brings forth the Messiah, who is snatched up to the throne of God (12:5).

One could point to many other instances of scriptural images taken over into the text of the *Hodayoth*, but one more striking example will suffice. In 1 QH 8:1–12 we have a rather mysterious description of a holy plant that is planted by God in a garden where there are trees and a well. The phrase 'holy sprout' (Mansoor's trans.) is used of it in 8:10. The Hebrew is *neṭer qodeš* (the first vowel in *qodeš* has to be restored in the text, but it is an obvious emendation). The word *neṭer* is the same as that used in Isaiah 11:1b for the 'branch' which is to grow out of the root of Jesse. Delcor claims that in the description as a whole we have echoes both of the tree of life of Genesis 2–3 and of the trees with healing leaves of Ezekiel 47:1–12. But of course the whole point of the picture is to emphasize the messianic nature of the Qumran community. The community can be described as itself the 'holy sprout' because it is destined to be the milieu in which the Messiah will appear. John the Divine can use this language when he describes Jesus Christ as 'the Root of David' in Revelation 5:5. The *Hodayoth* also use the technique of applying the language of scripture to both the leader and the community without explicit citation. We have already noted some examples of this on pp. 28–9 above.

As in the case of the *Psalms of Solomon*, so with the *Hodayoth* we can say that though their technique is similar to that of John the Divine they lack something of his inspiration. They are more eschatological than the *Psalms of Solomon*, in the sense that their authors are convinced that the critical time is very near. But in fact in the Qumran time-scheme nothing absolutely decisive has yet taken place. The Teacher of Righteousness has indeed come and put their feet on the right path, but the eschatological battle has not yet begun, and no Messiah has as yet appeared. For John the Divine it is very different: the Messiah has appeared; he has in principle conquered the forces of evil, and the last great conflict between God-in-Christ and Satan is already in full swing. This gives to his imagery a point and significance that is lacking in the other two works.

When we look in the rest of the New Testament for parallels to the way in which John the Divine uses scripture, we must confess that there is almost nothing to be found. We have said that in Revelation scriptural language is taken over without explicit citation, and also that scriptural images are incorporated into the narrative without acknowledgement. We can find parallels to the first of these features: in the poetic prophetic chapters in Luke's Gospel where the infancy narratives of both the Baptist and Jesus are to be found, scripture is sometimes used without explicit citation or any distinct claim that it is being fulfilled. Thus Mary's song of praise (the Magnificat) in Luke 1:46–55 is certainly modelled on Hannah's song of thanksgiving in 1 Samuel 2:1–10, in much the same way that the vision of God in Revelation 4 is modelled on Isaiah 6 and Ezekiel 1. But there is an absence of scriptural symbolism in Luke. Similarly, in the song of Zechariah in Luke 1:68–9 and also in Simeon's song in 2:29–32 (the Benedictus and the Nunc Dimittis respectively) we find scripture used without acknowledgement. Luke 1:76 quotes Isaiah 40:3 and 1:79 quotes Isaiah 9:2. Similarly, in 2:32 we have clear echoes of Isaiah 42:6 and 49:6. But these are almost explicitly claims for messianic fulfilment of prophecy, since they are all addressed either to the forerunner of the Messiah or to the Messiah himself.

In the same way in the apocalyptic chapter of Mark's Gospel, chapter 13, we find scriptural language being used to describe what is to happen just before the parousia. See Mark 13:24–5, which echoes Isaiah 13:10, etc. This is reproduced in Matthew 24:29f. Perhaps a nearer approximation to John the Divine's use of scriptural symbols is to be found in the bizarre phrase, 'the desolating sacrilege', in Mark 13:14. This phrase, which must have seemed sheer nonsense to the average educated Greek speaker, goes back to the Book of Daniel, where it occurs in one form or another three times: Daniel 9:27; 11:31; 12:11. We also meet it in 1 Maccabees 1:54. It refers in these places to the deliberate desecration of the temple in Jerusalem which took place in 168 BC when the Greek imperial authority placed on the altar in the temple in Jerusalem an image of Zeus Olympios. In Hebrew the words *šikkuṭ šōmēm* were probably originally a deliberate caricature of the Hebrew for Zeus Olympios, which would be *ba'al šāmaim*: instead of *ba'al* ('lord') they read *šikkuṭ* ('abomination'); and instead of *šamaim* ('heavens') they read *šomēm* ('desolating or appalling'). It rapidly became an accepted phrase among pious Jews for pagan desecration of the temple, as its use in 1 Maccabees, perhaps sixty years later than the Book of Daniel, shows. In Mark it refers to some mysterious act of appalling desecration to be expected as a sign of the approaching parousia. Many editors suggest that this passage was originally inspired by the declared intention of the emperor Gaius in AD 42 to set up his own image in the temple in Jerusalem, a plan that was only frustrated by the assassination of Gaius in the same year. Matthew reproduces this cryptic formula (Matt. 24:15), but it is too much for Luke. He interprets it in terms of the sack of Jerusalem by Titus in AD 70; see Luke 21:20. Both Matthew and Mark draw attention to the fact that they are using cryptic language. Mark writes 'let the reader understand', and Matthew says in addition that 'the desolating sacrilege' was 'spoken of by the prophet Daniel'.

It is most unlikely that either Mark or Matthew was ignorant of the original meaning of this phrase in the Book of Daniel. They must have known about the notorious desecration of the temple by Antiochus Epiphanes. They are therefore deliberately introducing a scriptural cryptogram into their narrative without claiming that it is a case of simple fulfilment of scripture, very much as John the Divine does with his symbols. In fact we do not find this cryptogram used in Revelation: it was not relevant, since Christians had no use for a material temple. But the language of Mark and Matthew reminds us of John the Divine's language when he does use cryptograms, as he does in 13:17–18 in connection with the number of the beast, and with the succession of kings in 17:9–11. However, the very fact that we can only produce such feeble and indirect parallels in the New Testament to the technique of using scripture in Revelation demonstrates clearly how very remarkable and idiosyncratic it is.

If we were to go through the entire Apocalypse pointing out where there are scriptural images and where scriptural language is employed, it would take up far more space than we can possibly allow ourselves here. We will therefore be content with taking a sample passage, the vision of the risen Christ in Revelation 1:12–18, showing what it owes to scripture. It is an excellent passage for our purpose. We will first reproduce it putting in italics words that echo scripture:

> Then I turned to see the voice that was speaking to me, and on turning I saw seven *golden lampstands*, and in the midst of the lampstands *one like a son of man, clothed with a long robe* and with *a golden girdle round his breast; his head and his hair were white as white wool, white as snow; his eyes were like a flame of fire, his feet were like burnished bronze*, refined as in a furnace, and *his voice was like the sound of many waters*; in his right hand he held seven stars, *from his mouth issued a sharp two-edged sword*, and his face was like the sun shining in full strength. When I saw him, I *fell at his feet as though dead*. But *he laid his right hand upon me*, saying, '*Fear not, I am the first and the last* and *the living one*; I died, and behold I am alive for evermore, and I have the keys of Death and Hades'.

In verse 12 the seven *golden lampstands* come from Zechariah 4:2f.; the *one like a son of man* comes from Daniel 7:13, where it is applied to the mysterious figure who appears before God at the end of the age. The *long robe* in verse 13 comes from Ezekiel 9:2, 11, where it represents the LXX rendering of a phrase in Hebrew which is more accurately translated 'linen'. He appears to be a recording angel, whose task is to record the names of those who are to be slaughtered for their sins. The *golden girdle* which Christ wears comes from Daniel 10:5, where it is worn by an angel. In verse 14 the description of the risen Christ as having *hair white as wool, white as snow* comes from Daniel 7:9 where it forms part of a description of an appearance of God. The phrase *his eyes were like a flame of fire* brings us back to the description of the angel in Daniel 10:6, as also his *feet of burnished bronze*. Still in verse 15, we find that the voice of the being in the vision is *like the sound of many waters*, which comes from Ezekiel 1:24, where it describes the sound of the angels accompanying the chariot vision of God; and in Ezekiel 43:2 it describes the sound of the glory of God himself coming from the east and re-entering the temple. The *sharp sword issuing from his mouth* comes from Isaiah 49:2, where it belongs to the servant of the Lord, and may echo Isaiah 11:4, where it is an attribute of the Messiah. John the Divine, when he sees this vision, *falls at the feet* of the risen Christ *as though dead*; this is reminiscent of Daniel's reaction to his vision of an angel: when he sees the angel he 'fell on (his) face in a deep sleep with (his) face to the ground' (Dan. 10:9). Christ touches John and says *Fear not*, as the angel does to Daniel in Daniel 10:10, 12; Christ's words *I am the first and the last* come from Isaiah 44:6, where they are uttered by God, and *the living one* in verse 18 may be a reference to the divine name. In Exodus 3:14 Moses asks God to disclose his name; in the Hebrew God replies: 'I will be who I will be', or perhaps 'I am who I am'; but the LXX translates this with 'I am he who is'.

Fourteen allusions to scripture in seven verses! Nor can we say that they are straightforward proof-texts wherein John sees scriptural prophecies fulfilled in Jesus Christ. On the contrary, his use of scripture here is very subtle: the various attributes, words and actions of the risen Christ are drawn from descriptions of angels, from the mysterious 'son of man' figure in Daniel 7, and from descriptions of God himself. John the Divine is clearly master of scripture: he is like an artist laying on his paints in order to bring about the effect he requires. But we cannot on the other hand dismiss the use of scripture as if it was purely illustrative with no theological implications. When John uses of Christ language used in scripture of an angel, he means that Christ represents the activity of God, as does the angelic ministry in scripture. When he calls him 'one like a son of man' he means to claim for Christ everything that Jewish tradition believed of the mysterious figure in the Book of Daniel. And certainly when he uses of Christ language which in scripture is applied to God, he means that Christ has divine status; he belongs to the dimension of God and not of creatures.

Schlatter (p. 36) maintains that this vision is formally a combination of the vision of the angel in Daniel 10 and the description of the cherubim in Ezekiel 1:7, 24, but this seems unduly to limit the scope of St John the Divine. It would be better to say that the vision is based on the appearance of the angel in Daniel 10 and the chariot vision in Ezekiel 1; but that it is enriched with significant details from other parts of scripture. Indeed these seven verses neatly bear out Jenkins's statement that the books of scripture most used in Revelation are Daniel, Ezekiel, Jeremiah, Isaiah, Zechariah, Psalms and Exodus (p. 15); since in this passage we have discovered echoes of all these books except Jeremiah and Psalms.

U. Vanni, writing in a work edited by J. Lambrecht, claims that John's usage of scripture varies from the strictly literal to pure reminiscence (p. 31). This seems to me to be analysing John the Divine's technique in a way that does not do him justice. I doubt if John is ever strictly literal, in the sense that he is like Matthew when he writes 'this was done in order that the scripture might be fulfilled', etc. Nor do I believe that he ever indulges in a purely reminiscent use of scripture, as I might do with Shelley's poem if I said that on a walk I had heard a lark pouring out its full heart. His references to scripture are always significant. Jenkins, I believe, is right when he points out that John the Divine uses Balaam and Jezebel in 2:14, 20 purely as types (p. 125). And Schlatter (p. 52) well maintains that John has no scruple about using even books in scripture that were on the very edge of the canon, for his great image of the church as the bride in 21:2 is taken from the Song of Songs.

The distribution table cited above from Jenkins for Revelation's use of the books of scripture is interesting. The most used books are Daniel, Ezekiel, Jeremiah, Isaiah, Zechariah, Psalms and Exodus, in that order of frequency. We can well understand why Daniel and Ezekiel should come first. Daniel is really the only book in the Jewish canon that is wholly apocalyptic, and John the Divine is writing an apocalypse. Moreover, in Daniel it is claimed that the prophet was informed about God's long-term plans in history. Revelation is a book much concerned about just that. Ezekiel would be important to John the Divine because Ezekiel had a vision in which he actually in some mysterious sense saw God, and God manifested 'a likeness as it were of a human form' (Ezek. 1:26). John the Divine believed that God had in Christ revealed himself to mankind more directly and intimately than ever before. The prominence of Isaiah and Psalms in Revelation needs no elaborate explanation: as we have seen throughout this work, these are the parts of scripture most favoured by those who hold a christocentric interpretation of the Jewish bible. Zechariah, whether we mean Proto-Zechariah or Deutero-Zechariah (a distinction unknown to the author of Revelation), is one of the sources of apocalyptic.

This leaves Jeremiah: at first sight it seems puzzling that this book should figure so largely in Revelation. If we were thinking in modern terms we would no doubt point out that in Jeremiah we find an unequalled intimacy and frankness between the prophet and God, which might well point forward to the close intimacy between God and man implied by the incarnation. But there is no evidence that any such thought occurred to the author of Revelation. When we look at the actual passages from Jeremiah used in Revelation we see at once why this book actually takes priority of Isaiah in the distribution table of Revelation. John the Divine has used the last two chapters of the Book of Jeremiah, 50—51, very extensively indeed in writing chapters 17 and 18 of Revelation. These last chapters of Jeremiah, which scholars believe not to have been written by the prophet, are a tremendous denunciation of judgement upon Babylon. John the Divine adapts them when he writes his judgement scene and taunt song on the Babylon of his day, the Roman Empire. But even apart from this, John the Divine seems to use Jeremiah as the prophet of judgement upon the nations, which in one sense he was. Much of John's material concerns the austerer side of God, his judgement and his wrath; there is no doubt that there is plenty of material in Jeremiah which represents this side of God's nature, and John the Divine makes free use of it.

Of all the writers of the New Testament, John the Divine is the one who seems to be most at home with the Hebrew text of the bible, and the least attached to the LXX. Swete (p. cliv) believes that he used the Alexandrian text of the LXX when he did use it; but this conclusion has not been confirmed by subsequent scholarship. Charles writes: 'John translated directly from the Old Testament text. He did not quote from any Greek version, though he was influenced in his renderings by the LXX and by another later Greek version' (p. lxvi). This is a little misleading, as John the Divine never, strictly speaking, quotes scripture at all. Since Charles wrote, it has become apparent that there was more than one alternative Greek translation to the LXX circulating during the first century AD. Lohmeyer says that John the Divine is quite capable of translating direct from the Hebrew. He often uses a non-LXX version of the Greek. He uses scripture with absolute freedom, hence the absence of formal quotations (p. 195). It is Trudinger who has made the most extensive examination of the use of the text of scripture in Revelation, and his conclusions are worth recording. They are four in number: (a) the author relies on Semitic sources rather than on Greek (p. 84), i.e. Hebrew and

Aramaic. (b) Many allusions to scripture are closest to the Aramaic targumic tradition (p. 86). John follows the Palestinian Targums sometimes against the MT and the LXX. (c) Some scriptural allusions seem to be influenced by a knowledge of the midrashim on scripture (p. 87) and (d) occasionally the author seems to be following a text of the MT closer to that used by Qumran than to the MT (p. 89). But this last point is disputable. Trudinger's conclusion is that the author was 'steeped in the Palestinian synagogue tradition' (p. 88). The textual situation as a whole is well summed up by Sweet: 'It appears that (John the Divine) normally had in mind the Hebrew text rather than the LXX, but he shows knowledge of both the Greek interpretations of the Hebrew represented by the LXX and the Aramaic interpretation used in the synagogue, found in the expanded paraphrases called Targums' (p. 40).

This comment may suitably introduce us to the question of John the Divine's knowledge and employment of traditional Jewish exegesis of scripture. As we might expect, there is more evidence in Revelation of a knowledge of Jewish exegetical tradition than in any other book of the New Testament. Indeed, one is tempted to say that Revelation shows more signs of the influence of Jewish exegetical tradition than do all the rest of the books of the New Testament put together! The richest source of information on this point is Adolf Schlatter's book written in 1912; one's only problem is what to leave out. He claims that the 'elders' in the great vision of God in heaven in 4:4 come from rabbinic tradition (influenced perhaps, one might conjecture, by Isaiah 24:23c); see Schlatter, p. 15. The detail that they have crowns on their heads is also taken from rabbinic tradition. Schlatter believes that John the Divine was in touch with the 'secret' tradition of interpreting Ezekiel (p. 16). This is a little-known area of Jewish speculation. In later times the rabbis condemned those who tried to gain direct access to God by means of speculations based on Ezekiel's chariot vision, and forbade anyone to attempt to interpret that chapter. There probably did exist in the first century AD a school of '*merkaba* mysticism' (*merkaba* is the Hebrew for 'chariot') but very little is known about it.

The seven angels who stand before God in Revelation 8:2 are found in Tobit 12:15 in the Apocrypha (Schlatter p. 23). The sea of glass in 4:6 is also found in the *Mekhilta*, one of the earliest rabbinic treatises extant. It is said that when the waters were held back as Israel crossed the Red Sea they became as glass (Schlatter p. 24). In Revelation 3:12 Christ promises that he will write his 'own new name' on him. Schlatter (p. 42) points out that in the *Pesikta de Rab Kahana* (a collection of addresses given on festal occasions by this famous rabbi) it is claimed that the Messiah will be given a new name. In Revelation 2:17 we have a reference to the 'hidden manna'. This also figures in rabbinic speculation (Schlatter p. 59). He suggests that the mention of 'the teaching of Balaam' in 2:14 may mean Greek philosophy, for there is some evidence that this phrase was used by the rabbis for philosophy as a rival to Judaism (p. 65). Schlatter has interesting light to throw on the strange detail in 12:15 whereby the dragon 'poured water like a river out of his mouth to sweep away' the woman with her child. There is a rabbinic story that Abraham on his way to Mount Moriah was nearly drowned by a stream which Satan launched against him (p. 79). In Revelation chapters 8 and 9 we see a series of plagues inflicted on the pagan world reminiscent of the plagues of Egypt. Schlatter (p. 84) notes that according to the rabbis God would execute on Rome (under the code name of Edom) all the plagues which he had poured on Pharaoh. In Revelation 16:12 horsemen from across the Euphrates lead the kings of the East in an attack on the Roman Empire. The rabbis expected, says Schlatter (pp. 86–7), that the Persian Empire would ultimately overthrow the Roman Empire (it looked as if it was going to happen in actual fact during the opening years of the seventh century AD). Then in Revelation 20:8 Gog and Magog appear as two Satanic enemies of the elect, not as they are in Ezekiel 38:2, the name of a prince of the Gentiles and his land respectively. This transposition, says Schlatter (p. 94) is found in the *Mekhilta*. The detail we remarked on on p. 159, of a gate made of a single pearl in Revelation 21:21, can be found in the tradition of Rabbi Johanan, a distinguished rabbi of the second century AD (Schlatter p. 102).

We pass to R. H. Charles's massive commentary: in his introduction p. lxv he gives us a detailed examination of chapter 6 of Revelation in the light of traditional exegesis. He says that the detail in 6:9 whereby the souls of the martyrs are seen under the altar is rabbinic. Martyrdom was a sacrifice, hence the altar; and the existence of an altar in heaven is of course a well-attested feature of rabbinic speculation. In 6:11 we are told that the consummation can only be brought about when the roll of martyrs is completed. Charles draws our attention to parallels to this in 1 Enoch and 4 Ezra. The 'white robes' in the same verse signify 'spiritual bodies', according to Charles; this detail can be found in 1 Enoch and in *The Ascension of Isaiah*, a work probably of the early second century AD.

Martin McNamara in his book *Targum and Testament* finds an interesting parallel to the concept of 'the second death' in Revelation 2:11; 20:6, which is not found in scripture. In the Fragmentary Targum on Deuteronomy 33:6 Moses prays: 'Let Reuben live in this world and not die in the second death, in which death the wicked die in the world to come' (McNamara p. 148). And he believes that the picture of the warring Messiah in Revelation 19:11f. is influenced by the Palestinian Targum on Genesis 49:10f. It presents a picture of one whose garments have been rolled in blood. He writes (p. 141): 'The figure of Christ we meet in Apoc. 19:11f. is the same as the one of the Palestinian Targum. The Apocalypse here, as in many other places, seems to be dependent on targumic tradition in its penetration of the Christian mystery.' We referred to this passage above on pp. 160–61, and we would still maintain that there is a much more specifically Christian message here than Father McNamara seems to allow. The blood on the Messiah's garment is his own blood. The war waged by the Lamb against the dragon is carried on by means of the cross.

Last of all we should pay attention to Court's reference to the Nero Redivivus myth in 13:3; 17:9–11 (p. 129). He points out that this myth is also found in the Sibylline Oracles. The legend was that Nero, who had in actual historical fact committed suicide in a villa near Rome in AD 68, would return from across the Euphrates and conquer the empire. When Domitian came to the throne in AD 81 he soon proved himself to be as ruthless a tyrant as Nero was. The Roman poet Juvenal, writing later in the reign of Trajan, calls him 'a bald version of Nero'. John the Divine has certainly made use of this legend. This raises the nice question of how far the author of Revelation used sources from outside Judaism and Christianity for his work. Schlatter (p. 105) believes that he had no such outside source. But others (e.g. Charles) have maintained that he did not scruple to take some of his symbols from pagan sources. It certainly looks very much as if the image of the 'woman clothed with the sun, with the moon under her feet' is borrowed from pagan mythology. Her child is snatched up to heaven. We recollect that Domitian's baby son, who died in infancy, was immediately deified by the Senate. Does this not suggest that if, as many believe, John the Divine wrote most of his work during the reign of Domitian, he is in 12:5 deliberately challenging the cult of the imperial infant? At any rate the question may remain open. John the Divine was so completely master of his material that there is nothing incompatible with what we know of his technique in the suggestion that he has occasionally incorporated pagan as well as Judaeo-Christian materials into his work.

Schlatter (pp. 104–5) claims that as far as following traditional exegesis was concerned, John the Divine was extremely hospitable to the *haggada* but rejected the *halaka*, i.e. he was ready to accept traditional exposition and embroidery of scriptural narrative, but rejected the traditional application of the Torah to the needs of daily life. This is hardly a sufficiently radical way of describing the situation: John the Divine was a Christian and therefore had no need of the Torah as a guide to daily life. What interested him was an exposition of scripture in terms of the career and significance of Jesus Christ. Since he uses scriptural language and images so frequently in his work, it is inevitable that he commits himself again and again to one tradition or another of explaining this or that passage of scripture. *Halaka* as such therefore would not come within the range of his vision and *haggada* only as far as it affects those passages in scripture which interest him. This amounts to something different from a simple decision to reject *halaka* and employ *haggada*. A good deal of *haggada* would seem quite mistaken or irrelevant to him, as for instance the widely attested rabbinic belief that Abraham was granted an oral knowledge of the entire Torah. John the Divine's criterion for the understanding of scripture was not 'Is it *haggada* or *halaka*?' but 'How far is it relevant to Jesus Christ?'

Elisabeth Fiorenze (Lambrecht p. 126) makes the interesting suggestion that John the Divine 'deliberately has chosen the title *apokalupsis Iēsou Christou* ('apocalypse of Jesus Christ') in order to characterize his own experience as a Christian prophetic experience similar to the call-experience of Paul'. We may recall that Paul in Galatians 1:16 says that God 'revealed' his Son in himself when he called him. This is a significant observation, but we should not conclude that therefore John's visions were charismatic in the sense of being arbitrary or subjectively determined. Though Paul claimed to be a *pneumatikos* and to have experienced revelations (2 Cor. 12:1), his method of expounding scripture was neither arbitrary nor subjective, and neither was that of the author of Revelation. Indeed the theological assumptions behind his exposition are very much the same as Paul's. What distinguishes him so sharply from Paul as from all other New Testament writers is his method of setting forth this exposition. And this in turn is no doubt due to the fact that he was doing what no other writer of the New Testament consciously does: he was writing an apocalypse.

The apocalyptist used symbols. This perhaps more than any other cause accounts for John the Divine using the technique he did use. Charles (pp. cvi–cvii) believes that he was compelled to use symbols because of the intensity of the experience which he had undergone: 'The more exalted and intense the experience, the more incapable it becomes of a literal description.' But is this necessarily the case? We have no reason to think that Paul's experience was any less intense. He tells us in 2 Corinthians 12:4 that in one of his experiences he 'heard things that cannot be told, which man may not utter', but this did not lead him to write an apocalyptic work instead of a series of letters to the churches with whom he had relations. It seems more in accordance with the evidence to conclude that John the Divine's symbolic technique is connected with the literary genre which he adopted rather than with any difficulty of expression which he may have felt. He has no more difficulty in putting into words his beliefs about God than has anyone who undertakes the perilous task of attempting to express the ultimate mystery.

One question should be faced before we leave the subject of the Apocalypse: John the Divine is so free and creative in his use of scripture that we are driven occasionally to wonder whether he really regarded scripture as inspired. We have noted above (p. 162) Sweet's admirable phrase for the way John the Divine uses scripture: 'creative freedom'. Does this mean that he could do anything he liked with scripture, make it serve any purpose which he chose, regardless of what it 'really meant'? This is the sort of question which we could relevantly ask in connection with almost any method of interpreting scripture. We could certainly put it to Philo: when we see how he allegorizes the Pentateuch we cannot be blamed for concluding that Philo could use his allegorical method to make his text say absolutely anything he liked. One could make very much the same judgement about a great deal of rabbinic exegesis: so far-fetched do their methods seem to us of applying scripture to the problems with which they were concerned, that we are often inclined to conjecture that they reached the conclusions first and harnessed their technique of scripture interpretation to the conclusions afterwards.

But we would be mistaken if we made such a judgement about either Philo or the rabbis or John the Divine. The ultimate rationale of any method of scripture interpretation depends on the theological assumptions which the interpreter brings to his text: grant these assumptions and the interpretative conclusions follow. Our difficulty lies in accepting the assumptions of *any* school of interpretation in first-century Judaism or Christianity, a difficulty which we must examine carefully in the ensuing chapters. It must be enough to say here that John the Divine did not consciously regard the Jewish scriptures as material over which he had complete authority. He was a prophet, and the prophets respected the work of their predecessors. Early Christians subsumed almost everything in scripture under the category of prophecy: Moses and David were prophets, just as much as any of the authors of the books which we today regard as prophetic. There were some themes which John the Divine would *not* find in scripture: a secret tradition of salvation by *gnōsis* reserved only for the elect, for example: a licence granted by God to the elect to ignore all moral sanctions; or divinely authorized permission to Christians to compromise with the emperor cult so as to avoid persecution; or encouragement to worship angels in the same way as the Lamb was to be worshipped. In short, John's apparent mastery of his scriptural material is an indication of his literary and theological genius, not of his freedom from all obligation to the authority of scripture.

Can we find any modern parallels to the technique of composition used by John the Divine? Beasley-Murray has suggested one (p. 16): 'The closest modern parallel to this mode of communication is the political cartoon.' This is a lively and significant parallel, but it only takes us a certain way: John does not deliberately exaggerate as the cartoonist does, though he certainly simplifies the issues. It is not surprising that his book has inspired some of the most successful examples of Christian visual art through the ages. Anyone who finds himself in Angers in France ought to visit the castle there where a wonderful series of tapestries illustrating the Apocalypse is preserved. They were woven early in the fifteenth century and have preserved their colours amazingly. The weaver who designed them has exactly captured the spirit of the Apocalypse. Perhaps another modern parallel might be the works of Franz Kafka: anyone who has read his books *The Trial* and *The Castle* will have the same sense of a half-glimpsed world conveyed by allegory, symbol and cryptic narrative that we encounter when we read the Revelation. But Kafka's world is more elusive, more complicated perhaps, and certainly a great deal darker and gloomier and more irrational than John's. A third example might be found in the use which Charles Williams makes of the *Mabinogion* (the corpus of Welsh legend founded on the Arthurian theme) in his novels and his poetry. The events of contemporary life are illumined and interpreted in the light of a universe of discourse which comes from outside and often seems strange and inexplicable.

But the truth is that John the Divine's work is unique. Others have written apocalypses, but no one has written an apocalypse like this. Difficult and bizarre though it often seems to us, an understanding of how he uses scripture can illuminate his work. It is worth while making the effort to follow him here, even if at the end we are still left marvelling at his power and literary genius.

It may seem to some out of proportion that, after having devoted a hundred pages to the central documents of the New Testament, Paul, the Synoptic writers, Hebrews, the Pauline school, I should then go on to devote as many as forty pages to what most people would regard as the less important writings, the Pastorals, the Catholic Epistles and the Revelation. But this has been done deliberately: much more attention has been devoted to the use of scripture in the first group of writings. The usage in the 'minor' works has engaged considerably less of the attention of scholars. My treatment has been by way of redressing the balance: it has proved, I believe, that some of the most interesting questions in connection with our whole subject have come up for consideration in our last forty pages. We must now turn to the theological implications for us today of what we have observed about how the New Testament writers use scripture.

9

THE NEW TESTAMENT INTERPRETATION
AND OURS

We have now reached what may be called a watershed in this work. We have finished our account of how the various writers in the New Testament interpreted scripture. Henceforth we must devote ourselves to the question which must have been in our minds frequently during the foregoing account: what sense can we today make of the way in which the New Testament writers interpret scripture? From now on we may freely use the phrase 'the Old Testament' for the Hebrew scriptures (including whatever books written in the intertestamental period which we may think relevant), for we are now looking at the question from the point of view of today.

Hermeneutics

Before we come down to details, however, it is necessary to say something about the topic of hermeneutics as a whole, for that is indeed the technical name for the subject-matter of this book. Hermeneutics is strictly the study of how any given text is to be interpreted; but we find ourselves in an exceptionally complicated situation. We are not merely concerned with the interpretation of the text of the bible. We are interested in the way in which one set of writers in the bible interpreted another set. Not only so, we must in addition ask ourselves how we understand their interpretation. Thus we are faced in fact with a fourfold problem, which we may set out under the following scheme:

1 What was the meaning of the original author of any given Old Testament text, and what are his presuppositions?

2 How was any given Old Testament text understood by the exegetical tradition of the period between its being committed to writing and the first century AD, and what were the presuppositions of that tradition?

3 How did any given New Testament writer interpret any given Old Testament text, and what are his presuppositions?

4 What sense are modern Christians to make (a) of any given Old Testament text, and (b) of the interpretation advanced by

any given New Testament writer to any given Old Testament text, and what are our presuppositions?

As set out in this way, the task seems impossibly complicated. Fortunately, however, it is simpler in practice. In the first place, large sections of the Old Testament are unnoticed by any New Testament writers, and can for practical purposes be ignored, except under the heading of question 4(a). For example, the New Testament writers show almost no interest in the Book of Esther or the Song of Solomon or Ecclesiastes, and very little interest in the Books of Chronicles, Ezra–Nehemiah, Job and Ruth. Some of the minor prophets such as Nahum, Obadiah and Zephaniah are virtually ignored. Again, though there are, as we have seen above, differences between the ways in which the various New Testament writers understand the Old Testament, there is a very wide area of agreement among them. To this the only apparent exception is the Book of Revelation and this may well be attributed more to the author's different technique than to any great difference in his underlying theological approach. Of the four groups of questions listed above, 4 is certainly the most difficult, since it launches us into the middle of one of the most keenly disputed theological topics in our modern situation. But we may not avoid it if this book is to be anything more than a purely historical account. We cannot completely separate question 4(a) from 4(b). If we were compelled to conclude that the way in which the New Testament writers understood the Old Testament has *nothing* in common with the way in which we must understand it (a position to which Bultmann came perilously close), then the two parts of the Christian bible would fall apart, and we would find it almost impossible to hold any consistent Christian theology at all.

Perhaps we can best illustrate the scope of our hermeneutical problem by taking one text as an example and attempting to apply and answer all four groups of questions in respect of it. A good test instance is Isaiah 7:14:

> Therefore the Lord himself will give you a sign. Behold, a young woman shall conceive and bear a son, and shall call his name Immanuel.

Question 1: The original meaning of this text is by no means clear, but it must have had some relation to the state of affairs in Judah at the time of Ahaz. The son who is to be born may be the prophet's own child. His birth is to herald a new stage in Judah's history, in which perhaps God's presence is to be more clearly recognized than previously. If we consider the presuppositions of this text, we must take into consideration the significance of the prophetic sign as signalling the beginning of a series of events which God has already decreed.

Question 2: In the period between the eighth century BC and the time of the writing of the New Testament this text probably acquired messianic overtones. It is possible that even before the writing of the New Testament it was understood by some tradition in Judaism as indicating a virginal conception for the Messiah. The presuppositions of this period were that whatever the prophet uttered must be fulfilled sooner or later, and that Isaiah in particular had a peculiarly clear knowledge of what was to happen in the future messianic era.

Question 3: This text is interpreted in Matthew 1:22–3 as prophesying the birth of Jesus from the Virgin Mary. The name 'Immanuel' is understood as indicating the intimacy and directness of what later theology called the incarnation. Matthew's presupposition is that the prophet Isaiah was granted a miraculous foreknowledge of the events of Jesus' life, and also that Jesus fulfilled in his life and ministry a messianic programme which can be traced in the writings of the Old Testament prophets.

Question 4(a): We must revert to the answer which we gave to Question 1. The primary meaning of this text must be identical with its meaning as intended by the original author, as far as that can be ascertained. But we might suggest a secondary meaning in the light of later tradition and later events: prophetic signs witness to God's action in history. This in its turn enables us to form an impression of God's character. The name 'God with us' is preeminently suitable to Jesus Christ, because we find in him the unique and normative revelation of God's character. As for Question 4(b), we must maintain that Isaiah did not intend to describe a virginal birth, probably not the birth of anyone who could legitimately be described as the Messiah either. The utmost we can concede to Matthew's interpretation is that at least he witnesses to the unique significance of the son who was to be born to Mary.

We could of course choose other texts to which we could give a less negative interpretation today (e.g. several verses from Isaiah 53), and others again which we would have to describe as being based on a misreading of the original (e.g. Hebrews' interpretation of Psalm 40:6b in Hebrews 10:5). But the text we have taken is probably a fair example, and witnesses eloquently to the difficulty of our task in these last three chapters.

However, our task is simplified by the fact that quite often much the same answer can be given to Questions 1 and 2, i.e. the traditional exegesis coincides with the original meaning of the text. This would apply, for instance, to a great deal of the prescriptions of the Torah, though we must admit that this does not help very much with our understanding of Christian interpretation, since this was not an area of scripture which held very much interest for early Christians. Again, on many occasions much the same answer can be given to Questions 3 and 4; that is, we today would agree with the New Testament interpretation of the text. A good instance would be Psalm 143:2b as interpreted by Paul in Galatians 2:16 and Romans 3:20. This enshrines the principle of justification by faith, which is the keystone of the Christian understanding of God known in Christ. Sometimes the answer to Question 2 will largely coincide with that of Question 3; in other words, the traditional exegesis and the Christian exegesis will prove to be much the same: an example occurs in Galatians 4:29, where Paul agrees with the traditional Jewish interpretation of the word *meṭaheq* in Genesis 21:9. It is taken to mean 'persecute', a meaning which it certainly did not bear in the original context.

There are also occasions when the answer to Question 1 approximates to that given to Question 3. In a very general sense this might be said to apply to Genesis 15:6, cited in Galatians 3:6, Romans 4:3. Paul claims that Abraham lived by faith rather than by Torah observance. It is probable that when Genesis 15 was written the people's relation to God was closer to a faith relationship than to the relationship of Torah observance which became the rule after the exile. We moderns tend to claim that the answer to Question 1 and the answer to Question 4(a) must always be the same: our understanding of the Old Testament text must always consist in as close an approximation as possible to the meaning of the original as far as it can be ascertained. But such a claim cannot always be substantiated. In the first place, as Christians we will often see more in an Old Testament text than the author would have seen at the time: for example, Habakkuk 2:4b, 'But the righteous shall live by his faith', takes on a deeper meaning in the context of the emphasis on Torah observance which became the norm later, and even more in the light of the Christian understanding of justification by faith. Similarly, a large part of the fourth servant song (Isaiah 52:13—53:12) gains immensely in significance in the light of Jesus Christ. This factor might be described in the traditional phrase the *sensus plenior*, the fuller sense of the text seen in the context of salvation history. But the phrase has been much misused, so as to read into Old Testament texts ideas which could not possibly have occurred to their authors and which often have little enough connection with anything except the particular doctrine which the Christian interpreter wishes to extract from the text. An instance of the misuse of the *sensus plenior* is the text from Ezekiel 44:2, 'This gate shall remain shut', which medieval interpreters applied to the womb of the Blessed Virgin.

In the second place, though we moderns may think that we can recapture the original meaning of the Old Testament text, we cannot by any means invariably integrate that meaning into our theology of the Old Testament. This is the way in which we differ most profoundly from the two groups represented by Questions 2 and 3, i.e. from traditional Jewish commentators and also from New Testament interpreters. Both those groups regarded the scriptures as divinely inspired and therefore inerrant; everything in scripture had to be internally consistent and compatible with contemporary religious opinion, Jewish and Christian respectively. Thus, although we may imagine that we have a great advantage over both traditional Jewish and traditional Christian exegesis, in that we can attempt to understand the original meaning of the Old Testament text without imposing a doctrinally motivated interpretation, we find ourselves by this very fact faced by a problem which they did not face. If there are parts of the Old Testament which we cannot accept and do not wish to integrate into our theology, what is to be our overall account of the Old Testament, and how do we justify our rejection of certain parts of it? This is a question which we try to answer in the next chapter.

New Testament Interpretation versus Modern

Von Rad claimed that 'there is in fact (in the New Testament) no normative interpretation of the Old Testament' (*Old Testament Theology*, vol. ii, Eng. trans., p. 409). This is true in the sense that no New Testament writer consciously sets out to give an authoritative Christian interpretation of scripture as a whole. The nearest we come to this is the argument of the Epistle to the Hebrews, and that involves the exegesis of only a relatively limited section of scripture. But we can say that all the writers of the New Testament had a great deal in common when it came to expounding scripture. They all needed to work out a theology of the Old Testament for themselves: what we call the Old Testament was their scripture. One of the earliest tenets of the Christian faith was that Christ had lived and died and risen again in fulfilment of the scriptures. They all saw the Old Testament as full of references to Christ, some absolutely explicit, as when the LXX used the word *christos*, others less obvious but nevertheless significant. As we have suggested in Chapter 2, the basic clues must have been given to them by Jesus himself. In his teaching the coming of the Kingdom brought with it the revelation of God. The adjustment which the earliest Christians made in view of Jesus' resurrection was that Jesus Christ was seen not only as the essential link with the coming Kingdom, but also as constituting in himself the revelation of God. This meant that they naturally tended to concentrate on those passages in the Old Testament in which the coming revelation of God was most clearly set out, not only admittedly 'messianic' passages, but also those which looked forward to the action of God in the end time or the coming age. Consequently much of their attention was concentrated on the prophets, with Isaiah as the most frequently quoted. This was because the Book of Isaiah contains the prophecies of the great prophet of the exile with their markedly eschatological flavour.

The second most popular source for quotations was the Psalter. This might seem to call for some explanation: most of the psalms are not very eschatological, and few can be rightly described as messianic. But the king is often called 'the anointed one' in the psalms of the period of the kingdom, and in the LXX this is rendered with *ho christos*, a phrase which would certainly catch the attention of an early Christian who read his scriptures in Greek. Moreover, as we have suggested on pp. 27f. above, Jesus himself may have seen in the righteous sufferer of the psalms a foreshadowing of his own role. It is even possible that before the rise of Christianity one tradition in Judaism may have been inclined to interpret the psalms in a messianic sense.

The early Christians were not much interested in the Torah as such, not at least in the prescriptions which form the great bulk of the Torah. They did of course quote the non-legal parts of the Pentateuch quite freely, especially Genesis and the songs at the end of Deuteronomy in chapters 32 and 33. The Book of Proverbs interested them in as far as its concept of wisdom could help in constructing their Christology; see especially Colossians 1:15–20. The Book of Daniel does not fit into any category and is used primarily for two purposes: it supplies the Son of Man title with which the early church could describe Jesus (building on the fact that he had used the phrase to refer to himself). And secondly, Daniel provides some of the most striking symbols in the Book of Revelation. The early Christians had no very strong interest in the historical books. Job served mostly to furnish them with misunderstood hints of resurrection.

What all the New Testament writers have in common as far as concerns the interpretation of scripture is a belief in salvation history and a christocentric approach. This in itself, as we have seen, resulted in an emphasis on the fulfilment of prophecy. Indeed, judging by the New Testament, we could say with some justification that early Christianity represented a 'back to the prophets' movement. They all believed that scripture can be effectively quoted in defence of their christocentric faith and hence that scripture is, so to speak, on their side. Luke is entirely justified in depicting Paul as arguing with the Jewish community in Rome on the basis of 'the law of Moses and the prophets' (Acts 28:23), as also in his claim that Paul was a prisoner 'because of the hope of Israel' (28:20). The earliest Christianity claimed to be based on what we would call the Old Testament scriptures. The writers of the New Testament would have been astonished at the suggestion that Christianity could afford to dispense with the Old Testament.

But we today are in a different situation. In the first place, we have a New Testament. Indeed, we incline quite rightly to give more authority to the New Testament than to the Old. In this respect of course there is nothing new about our situation: there has been something like an acknowledged New Testament ever since the end of the second century. But what is new about our situation is that we cannot unthinkingly adopt either the interpretation which the New Testament gives to the Old or the interpretation of the Old which the exegetical tradition of the Church has defended ever since the end of the second century. We have been in a different situation ever since the rise of biblical criticism 200 years ago.

In any case we in our day are no doubt as much influenced by our cultural environment as ever the New Testament writers were by theirs. Indeed, we might here draw an analogy between the New Testament writers' attitude to the Old Testament and our modern attitude to our bible as a whole. We tend, for example, to praise Moses as a broadminded man who did not suffer from colour prejudice, since he married an Ethiopian woman (see Num. 12:1 – I have heard this point seriously put forward in a synagogue sermon). Or we find the parable of the embezzling steward in Luke 16:1–9 unintelligible because we do not understand how the Torah in Jesus' day was made to square with the need to charge interest (see J. D. M. Derrett, *Law in the New Testament*, pp. 48f.). In a similar way the New Testament writers saw David as an inspired prophet well acquainted with the career of the Messiah-to-come, like their fellow early Christians. Sarah appeared as a pious female because she was closely associated with other figures of legendary piety such as Abraham. Lot appears as a bit of a prig because the author of 2 Peter was a bit of a prig (see 2 Peter 2:7–8). This is even more true of contemporary Jewish exegesis. One might perhaps make a nice distinction between Jewish exegesis intended for home consumption (Qumran and rabbinic) and Jewish exegesis intended to be read by educated Greeks and Romans as well as Jews (Philo and Josephus). It is conceivable that something like this distinction might be traced within the New Testament itself: Matthew, James and Revelation would be intended for home consumption; Paul was writing for educated (or semi-educated) Gentiles as well, and so *a fortiori* was John. But only when we reach such writers as Clement of Rome and the author of the *Epistle of Barnabas* do we find

Christian documents which in this respect can be compared to Philo and Josephus.

It is time, however, that we said explicitly why we today cannot accept the New Testament interpretation of the Old Testament *au pied de la lettre*. There are three main reasons, which we must illustrate from the pages of the New Testament:

1   We cannot accept the concept of a superhuman form of prediction divinely guaranteed. This concept was common to all Jews and all Christians by the first century AD: 'All scripture is inspired by God' (*theopneustos*) writes the author of 2 Timothy 3:16. Not every New Testament writer might express it like this exactly, but all agreed that the Old Testament prophets (who included Moses and David) had a miraculous knowledge of the future. This we moderns cannot accept. The reasons for this we cannot stay to explore, but they are connected with the influence of the Enlightenment on the mind of European man.

2   We cannot understand messianic prophecies in exactly the sense in which they were understood by the writers of the New Testament. This is not to say that we cannot use the argument from prophecy; but we cannot use it as clearly as the New Testament writers did. We cannot use it in order to prove that everything in Jesus' life happened 'according to the scriptures'. We have already seen an example of this in Matthew's treatment of Isaiah 7:14 (see pp. 179–80 above). Another clear example occurs in Matthew 2:18. We cannot possibly agree that Jeremiah 31:15 was fulfilled by the massacre of the innocents. The same argument applies to the occasions when New Testament writers trace a dialogue between God the Father and the pre-existent Son in the psalms. This is done on a lavish scale by the author of Hebrews in Hebrews 1:5–13. But we must insist today that Psalm 45:6–7 is not an address by God the Father to the pre-existent Son, nor is Psalm 102:25–7 (see Heb. 1:8–12). Paul is quite capable of this sort of exegesis also; see Romans 15:3, where he represents Psalm 69:9, 'The reproaches of those who reproached thee fell on me', as an utterance of the Son to the Father. We must maintain that this is not what the author of Psalm 69 meant. In the same way, John implies in John 5:35 that Psalm 132:17, 'I have prepared a lamp for my anointed', refers to the relation of John the Baptist to Jesus (see above, p. 124). We cannot possibly allow this. The author of Psalm 132 has no such thought in mind.

3   Much New Testament interpretation of the Old Testament misses its mark as far as we are concerned because what they regarded as history we must regard as legend or myth. To take a simple example, in Galatians 4:29 Paul writes: 'But as at that time he who was born according to the flesh persecuted him who was born according to the Spirit, so it is now.' Putting aside for our

purpose the question of whether it is legitimate to render $m^e taheq$ with 'persecuted' (see above, p. 44), this example does not convince us because we can have no confidence whatever that the events described in Genesis 21 have any relation to history at all. But unless Ishmael really did persecute Isaac, Paul's argument has no force. In the same way, on pp. 106–7 above we have suggested that according to the author of Hebrews he whom Moses saw in the burning bush was the pre-existent Christ (see Heb. 11:24–7). But if it is quite impossible to determine what historical event, if any, lies behind the story of the burning bush in Exodus 3, the author of Hebrews' claim loses its point. An example from the Fourth Gospel is also appropriate: in John 8:39–40, 56–8 Jesus is represented as making the claim that Abraham had seen him, or, as the Jews understand it, that he had seen Abraham (see above, p. 125). But we must regard Abraham as something less than legendary; it is by no means certain that there ever was such a person. He is about as historical as King Arthur. Hence the episode related in Genesis 18, on which John's exegesis is founded, cannot prove anything about Christ's pre-existent activity.

We could pursue this third point further. It is perhaps the way in which we differ most radically from all Christian and Jewish exegesis before the eighteenth century. We will content ourselves here with observing that all New Testament argument based on the *historicity* of characters belonging to the patriarchal age is invalid for us: whether they appeal to the example of Enoch, or Noah, or Abraham, or Melchisedech, as historical characters they cannot be regarded by us as credible. This is not to say that Abraham, for instance, may not be regarded as an example of faith in the same way as the Good Samaritan is an example of works. But when appeal is made to the historical significance of some action or utterance of a character encountered in Genesis, as for example the action of Melchisedech in blessing Abraham, we must refuse to accept it as valid.

Typology

When we apply these considerations to the question of typology in the New Testament, we find ourselves in a very similar position. For example, the clearest example of typology in Paul, the comparison between Israel's experience in the exodus and wilderness sojourn with the Corinthian church's experience of baptism and the Eucharist in 1 Corinthians 10:1–11, loses a great deal of its effectiveness in the light of our modern understanding of the Old Testament: perhaps the comparison with the crossing of the Red Sea may stand as a type of baptism, though our doubts as to whether there was any superhuman element in the event must considerably blunt the point of it. But the giving of the manna as superhuman food and the miraculous production of water from the rock must be regarded as legend and most unlikely to be sufficiently historical to give a genuine parallel to the bread and wine in the Eucharist. Paul has compounded our difficulty by introducing an element of haggadic legend which is not even to be found in scripture.

Another prominent piece of typology in the New Testament is the type of Jonah as the foreshadowing of the *triduum* and the Lord's resurrection. This type is found both in Paul (Rom. 10:5–9) and Matthew (Matt. 12:39–40; see above, pp. 36–8). Here too the question of historicity is vitally important. The critical understanding of the Book of Jonah assumes for good reasons that it is not an historical account at all, but a parable. In any case the exact period which Jonah spent in the fish's belly has no particular significance in the narrative. Later Jewish tradition embroidered this element in the story out of all proportion to the whole (see *The New Testament Interpretation of Scripture*, pp. 148f.). We must therefore conclude that the typology of Jonah has no real significance for the Lord's resurrection. It is an early Christian conceit, not original to Jesus, and depends largely on Jewish exegetical tradition which draws on sheer legend. Paul in fact uses this piece of *haggada* in order to assist his astonishing claim that Deuteronomy 30:12–14 is really concerned, not with strict observance of the Torah, as we might imagine, but with the righteousness of faith. We may well admire his virtuosity, but we can hardly accept his conclusion.

We take another example of typology from 1 Peter 3:21. Here Noah's ark is represented as a type of the church: in both salvation is received for a special group by means of water. Despite the widespread use, during all periods of the church's history, of the ark for the type of the church, we cannot today accept this in the way in which the author of 1 Peter understood it. The story of Noah is not even legend. . . The best we can say of it is that the ark as a *symbol* of the church may be effective enough. We cannot admit that in the time of Noah we see God acting in the same way as he did in Christ, because we cannot possibly maintain that God did actually command Noah to build the ark. In much the same way we can hardly be impressed by the statement in Jude 5 that Jesus saved the people from the land of Egypt. Perhaps if he had said, as the author of Wisdom 18:14–15 implies, that the divine Word had saved the people from Egypt, we might make some sense of it. But to attribute the name of an historical character, Jesus of Nazareth, to the divine being who was behind the exodus is to strain our credulity to breaking point.

At the same time we should not dismiss typology out of hand as a completely outdated method of scriptural exegesis. There are examples of it in the New Testament which can still be regarded as meaningful: in Romans 10:16, for instance, Paul quotes Isaiah 53:1: 'Lord, who has believed what he has heard from us?' No doubt Paul envisaged the prophet as referring to the message about the crucified Messiah. But we can perfectly legitimately trace a connection here: the true significance of the suffering servant in God's design was understood by almost none of his contemporaries and affords a true parallel to the reception given to the message of the crucified Messiah in Paul's day. Exactly the same point is made by the author of the Fourth Gospel at John 12:38f. (For a full discussion of the Pauline passage see above, pp. 56f.) We need not do as Paul did, and imagine that the historical Isaiah knew about the crucifixion, but the correspondence is genuine enough.

Von Rad, whom no one could accuse of a slavish biblical literalism, is ready to accept that the figure of Joseph provides a faint type of Christ (see (2) p. 369). Certainly Joseph is portrayed in this light in Stephen's speech in Acts 7:9f. And here perhaps the historical objection is not so impassable, since the story of a righteous man rejected by his own was certainly a product of Israel's faith, and the actual question as to whether it ever happened does not alter the validity of the type.

Baker (op. cit., pp. 255, 259, 266–7) has a useful discussion of typology. The essence of typology, he says, lies in the assumption that God acts consistently, and he claims that for a typological exegesis to be valid two conditions must be fulfilled: the events in the Old Testament claimed as a type must be historical, and there must be a real correspondence: 'Typology is generally historical, whereas allegory is fanciful' (p. 259). We may well agree with this: typology depends on what the Old Testament calls God's 'emet, his reliability or truth. God does not exhibit a radically different character at different epochs in history. If, therefore, we recognize God's character in the life of Jesus Christ, it is quite reasonable to expect the same character to be revealed in at least some of the events in the old dispensation. This is precisely typology. But must it be revealed in events? If we are to do justice to the Old Testament must we not admit that sometimes God's character is revealed in what Israel believed happened, even if we today may have our doubts as to whether it did actually happen? In other words, in some circumstances the Old Testament type may be more the product of Israel's faith. We shall be returning to this theme in a subsequent chapter, but we should perhaps ask at this point: how is it that we can accept Joseph as in some respect a type of Christ, whereas we reject Paul's typology of the manna and the water from the rock? The answer must surely lie in the quality of the type: in Joseph we have a human character imagined as undergoing an experience (rejection by his own and subsequent vindication) which we see reproduced in the life, death and resurrection of Jesus Christ. If both stories are claimed as examples of God's design of salvation in history, the typology holds, even if Joseph never existed. The story, at least as related in Genesis, indicates that some in Israel had some notion of how God acts, even though God's design was much more fully exhibited in Jesus Christ. But for Paul the point of the typology between the wilderness events and the sacraments (if we may be permitted a term which is strictly anachronistic) was the remarkable similarity between the mode of the Lord's presence among his people under the old dispensation and the new. Since we can have no confidence that the Lord really did use this mode in the old dispensation, the typology loses its point for us. The most we could say is that Israel of old had the belief that their fathers were somehow miraculously sustained in the wilderness. Because it is a typology of things rather than persons it ceases to be very meaningful to us.

Our Debt to New Testament Interpretation

Thus there is not complete discontinuity between the New Testament interpretation of scripture and our interpretation of the Old Testament. Without working out a full account of how we can best relate ourselves to the New Testament interpretation, a subject we consider in Chapter 11, we can at this point indicate at least what difference the New Testament interpretation makes to the modern Christian's understanding of the Old Testament. We find that this is best summed up under four heads:

1   The New Testament makes it easier, not more difficult, for us to understand the Old Testament. This is because the New Testament writers have in a sense done our homework for us: they have provided us with a Christian bible which they did not have. They had the more difficult, but absolutely essential, task of writing a Christian interpretation of the Old Testament. They have shown (sometimes despite themselves) how Christianity is linked to the Jewish scriptures. They had to try to find Christ in the Old Testament. We only have to relate the revelation recorded in the Old Testament to the revelation in Christ as recounted by them. In other words, because in the New Testament they have given us an account of God's revelation of himself under the Christian dispensation, we are now in a position to find a basically Christian approach to the Old Testament. Difficult as this task is

in many ways, it would have been quite impossible without the New Testament.

2   We are not under any obligation to accept any given instance of a New Testament interpretation of the Old Testament just because it is in the New Testament. We have already shown how such passages as Matthew 1:22–3 and 1 Corinthians 10:1–11 cannot be understood by us in the sense in which they were intended by their respective authors. Perhaps another example, this time from the Fourth Gospel, may help to make this clear. We have claimed that in John 1:29–51 we have an extensive Johannine midrash on Jacob's vision at Bethel recounted in Genesis 28 (see above, p. 123). Here John presents Christ as the ladder and also as the figure who stood at the head of the ladder. To be quite accurate, he probably meant that the pre-existent Word was the figure at the head of the ladder, and the incarnate Word was himself the ladder between heaven and earth. Now in as far as Genesis 28 witnesses to a desire for a living link between God and man at the period when it was written (perhaps the eighth century BC), and the conviction that such a thing was within the scope of God's design for his people, it can be said to have been fulfilled in Christ. But we can neither admit that the author of Genesis 28 had Jesus Christ in mind, nor can we be easily persuaded that Jesus himself actually interpreted Genesis 28 in this way.

3   The New Testament writers indicate those areas in the Old Testament which are most relevant to Christianity: the prophets, the psalms, some parts of the wisdom literature. This is in contrast to the prescriptions of the Torah, for example, or the Book of Esther (that favourite with the rabbis). This does not mean that we cannot find other areas in the Old Testament relevant which the New Testament writers largely ignore, the Book of Job, perhaps, or a chapter such as Hosea 11, which is totally ignored by the New Testament writers with the exception of Matthew 2:15, and he offers an exegesis which seems to us far-fetched. Indeed, one could write a whole monograph on books of the Old Testament which New Testament writers and modern scholars unite in admiring, but for very different reasons. The Book of Jonah would be one such, and perhaps the Book of Daniel another. In this category might also come Amos' prophecy. But on the whole it is reasonable to claim that the New Testament writers have fairly indicated to us the relevant target area in the Old Testament.

4   There is one other way in which the New Testament writers provide us with an essential service: they selected from the Old Testament those symbols and images which have proved most

effective in the understanding and presentation of the Christian gospel: the Lamb, the Word of God, the Son of God, the Second Adam, the Dragon, the Bridegroom, the High Priest, the Lion of Judah, the Bride of Christ. These symbols and many others were first used in a Christian context by the writers of the New Testament, and have proved their lasting value ever since. It is indeed in this respect that the astonishing virtuosity of John the Divine becomes most apparent. Virtually none of the disclaimers about the New Testament interpretation of scripture which we have made in this chapter apply to his work. This is because he does not adopt the schema of prophecy and fulfilment. He never says anything like Matthew's 'All this took place to fulfil what the Lord had spoken by the prophet. . .' He simply uses Old Testament imagery and symbolism with the supreme confidence of a great artist and we see its complete appropriateness. The only time we find it difficult to follow him is when we have doubts about his theology. His use of the Old Testament is always effective and never contrived.

The Historical Development of Scriptural Exegesis

In this chapter we have been considering both the New Testament interpretation of scripture and our assessment of it today. Something should be said about the many centuries of interpretation that intervened. It is relevant first to look briefly at how Judaism's interpretation developed, in order to afford a useful comparison with the parallel Christian development.

From at least about the middle of the second century before Christ, Judaism has been consciously Torah-centric religion, interpreting everything in its bible in terms of the centrality of the Torah. The tradition of scriptural exegesis has existed from long before the second century BC, since it is found within scripture itself. But the significant feature about orthodox Judaism is that there has never been a serious break in that tradition of exegesis. First there was the 'great synagogue', then came the Mishna, then the Talmud, then the great medieval commentators such as Rashi and Maimonides, and so on up to the scriptural exegesis of the latest modern rabbi. In this process the Jewish bible has been very considerably modified: targum, midrash and *haggada* have all combined to present a harmonious picture of scripture in which historical perspective is almost entirely ignored. The desire to make scripture meet current religious needs and to present it in contemporary terms has very often ended by transforming it almost out of recognition. Legend and harmonization have buried a great deal of the reality of scripture. An historical outline has survived, indeed: exodus, covenant on Sinai, occupation of

Canaan, the monarchy, the division of the kingdom, the disappearance of the northern kingdom, the Babylonian exile and return. These have indeed survived, but much else was transformed: such characters as Abraham, Moses, Aaron, Miriam, Samuel, David, Elijah, Solomon were almost obliterated as historical figures, in as far as the first four were ever historical figures. As they appear in orthodox Judaism they bear very little relation to what can be recovered of their actual history. When we come to the period of what Christians would regard as the most significant history, the period of the classical prophets, remarkably little was utilized by the religious tradition. Sometimes, it is true, the rabbis surprise and delight us by their understanding of the great prophets but too often these great figures have been buried under the accretions of later tradition.

As far as we can judge, up to AD 70 this process of accommodating scripture to contemporary sentiment continued unchecked by any firm attempt to impose a standard of orthodoxy. The fall of Jerusalem and the rise of Christianity changed all that. Rabbinic orthodoxy made its appearance and from now on religious tradition was guided by an anti-Christian, anti-speculative direction. For this Christianity itself is partly to blame; the abusive hostility of the Christian fathers, and the vile persecuting policy of the Constantinian empire, ensured that Christianity and Judaism should be divided through the centuries by a barrier of mutual hatred. The emergence of an orthodox tradition in Judaism did not mean a better appreciation of the meaning of scripture or any attempt to get back to the bible. There *was* a sort of 'back to the bible' movement in Judaism in the eighth century AD. This produced the sect known as the Karaites. But it was just as Torah-centric as orthodox Judaism and only ended by producing its own *halaka*.

One might institute an interesting comparison between modern orthodox Judaism and the Roman Catholic Church as it presented itself to the world between Vatican I and Vatican II. In both, religious sentiment gave the impression of having pretty well freed itself from scripture, but was kept under control by religious authority. In neither is regard given to modern methods of deciding what is history, and what is not. In both there was a real danger that the evolution of tradition would end by burying altogether the original history and the original characters of scripture. It is therefore not wholly accurate to describe Jews as 'the people of the book' because religious tradition has enabled them to avoid the impact of at least certain important elements in the book in question. Of course there are also immense differences between orthodox Judaism and the Roman Catholic Church in the inter-

Vatican period, not least in the method by which authority is imposed.

There can be no doubt that the Christian exegetical tradition developed for several centuries in a way very like that of Judaism. The bible was interpreted in terms of credal orthodoxy: complete harmonization was universally accepted. Biblical characters underwent the process of standardization, becoming either plaster saints or stage villains. But certain features in the tradition caused the development gradually to diverge from the pattern of Judaism. One was the failure to translate the bible into the new languages of the Roman Empire or the Germanic and Scandinavian languages of the converted barbarians. This meant that the bible, far from being made contemporary by a process of targumizing, remained doubly remote, in the case of the Old Testament trebly remote. Consequently at the Reformation there could be a 'back to the bible' movement. Orthodox Judaism has never got sufficiently removed from its bible to be able to break the bonds of *halaka* and *midrash*. If the Christian church in the dark ages had targumized its bible into the Romance languages, and into the languages of the northern peoples, and if its scholars had maintained contact with the Old Testament in Hebrew and the New Testament in Greek, we might still today be in the position of Orthodox Judaism; that is, we might be unable to establish contact with large areas of the real bible because the interpreted bible eclipsed it. As it was, when the Western Church rediscovered the Hebrew and Greek bible, it came as a surprise.

In the first century of our era Christianity freed itself from the Jewish exegetical tradition because of the life and teaching of Jesus. His originality launched what was at first a new stream of tradition within Judaism and enabled it to leap over the fence of the Law and establish communication with the Gentile world. After his resurrection Christians could still know God in Christ in the Spirit, and this constituted a potential defence against legalism and biblicism. Not that the church did not at various times and in various places fall into both these errors. But there was always the appeal to the tradition of Jesus Christ in the Spirit, a more definite, more historical, more three-dimensional figure than Moses could ever be.

The other important figure in the development of early Christianity was Paul. Paul was no super-rabbi, anxious only to divert the tradition which he inherited in the direction of a messianic Judaism. Certainly before his conversion he must have been in contact with elements in Judaism which predisposed him towards the Christianity which he embraced. He probably already held that the psalms and the latter prophets should be interpreted messianically. He already had an interest in wisdom speculation.

He must have had some contact with the apocalyptic tradition.
But cutting across all these traditions was the historical figure of
Jesus Christ and above all there was the crucifixion of the Messiah.
It was the cross more than anything else that disorientated Judaism
for Paul, and this it is that makes it impossible to regard Paul
merely as a Christianized rabbi. And with the cross was closely
bound up the doctrine of justification by faith, something that
certainly goes back to Jesus himself.

These two disorientating elements in Christianity were brought
together by Paul, and rightly, for they are integral to each other;
unless we realize this, Paul's sentence will be completely mysti-
fying to us: 'If justification were through the law, then Christ died
to no purpose' (Gal. 2:21). We now know that justification by
faith was not peculiar to Christianity. It is found in the *Hodayoth*,
and in the hymn in the *Manual of Discipline* in the Qumran
documents. Moreover, the religion of the great prophets from
Amos to the Second Isaiah, being a religion more of faith than
of Torah observance, allowed implicitly for justification by faith.
There was bound to be a clash ultimately when after the exile
Judaism became more and more narrowly Torah-centric. That
clash did not appear in Qumran because justification by faith only
emerges in the devotional life of its leaders and was not allowed
to interfere with the Torah-centric nature of their religion. Justification by faith emerged as essential to Christianity because it was
an important part of Jesus' teaching, and because the cross, as
expounded by Paul and John, made a doctrine of justification by
faith necessary. The cross was the turning upside down of previous
notions about God, and justification by faith was the disorientating
of previous notions about merit and reward. Justification by faith,
closely connected with the doctrine of the cross, has remained
ever since in Christianity to be a disturbing, disorientating, destab-
ilizing influence. It has been ignored for long periods and the
cross has been largely ignored with it. Always it has returned to
be the gadfly, the warning, the grit in the oyster, the nuisance to
well-established ecclesiastics, as Søren Kierkegaard was a nuisance in his day and Ernst Käsemann is in ours – a nuisance, but
one that cannot be ignored for ever. Christianity thus has an
inbuilt capacity for profitably breaking tradition which Judaism
seems to lack.

Did Christianity actually divert a part of the stream of Jewish
exegetic tradition, so that Judaism was actually impoverished, and
potentially fruitful elements in Judaism were lost? It seems that
this did happen. It could well be maintained that certain important
elements in the Judaism of the first century AD were in fact
absorbed by Christianity in such a way that they were inevitably
rejected by Judaism. The putting of the quality of mercy or love

at the centre of the divine nature, the tendency towards universalism, the apprehension of distinctions within the godhead, justification by faith as an operative principle – all these were potentially present in Judaism but were exploited by Christianity. The consequence was that Judaism became a more monochrome and more exclusive religion. The rise of Christianity meant a diminution of Judaism.

Similarly, Christianity undoubtedly suffered as a result of its early divorce from the parent Judaism. An intimate knowledge of the Old Testament; a prophylactic against Mariolatry and undue veneration of the saints; above all an ability to resist the tide of monastic asceticism that engulfed the church from the fourth century onwards, creating a fundamentally unChristian prejudice against marriage and sex – all these potential advantages Christianity lost by its divorce from Judaism.

One could pursue this fascinating line of inquiry further. One could ask, for example, since the *aggiornamento* means that the Roman Catholic Church has repudiated the idea that scripture should be subordinated to religious tradition, what is the next step? Can Catholics, Protestants and Anglicans tackle together the task of appealing back to the bible without ignoring the church's tradition? Has the Eastern Orthodox Church, untouched by any reformation, a part to play in this? But we would be straying from our subject if we were to go any further. It must be enough to indicate that these questions remain to be answered.

10

WHAT IS THE OLD TESTAMENT?

We have now reached a point in this study where we are inescapably faced with the question: what is the Old Testament? We have concluded in the previous chapter that we today cannot simply take over unmodified the tradition of Old Testament exegesis used by the writers of the New Testament, though we see the need for finding something in common with them. We have also traced the course of Old Testament interpretation through the ages right up to the point where the advent of biblical criticism required a reorientation of attitude towards the Old Testament on the part of all thinking Christians. We must therefore make some attempt to answer the question: what does the Old Testament signify for Christians today?

Much has been written on this subject during the last fifty years. I have myself published a certain amount about it, and for a fuller and more technical account of my position I must refer the reader to *Studies in Paul's Technique and Theology*, chapter 12, and *The New Testament Interpretation of Scripture*, chapter 1. Here it will be sufficient if we examine the answer that one outstanding Old Testament scholar gave to this question, and also the answers given by a number of others. We must also come to some conclusions about the limits of the Old Testament. Nor must we fail to examine the literalistic way of interpreting the Old Testament, popularly called Fundamentalism.

The Answer of Orthodox Judaism

But first we must consider those who have the best right to be heard on the topic of what the Old Testament is, those who would claim to be the lineal descendants of the men who wrote the Old Testament, that is, the representatives of modern orthodox Judaism. An informed orthodox Jew today would claim that the centre of what for him is inspired scripture is the Torah, God's detailed presentation of the law by which he desired Israel to live, revealed to Moses on Sinai and committed to writing in the Pentateuch. All the rest of scripture is to be understood in the light of this Torah: the prophets are commentators on the Torah and judges and critics of Israel when Israel departed from observance of the Torah. The k^{e}tūbīm (Psalms, Proverbs, Job, etc.) are valuable in as far as they throw light on the Torah and Torah observance. Any other books in the Hebrew canon, such as Esther or Qoheleth (Ecclesiastes), are to be interpreted in terms of the Torah. The Torah is the supreme revelation; the rest of the scriptures, though inspired, are to be regarded as sharing in greater or lesser degrees of revelation. The Torah is always the criterion of scripture.

But orthodox Judaism, as we have seen, is not content to present its adherents with the bible alone. It considers that the tradition of exegesis which sprang from the scriptures is continuous with them and in some degree shares in their inspiration. So that midrash, Mishna, Talmud and medieval commentary are all to be studied with equal attention and reference. The Torah is indeed the centre and meaning of scripture; but scripture is incomplete without the ensuing exegetical tradition right up to the present day.

With some of this we have no quarrel. A great deal of what Christians call the Old Testament is concerned with the law of Moses and its observance. We do not need to go along with Paul in a passage such as Romans 10:5–8 when he argues that if scripture seems to be commending Torah observance it is really contrasting the way of law obedience with the way of faith obedience. Our difference from orthodox Judaism does not lie in denying the central position of the Torah in the Pentateuch, but in the question as to what is the true will of God for his people. And here we come up against the issue of the critical approach to the Old Testament. As long as Judaism holds that the Torah was given intact through Moses to the Jews, to be observed in all particulars until the age-to-come, we must dissent from them. Modern Jews may choose to obey the dietary laws for old times' sake, or for the sake of preserving the distinctive Hebrew culture, or for hygienic reasons. But we cannot hold that God desires them to do so or that he is grieved if they abandon detailed law observance.

Moreover, we cannot agree that the Torah was given entire in the time of Moses, or that detailed Torah observance has always characterized the religion of Israel. Critical study of the Old Testament shows that the Pentateuch is the product of a long process, that many of the dietary and ritual prescriptions have their origin in primitive folk-religion, and that none of the Torah as we have it was written down until hundreds of years after the time of Moses. In addition, Judaism as a religion centred on detailed Torah observance is a product of the post-exilic period. During the time of the great prophets (750–550 BC) there was nothing like the fully articulated law system which we have in the Pentateuch.

Most of the prophets do not consciously call Israel back to Torah observance as the phrase is understood in modern Judaism. We shall have to give a little more attention to the Torah in the next chapter; but this suffices to define the position of Christians today in relation to orthodox Judaism.

Two consequences follow from this: Judaism does not really hold a distinctive 'theology of the Old Testament'; and the Torah is not the only possible centre and significance of the Old Testament. Those who try to discover a theology of the Old Testament usually assume that the Old Testament as a whole must exhibit some unifying scheme or concept in the light of which it becomes a significant and more or less integrated body of writings. But Judaism does not attempt to do this, nor does it make such a claim. For Judaism the scriptures with the ensuing tradition (Mishna, Talmud, etc.) are intelligible. Jewish theologians would not be interested in working out a theology of the scriptures apart from such a context.

The second consequence is that the Torah is not necessarily or demonstrably the centre of the Old Testament. Or, to be more accurate, the true significance of the Old Testament does not demonstrably lie in its witness to the necessity of Torah observance. When Eichrodt writes that post-exilic Judaism 'turned the religion of Jahweh into a religion of observances' (p. 177), he is perhaps being less than fair to the best elements in the Judaism of the years 300 BC to AD 100, to the genuine devotion of the Pharisees, to the intense awareness of the need for God's grace shown by some of the leaders of the Qumran, to the underlying conviction of practising Jews that the covenant was God's gift and the Torah the supreme example of God's mercy. But there is enough truth in Eichrodt's dictum to justify us in saying that post-exilic Judaism did not do justice to some vitally important elements in the witness of the Old Testament. As a result of biblical criticism modern scholars actually know more about many parts of the Old Testament than either orthodox Judaism or traditional Christianity ever found out. When the prophets, the Books of Job, Jonah and Daniel, to take some very obvious examples, are no longer looked at through the spectacles of the Torah, they appear in a clearer, more real light. They yield all sorts of information that a Torah-centric approach obscures or misses altogether. Orthodox Judaism has no intrinsic right to possess the full significance of the Old Testament, and, as long as it clings to a traditional literalist approach, it will always fail to understand some of the deepest insights of its own scriptures. Whether the same thing can be said for a traditional Christian approach is a question we must face in the final chapter.

In the rest of this chapter we have three tasks before us: we must discuss some of the answers to our question given by some modern Christian experts on the Old Testament. We must consider the solution offered by modern Christian literalists. And we must examine the limits of the Old Testament, the canon and apocrypha.

The Answers of Some Modern Scholars

We begin, then, with G. von Rad. He thinks the New Testament is related to the Old Testament by the common bond of salvation history. In both, God is known through his acts. See (2) p. 338. See also Baker, p. 291: God is revealed through saving acts in history. But von Rad realizes that often the acts on which Israel's writers laid most emphasis are very obscure to us because of our doubts about their historicity. Thus the Exodus is the great archetypal act of salvation, but a conscientious scholar can say very little definite as to what actually took place. Consequently von Rad adds that very often what Israel treats as salvation history comes to us in the form of Israel's faith about God's acts in history. Of the earliest records von Rad writes: 'Here everything is shaped by faith; even the association of the events into a grand path of salvation is not merely historical record, but is itself already an acknowledgement of the leadership of God' (1, pp. 4–5). This is an important point to which we must return later. With the concept of salvation history goes of course the idea of revelation: God is revealed in his saving acts. The theology of the Old Testament consists in the revelation of Jahweh (1, p. 115). It is true that some of the prophets apparently look forward to a time when the reference back to the exodus event will be no longer necessary (e.g. Jer. 23:7; Isa. 43:16–20), but this does not mean that salvation history is dispensed with. Though von Rad speaks of revelation, it is not by any means a positivistic or automatic process: 'The commandment forbidding images is bound up with the hidden way in which Jahweh's revelation came about in cult and history' (1, p. 218). In other words, faith is needed to perceive God's acts in history quite as much as when we are dealing with historical events such as the exile in Babylon and the return as when we are considering the legendary period of the patriarchs and the wilderness sojourn.

Von Rad says quite clearly that the religion of the prophets was not centred on the Torah, at least as Torah observance was understood in the post-exilic period. That Torah was formulated after their time (2, p. 3): 'Yet they (the prophets) were not precursors of legalism; they did not reproach their fellows with not living their lives in obedience to law'. . . (2, p. 186). He holds therefore that in proclaiming their message the prophets outline a completely new state of affairs, Jahweh dealing directly with Israel in his free love (1, pp. 67–8). He adds another very important point about the prophets: they had an eschatological orientation. This does not mean that they expected 'the end of the world' but rather 'something final' (2, p. 114).

Von Rad points out that there is no focal point to the Old Testament as there is to the New Testament (2, p. 362). He concludes from this that the Old Testament can only be understood in the light of the New Testament, and that in effect the latter is the logical end of the former (Baker pp. 278, 282). This is a rather far-reaching claim. It is difficult, for example, to see how the legal parts of the Old Testament find their logical end in the New Testament, unless one accepts christocentric presuppositions. It is quite true that Christians claim that certain important parts of the Old Testament are only truly to be comprehended in the light of Christ, but it would be very difficult to substantiate this claim for every part of the Old Testament. Von Rad has some interesting remarks to make about the New Testament interpretation of the Old Testament. In the New Testament, he says, the Old Testament is no longer read as law, but as saving history (2, p. 328). But he adds that 'there can be no impartial proof for the legitimacy of the new interpretation given to the Old Testament in the New' (2, p. 333). His last word seems to be: 'Each Testament legitimates the other' (2, p. 386). This, I believe, is true, granted a christocentric presupposition. It certainly cannot be defended as an 'objective' conclusion from a study of both.

We next look briefly at the views of three other scholars, Eichrodt, Vriezen and Knight. Eichrodt takes the notion of covenant as the basic concept that makes sense of the Old Testament. Covenant is also the link with the New Testament. He is willing to describe this in terms of the response of the people of God to God's will, only finding its culmination in the New Testament not 'a self-contained dogmatic totality, but a real God becoming manifest in history' (pp. 13–15). This sounds very like von Rad's schema: God's will is made known to his people through salvation history. Eichrodt illuminates this a few pages later (p. 26) when he writes that what binds the Old Testament and the New Testament together is 'the irruption of the Kingdom of God into this world and its establishment here'. This too has a hint of salvation history, since presumably Jesus' coming proclaiming the advent of the Kingdom is the culmination of the process recorded in both the Old Testament and the New Testament. Eichrodt has some important remarks on a section of the Old Testament to which we have not yet given the attention it deserves, the wisdom writings. It was the impact of Greek culture, he says, that produced by way of reaction in Israel the emphasis on the divine wisdom.

And he adds that by the time the Book of Wisdom was written wisdom had definitely become an hypostasis within the godhead (pp. 85–6). In Ben Sira wisdom, in the form of the law, is the content of God's revelation. Indeed, the concept could cover both general revelation available to all men, and special revelation (pp. 90–91). This should help us in the next chapter when we relate ourselves to this part of the Old Testament.

Vriezen makes the interesting suggestion that it is the prophetic spirit which gives real unity to the Old Testament (p. 53; see also p. 101). This could no doubt be defended even when we consider the legal prescriptions in the Pentateuch on the grounds that many of them were written by people influenced by Hosea and Isaiah (Deuteronomy, at any rate). But one might have some doubts as to whether there is very much of the prophetic spirit in Leviticus, for example. And, at the other end of the historical process, we might well ask whether a book such as Daniel is not much more influenced by a zeal for the strict observance of the Torah than by any link with the great prophets. Vriezen also holds that 'the New Testament is the confirmation and crowning of the Old' (p. 28). On p. 89 we read that 'Christ fulfils the law in the sense that he actualizes the revelation that had been accorded to Israel, by making the Kingdom of God the basis and essence of his life'. Vriezen, however, admits that such a conclusion is not demonstrably true, since he writes: 'From the historical point of view the Talmud is just as legitimate a continuation of the Old Testament as the Gospel' (p. 121). But two pages later we read: 'The true heart of both the Old Testament and the New Testament is, therefore, the eschatological perspective.' We find, it seems, in Vriezen a strong desire to subsume the whole of the Old Testament under a Christian schema, not only those parts of it that fit easily into this, together with an awareness that such a schema cannot be substantiated on purely literary or historical grounds.

Knight is a scholar who goes further than any other critical commentator in claiming the Old Testament for Christianity. His opening quotation from N. W. Porteous is symptomatic of the whole of his book: 'For the biblical theologian neutrality would be unscientific' (p. 7). He puts strong emphasis on God as revealed in history; the central theme of the Old Testament is God's saving purpose for Israel (p. 18). 'God is known in his speech and in his acts' (p. 21). 'The conception of God as the living "God" is actually the characteristic conception which the Old Testament holds' (p. 42). He goes on to say that 'pictorial thinking is the essence of the whole biblical revelation' (p. 80), and adds (p. 89) that the Old Testament does not present us with any speculative ideas about God, only God in action. This is certainly true for most of the Old Testament, though the wisdom conception was the beginning of a philosophy of religion. But the reason is that until Israel encountered the challenge of Greek philosophy it had not occasion to use anything other than pictorial thinking about God. Once that challenge had been delivered, speculative thought and theology proper had to be worked out. Otherwise Israel's religion, like the religion of every other people affected by Greek culture, would have been absorbed by Greek thought.

Knight agrees with the point made by von Rad that what turned the exodus event into revelation was Israel's faith (p. 152): 'Before us in the Pentateuch lie God's action, Israel's response and the various interpreters' description of both, each conceivable only in terms of the other' (p. 158). Towards the end of his book Knight draws an elaborate parallel between the events of Israel's history and the events of Christ's life, finding in both a fivefold pattern. In Israel's history we can trace the exodus, the covenant on Sinai, Babylonian exile, return from exile and the day of the Lord (yet to come). This corresponds apparently to Jesus' birth, baptism and ministry, crucifixion, resurrection–ascension and parousia. This, it seems to me, is fanciful and even misleading. He has left out some events in Israel's history which Old Testament writers would consider to be of the greatest importance, such as the entry into Canaan and the covenant with David. Moreover, his scheme would not have appealed at all to New Testament writers. They take very little notice of the exile and return, for example. When we turn to his New Testament correlate we find it equally unsatisfactory: the circumstances of Jesus' birth are ignored by two of the four evangelists, and have no significance for Paul. Nor can we say that Jesus' baptism is much emphasized by anyone but the Synoptic writers. In fact such a theory of correspondence between Old Testament events and New Testament events can only be defended in terms of a theology which is heavily dependent on the traditional shape of Christian doctrine and the conclusions of modern scholarship about Israel's history, two presuppositions which make strange bedfellows.

For the rest we must content ourselves with picking out significant observations by individual scholars. J. N. Schofield, writing in the book edited by R. B. Laurin, well remarks that the true centre of the Old Testament is 'God as Creator and Saviour of the world' (p. 119). In the same work (p. 168) E. Jacob is quoted as holding that 'the New Testament is itself a theology of the Old Testament.' This is true as long as the indefinite article is retained before 'theology'. Christians have no right to claim that the New Testament is *the* theology of the Old Testament. B. Anderson has some interesting comments: the Old Testament, he says, makes a claim upon us, not because of ecclesiastical decisions in the past; not because of proof-texts about the Messiah; not because of any theory of divine authorship; but because 'the story defines our identity' (p. 43). If 'our' means 'our Christian identity', this is true. But we must also admit that the Old Testament defines the identity of Judaism. B. Anderson explores further the thought of God's activity being revealed in Israel's faith. He sees that we must distinguish between history as seen through the eyes of Israel's faith and history as it actually happened (p. 48). On the other hand, if you say the Old Testament is 'only a story' you reduce it to the status of a mental event (p. 53). So happenings in history tend to become symbols (of God?) rather than direct disclosures of God (p. 55). This is well worth saying. It is true that if all scriptural history were legendary, as for example is the case with the Hindu scriptures, we would be reduced to admitting that we were dealing only with mental events. But for Christians the most important events in Israel's history take place in the light of history: the career and teachings of the great prophets, the exile and return, and much of Israel's subsequent history up to the coming of Christ. Of course these historical events, including the events recorded in the New Testament, can only be viewed as salvation history in the light of Christian faith. But this does not mean that they were not events. Anderson's argument would be much more damaging to the doctrine of revelation of Judaism than to that of Christianity.

From this necessarily brief consideration of the views on the nature of the Old Testament held by various modern scholars we may at this point draw three conclusions, all of which will have to be elaborated in the next chapter, but which may be usefully stated here:

1   What is common to the Old Testament and the New Testament is that, in both, God is revealed in the course of salvation history. This is a link which practically everyone who has studied the subject from the Christian point of view insists on.

2   Running through the Old Testament prophets and through those parts of the Old Testament influenced by them is a sense of expectation, expressed in the form of eschatological statements, and verging towards the end of the prophetic period into apocalyptic. This is an element in the Old Testament which is indispensable to Christianity.

3   There is no one overall schema of thought into which the Old Testament can be honestly integrated. There is no harmonious 'theology of the Old Testament'. We cannot claim that everything in the Old Testament finds its fulfilment in the New Testament. The utmost we can claim is that certain vitally important elements in the Old Testament find their fulfilment in the New.

The Answer of Fundamentalism

We must now attempt to come to terms with a method of interpreting the Old Testament on the part of Christians which is not defended by any scholars of the slightest academic reputation, but which is pursued by very many Christians and is represented by a very large body of writing. I refer to the 'literalistic' approach to the Old Testament, popularly called 'Fundamentalism'. As we shall be seeing, this is by no means identical with either the New Testament interpretation of the Old Testament, or the traditional Christian approach, though it has elements in common with both.

Perhaps the best way to examine this approach is to take an actual instance of Old Testament interpretation by a 'literalistic' exegete. While I was collecting material for this book I was sent a sixty-page brochure published by the Crusade for World Revival (Walton on Thames, Surrey). It contained a series of daily notes for bible study by Selwyn Hughes, designed to be used for two consecutive months. The author covers the whole of the Book of Exodus in this period. His notes provide a very fair specimen of this type of exegesis. I will refer to the first and second months as i and ii respectively. The Arabic numerals refer to the days of the month.

Very early on we encounter a characteristic feature of literalistic interpretation of the Old Testament, a tendency to Christianize it, that is, to attribute Christian motives to Old Testament characters. Thus when Exodus 1:17 says that 'the midwives feared God and did not do as the king of Egypt commanded them', Hughes writes: 'Who shall they obey? The command of the king or the moral principles of Almighty God?' (i, 2). The difficulty with this piece of exegesis lies in the incongruity of treating a folk-tale as if it was a piece of solid historical testimony. It is like saying that Dick Whittington's decision to obey the bells and turn back to London with his cat was made on the highest moral principles. On the next day we find another feature, already implicit in his treatment of the incident of the midwives, a determination to read legendary narrative as if it was reliable historical record. This often has misleading, not to say ludicrous, consequences. The author of the notes relates the story of Moses' parents hiding him and his adoption by Pharaoh's daughter, and he draws from this a conclusion about God's providence: 'What quietly pulses through this intriguing passage is the remarkable providence of God. At every turn and in every single event, the Almighty is there to advance His purposes and thwart the evil intention of Pharaoh. The more we study God's providential acts in history, the more firm should be our faith in the overreaching sovereignty of God.' But if we have here not history but legend, we cannot honestly draw this conclusion from this passage. The utmost we can do is to draw a conclusion about the faith in God's sovereignty displayed by the author of Exodus.

On days 4 and 5 of the first month we run across an interesting phenomenon. Selwyn Hughes is dealing with Moses' killing of the Egyptian and subsequent flight narrated in Exodus 2:11–22. He blames Moses for this killing and says that because of it God's purposes for Israel were set back though not permanently frustrated. This shows that he does not join traditional Jewish commentators, and indeed New Testament writers as well, in regarding famous heroes of the Old Testament as more or less impeccable. Philo, for example, obviously does not regard Moses as at all culpable. Josephus omits the incident altogether. See Philo, *De Vita Mosis*, i, pp. 44–7; Josephus, *Antiquities*, ii, pp. 25–7; W. G. Braude, *The Midrash on the Psalms*, pp. 62–3. For a fuller discussion see *The Image of the Invisible God*, pp. 170–1, n. 26. The author of Hebrews probably considers Moses as innocent (see Heb. 11:27: 'not being afraid of the anger of the king'). We should no doubt applaud Mr Hughes in this respect, since he is determined to regard biblical characters as men and women of flesh and blood.

When he comes to deal with the incident of the burning bush in Exodus 3 (i, 7), Hughes goes out of his way to reject any attempt to rationalize this miracle; he quotes Dr Alexander Maclaren: 'I would rather believe in the supernatural than in the ridiculous.' There is a third alternative: this is not history but legend. We do not need either to believe in a miracle or to explain it in rationalistic terms. As for believing in the ridiculous, let us turn to the next example.

At i, 12 Hughes bravely expounds a very difficult passage, Exodus 4:24: 'At a lodging place on the way the Lord met him (Moses) and sought to kill him.' Then we read that Zipporah averted this by cutting off her son's foreskin, and touching Moses' feet with it, exclaiming: 'Surely you are a bridegroom of blood to me!' The critical scholar would certainly see here traces of some early apotropaic ritual, perhaps in connection with a fertility rite. But such an option is not open to the literalist. Hughes comments: 'Hebrew scholars interpreting the original Hebrew here, indicate it means that God brought a serious sickness upon Moses because of the fact that he had failed to circumcise his son. . . God's anger was, however, turned away once circumcision was enacted, and Moses recovers and continues his journey.' Even if this is the meaning, which is by no means clear, the necessity to accept this as a divinely inspired account of what God did has resulted in the commentator holding a distinctly sub-Christian doctrine of God: a God who can intend to kill Moses because he has not carried out a purely ritual ceremony, and whose anger is removed by the enactment of the ceremony, is not the God revealed in Jesus Christ. There is something absurd, even pathetic, in the spectacle of a devout Christian attempting to present this crude and early picture of God in terms of the God known in the New Testament.

At i, 18 and 19 we find ourselves faced with another difficulty. Selwyn Hughes is dealing with the ten plagues, culminating in the death of the firstborn. Never at any point does he raise the question which might well be very prominent in the mind of a Christian today: how can we justify God for inflicting these dreadful plagues, most of all the slaughter of the firstborn, on *all* the Egyptians, whereas it was Pharaoh who was primarily responsible, or at the very most Pharaoh's servants? The people of Egypt as a whole can hardly be held responsible for Pharaoh's misdeeds, but it was they who had to suffer. One could imagine various answers that could be made to this, even on literalist presuppositions: the people really were guilty, at least of idolatry (roughly what the author of the Book of Wisdom says); the plagues were not *punishment* on those who were not guilty, only suffering caused by Pharaoh's sin. The astonishing thing is that Hughes never even raises the question. A literalist exegesis is always in danger of missing the really important issues.

Next comes something which is very significant; a cross-connection is traced between a legal prescription in Exodus and the atoning death of Christ. In i, 22 Hughes draws attention to Exodus 12:46, where it is directed that not a bone of the passover lamb should be broken. He writes: 'Deeply symbolical, the full significance of which would not be known by Israel at that time, was the fact that not a bone of the passover lamb was to be broken. This was fulfilled in the death of our Lord', and he refers to John 19:36. Here Hughes is of course entirely in line with Johannine interpretation and with the tradition of the entire church up until the present day (and indeed he draws an admirable moral that we should carefully observe the great feasts of the church). But the implication is that this ritual prescription was given to Israel not for any reason at the time, but for the benefit of Christians hundreds of years later. Many Christians today find this incredible.

We may join with this a number of comments which follow on the incidents of the wilderness sojourn and the furniture of the tabernacle. Hughes employs allegorical exegesis extensively in order to connect them with the life, death and resurrection of Christ. Thus in i, 27 the incident at Marah (Exod. 15:22–7), wherein Moses throws a tree into a bitter pool in order to make it sweet, is treated as a lesson given by God: 'What possible truth could God be trying to teach his people by this incident?. . . The placing of the tree in the bitter waters is a beautiful picture of

God's involvement in our lives through the power of His Cross.'
Now as a fanciful analogy, or devotional conceit, this might pass.
But we cannot allow that this interpretation, confirmed though it
is by ample patristic authority, was intended by God, or that it is
the true meaning of the passage. It is hardly even a type of the
cross, for nobody suffers. It is allegory pure and simple and, as
such, purely subjective.

Hughes follows this up in ii, 8–15 in a determined allegorizing
of the furniture of the tabernacle as described in Exodus 25–7:
the ark 'typifies most effectively the person of our Lord Jesus
Christ' (ii, 8); the shewbread typifies the death, resurrection and
risen life of Jesus Christ (ii, 9). The menorah or golden lampstand
has the same function (ii, 10). The colours of the curtains typify
Christ's two natures as God and man (ii, 11). The goatskin cover-
ings for the roof of the tent typify our Lord's substitutionary death
(through the image of the scapegoat, ii, 12), and so on. Mr Hughes
is determined to find a christological significance in every detail,
no matter how far-fetched it be. Indeed it is no longer appropriate
to describe this as literalism. It is a highly allegorical exegesis of
which Origen himself would be proud. It has nothing to do with
the real meaning of the passage. A British Israelite could as
legitimately interpret these chapters as typifying the Queen's
coronation or the Falklands campaign.

In ii, 5 we have an interesting treatment of the sanitary ceremonial and civil legislation which we find in Exodus 21 and 23.
Hughes implies that God is here providing Israel with a culture
suitable to their geographical and historical environment.
'Cultural rules for specific cultures must be very explicit and
because they are explicit, they are not always appreciated by
people of a different culture and a different time.' This raises
many questions: Hughes seems to imply that God deliberately
prescribed these rules and intended Israel to obey them, a view
which, I believe, neither St Paul nor the author of the Fourth
Gospel held, though the author of Hebrews comes close to it. We
might also ask: why did God not prescribe a culture for the new
people of God? Mr Hughes might find it difficult on his own
premises to answer the question of a modern orthodox Jew: 'Since
you believe that God prescribed them, why do you not obey
them?'

We will content ourselves with noting three more details in Mr
Hughes's commentary. In ii, 22 he deals with the episode of the
golden calf narrated in Exodus 31 and 32. He calls the golden
calf 'a replica of an Egyptian god'. This shows really remarkable
ignorance, or rather ignoring, of evidence about Baal worship
which is available in any modern work on the background to
the Old Testament. He does not apparently realize that Israel

worshipped Jahweh under the image of the bull – or he chooses to ignore the evidence. I cannot see that his view of divine inspiration of the Old Testament would necessarily be impaired by this understanding of the passage. Next we look at ii, 23, where Hughes takes issue with Alfred North Whitehead. He is dealing with the incident of Moses' intercession. Moses offers himself as a victim of God's anger over the sin of the golden calf (Exod. 32:30–38). Hughes writes: 'A famous philosopher, Alfred North Whitehead, claimed that he rejected the God of the Old Testament because he was a being of such stern moralism, inflexible, unbending and lacking in compassion. He must have neglected to read this section, for here in the account of Moses' intercession with God, the Almighty is seen to be extremely sensitive to the failure of his people and shows himself to be full of compassion.' On the contrary, if we interpret this passage as a true and literal description of God's behaviour, God is not shown to be particularly merciful. All he does is to reject the suggestion that he should destroy Moses instead of Israel, which would be an act of gross injustice. He is still determined to punish Israel, and does so. It is Moses who is merciful, more merciful in fact than Jahweh. If both Alfred Whitehead and Selwyn Hughes had realized that much finer and more nearly Christian conceptions of God are to be found in the later parts of the Old Testament, they would have been the better theologians.

Finally we note a piece of striking naivety: at ii, 26 Hughes is expounding Exodus 34:29–35; he says: 'The Almighty wrote out for him (Moses) a second copy of the Ten Commandments.' A patristic commentator would at least have been careful to say that of course God did not write them himself, he caused them to appear. Rabbinic tradition envisaged Moses as writing at God's (or the angels') dictation. But Hughes is quite content to say that God wrote them *tout court*.

This close examination of a 'literalistic' or Fundamentalist exposition of a very important book of the Old Testament has surely shown how impossible such an approach must be for any educated and intellectually honest Christian. Quite apart from the immense historical questions which this type of exegesis simply ignores, it encounters all sorts of insuperable theological problems. Its most serious defect is that it ends by accepting a sub-Christian understanding of God. This always happens when the Old Testament is treated as having exactly the same authority for Christians as the New. Secondly, the determination to treat everything in the Old Testament as *literal* truth means a much too close approximation to the orthodox Jewish understanding of the Old Testament. Only tendentiously christocentric exegesis distinguishes 'Fundamentalists' from Jews. And thirdly, this approach has very often to fall back on purely arbitrary allegorical exegesis. If one is determined *both* to take everything in the Old Testament as historical fact *and* to find a Christian meaning everywhere, one can only fall back on allegory. In fact a Fundamentalist exegesis indicates intellectual bankruptcy.

The Apocrypha

We now devote some consideration to the canon of the Old Testament, and this means taking account of the Apocrypha. It is undoubted that the Old Testament canon as those outside the Roman Catholic Church hold it, is identical with the canon as laid down by the Jews after the times of Jesus. It is held by some experts that this decision was only made at the Synod of Jamnia in about AD 100, a conference dominated by the pharisaic party. As we shall be seeing, this appears to be the canon recognized by the writers of the New Testament. But the early church up until the year 400 generally followed the wider Alexandrian canon, that is, the collection of books found in the LXX. The disputed books are roughly those found in the LXX but not in the Hebrew canon. Jerome, late in the fourth century when he had learned Hebrew and realized that the Hebrew canon was different, made strenuous efforts to persuade the church to revert to it and to abandon the Alexandrian canon. Several Greek fathers also questioned the canonicity of the books now known as the Apocrypha, e.g. Gregory Nazianzen and Epiphanius. Jerome's efforts were unsuccessful as far as concerns the Western Church which went on using the Apocrypha and treating it as canonical until the Reformation. The Eastern Church on the whole followed suit, but at the Synod of Jerusalem in 1677 all but four of the apocryphal books were rejected, Tobit, Judith, Ecclesiasticus (Wisdom of Ben Sira) and Wisdom. The Reformers represented a reaction against the Apocrypha and in favour of the Hebrew canon. This was no doubt because, having rejected the authority of the medieval church, they needed a cut-and-dried bible. The Alexandrian canon had blurred edges. Their rejection of the Apocrypha was also caused by the fact that some practices which the Reformers disliked had been justified by appeal to the Apocrypha, e.g. prayer for the dead by appeal to 2 Maccabees 12:40–46. Part of the inspiration for the Reformation came from the rediscovery of Hebrew by Christians. A Hebrew Old Testament could more easily be defended as a verbally inspired whole. The Council of Trent officially committed the Roman Catholic Church to accepting the apocryphal books as a full part of the Old Testament canon.

Zarb has some judicious remarks about the emergence of the canon (p. xxxi). He claims that the action of the church in recognizing the canon of scripture does not itself constitute the canon; it is merely a *sine qua non* of canonicity. This is particularly true of the Old Testament canon, since it was already pre-selected for the Christian church by Judaism. Zarb also speculates as to the criteria by which the Old Testament canon was fixed in the Jamnia period. He distinguishes four (p. 72): (a) A book must agree with the Pentateuch; (b) it must show antiquity, that is, it must have been written not later than the time of Ezra; (c) it must have originally been written in Hebrew; (d) it must have a Palestinian origin. Of course in the light of critical study we know that some of these criteria were not actually met by some books that were recognized as canonical. Daniel is much later than Ezra (and is written partly in Aramaic), but claims to have been written early in the Persian period. The Song of Solomon has no connection whatever with the Torah, but could be made to appear to have some connection by means of allegorical exegesis. The Book of Ezekiel was probably written in Babylon, as were the oracles of the Second Isaiah. We could also point to some books which seem to be altogether outside the sphere of the relation between God and Israel, notably the Book of Job. No doubt it was allowed to pass as belonging supposedly to a pre-Torah period. Anyway, the rabbis gave Job a pedigree that connected him with the patriarchs. The criteria are therefore only a rough and ready guide. A large part of scripture had to be accepted by the Judaism of the AD post-70 period simply because it was there and had already been accepted for centuries.

Once a critical approach to scripture has been accepted, the distinction between the canonical and the apocryphal books of the Old Testament loses most of its significance and all its controversial bitterness. It is true that the Apocrypha as a whole is not a body of writings that fits very easily into a christocentric understanding of scripture. This is because all of it was written during the period when Judaism was becoming increasingly Torah-centric. The Books of the Maccabees celebrate the endurance and victory of those who were willing to offer their lives in defence of the Torah. The Book of Tobit assumes a life of Torah observance as the ideal for devout Jews. Even books which contain a great deal of material that appealed to Christians, such as Ben Sira and Wisdom, take it for granted that the Torah lies at the centre of Israel's religion. The rise of biblical criticism meant that the Apocrypha came once more into favour with Protestant scholars (Roman Catholic scholars being severely handicapped in their use of critical methods by church authority), because the Apocrypha provides invaluable evidence about the historical and cultural circumstances in which all the books of the Old Testament were preserved, studied and handed on, and about the circumstances in which some of them (such as Qoheleth, parts of Proverbs and Daniel) were actually composed. It also throws welcome light on what would otherwise have been an obscure period in Israel's history, a period, moreover, which is increasingly proving to have been of vital importance for the circumstances in which Jesus lived and worked. If we judge the books of the Apocrypha of the Old Testament, as we must today, not by the standard of infallible and inspired scripture but as a witness to the religious life of the period in which they were composed, we shall welcome them. But we will readily admit with the Reformers that they are more redolent of the law than of the prophets. Only if one is anxious to confer the accolade of 'inspired' on certain books, and refuse it to others, will one be very much concerned whether any given book is in the canon of the Old Testament or not. Zarb's efforts therefore to prove that because one can find echoes of some apocryphal books in the New Testament (notably the Book of Wisdom), those books must be inspired scripture (pp. 117f.), are quite beside the point. Fussiness about the Apocrypha, whether pro or con, is a sign that the lesson of biblical criticism has not been learned. Protestants should not repudiate the Apocrypha. Roman Catholics should not insist that it be treated as inspired scripture. It fades off imperceptibly into entirely non-canonical intertestamental literature; for example, are Maccabees 3 and 4 part of the Apocrypha or not? They are normally printed in the LXX, but not in vernacular versions of the bible, even Roman Catholic ones. Some books which never achieved even the status of entering the Apocrypha are of greater significance than some books which are firmly ensconced in the Hebrew canon; e.g. the Book of Enoch is more important for our understanding of Israel's development than is the Book of Esther.

Even in the medieval West there were always some people who had doubts about the Apocrypha, or at least knew that others had doubts. Zarb (pp. 228–30) cites a sermon of Thomas Aquinas in which he justifies the inclusion of many of the Old Testament books, especially the Hagiographa (k^etūbīm), on quite extrinsic grounds, that have nothing to do with inspiration, or salvation history, or indeed theology, e.g. that they teach the cardinal virtues, or that they teach the active and passive virtues. Job is useful, he suggests, because it gives an example of a liar exposed (Satan presumably!). I remember when I was on a panel in South India charged with the task of translating the Apocrypha into Telugu, one of the members of our group was a venerable and learned retired Baptist minister. As an Indian belonging to a strongly Protestant church, he had never even heard of the Apocrypha. We asked him to translate the Book of Tobit. He came to our first meeting full of enthusiasm for the book: 'Why were we not told about this book?' he asked. 'It contains excellent Christian teaching about marriage.' It does of course contain very sound teaching on this subject, but it is part of the Jewish rather than the Christian heritage.

Is there any evidence that the writers of the New Testament had any doubts or queries about the canon of scripture? We would hardly expect this *a priori*, since the books that were on the borderline would not have appealed very much to Christians. Song of Songs, Qoheleth, Chronicles do not figure largely among Christian testimony lists. No New Testament writers display the slightest scruple in using a Greek translation of scripture which is often far from the original Hebrew. One cannot help suspecting that some of the veneration for the LXX which is found in the *Letter of Aristeas* and in Philo had rubbed off on the writers of the New Testament. As is so often the case, the great exception here is John the Divine, who shows no fondness for the LXX. Of course very often the parts of scripture which the New Testament writers quote appear to be self-authenticating: they consist of either direct speech by God or inspired writing by acknowledged prophets. The psalms would be regarded as the work of David, himself an inspired prophet; and of course Moses would be regarded as the author of the entire Pentateuch (see Rom. 10:5: 'Moses writes . . . ', quoting Lev. 18:5). We can point to a few places where citations of the *ketūbīm* might seem to raise questions about the canon. For instance, there is an echo of Job 41:11, as we have seen (see p. 48 above), in Romans 11:35. But this was certainly part of an already existing conflated citation. There are echoes of the Book of Wisdom in both Paul and Hebrews (and perhaps the Fourth Gospel). I think these are literary borrowings. We never have a formal quotation of a non-canonical book. The one exception could be said to prove the rule: Jude 14 quotes the Book of Enoch. But the author of 2 Peter, though he models himself on Jude's letter, deliberately omits the reference to Enoch.

I do not believe that Paul, or anyone else, ever quotes from unknown works which he regards as scriptural. This suggestion is a favourite resort of scholars when a New Testament writer quotes as scripture some passage that cannot be found in canonical scripture. See 1 Corinthians 2:9 (and my extensive examination of this in *The New Testament Interpretation of Scripture*, chapter 2); John 7:38; James 4:5. The supposition of an unknown apocryphal book is too easy a solution. In all cases, I believe, the alleged apocryphal citation will prove to be an elaborate midrash on one or more passages of canonical scripture. In this respect, as we have seen, John the Divine is a law to himself. He never quotes explicitly, but uses symbols from all parts of scripture and from outside scripture.

The New Testament writers are conscious of *hai graphai*, scripture, as a definite body of literature marked out from all other literature. This is clear from the references in Paul (e.g. Rom. 15:4); John (e.g. John 10:35); the Pastoral Epistles (2 Tim. 3:16); 1 Peter (1:10–12); and 2 Peter (1:19–21). Whether there are, as some scholars maintain, any passages where Paul buttresses his argument by quotations deliberately taken in rabbinic fashion from the three sections of scripture – the law, the prophets and the writings – I am inclined to doubt. If he did, he did not make much capital out of it.

Despite the openmindedness of Protestant scholars about the Apocrypha, one can sometimes detect something of an animus against it in their works. Knight, for example, says (p. 213) that the intertestamental literature really adds nothing to revelation, but rather obscures it, because four of his five 'moments' of revelation were already over when it was written, and the looking forward to 'the Day' is not in evidence. And Eichrodt (p. 35) says in effect that intertestamental Judaism is not important, as 'Jesus made almost exclusive use of the Old Testament canon'. These are rash statements. During the period in which the Apocrypha was written the most far-reaching events for Israel's future development took place, the contact with Greek culture, the Antiochean persecution, the violent reaction against Gentile influence, and the consequent fencing of the law. We cannot possibly understand the life and teaching of Jesus, on which the New Testament is founded, unless we understand the historical and cultural influences that conditioned the society in which he grew up. But these influences are reflected in the Apocrypha and the intertestamental literature. Such features of Jesus' life situation as the parties of the Pharisees, of the Zealots and of the Essenes, all of whom certainly played a part in his culture, are reflected and explained in this literature. Though Jesus to some extent, and after him the early church, appealed back to the prophets, he and the first Christians did not escape from the cultural influences among which they lived. As Karl Rahner so finely says, if God is to appear in our world, he must be part of it. Without the intertestamental literature we would be painfully ignorant of the background and intellectual presuppositions of him who is for Christians the supreme revelation of God. To claim that this literature has no significance for God's revelation of himself is shortsighted in the extreme.

11

THE OLD TESTAMENT IN THE CHURCH TODAY

Do we need the Old Testament?

The first point to make is that Christians need the Old Testament. One still encounters the occasional believing Christian who betrays Marcionite tendencies by declaring that 'he does not believe in the Old Testament', or that the Old Testament ought not to be read in church, or that the God of the Old Testament is an angry tyrant as compared to the loving God of the New Testament. Such attitudes often represent a most understandable reaction against literalistic teaching about the Old Testament. As we have seen, if the Old Testament is treated as equally authoritative with the New Testament, a sub-Christian conception of God results. Indeed, it is often a conception of God that is below the finest conceptions found within the Old Testament itself. It must be admitted that the present custom in the Church of England of encouraging the reader of the Old Testament lesson in the liturgy to exclaim 'this is the word of God' at the end of the lesson is only too likely to encourage mistaken attitudes towards the Old Testament on the part of those who listen, thinking and unthinking alike. The thinking Christians will be tempted to become Marcionites and the unthinking will be merely muddled. At the same time, the extensive growth in this generation of the habit of making the Eucharist the only service which the faithful are expected to attend on a Sunday may mean a form of creeping Marcionism in the Church of the West. Not many congregations will stand the regular reading of three portions of scripture at the liturgy; where the choice is between Old Testament lection and epistle, in nine cases out of ten the epistle lection will be chosen. The remedy for this is not the abolition of the Sunday Eucharist, but the appointment of a lectionary so arranged that a reasonable amount of the Old Testament must be read in the course of the year.

A more sophisticated way of opposing the use of the Old Testament among Christians is found in countries where Christianity is a relatively recent arrival, and where a religion already exists with scriptures of high spiritual and literary value. In such circumstances the plea is often made that the scriptures of the indigenous religion should be used as a *praeparatio evangelica* rather than the Old Testament. Thus the *Bhagavad Gita* might be read in India before the Gospel instead of a passage from the Old Testament. We must not refuse to consider the claims of any scripture or any culture *a priori*, least of all a document of such venerable lineage and spiritual depth as the *Bhagavad Gita*; but such scriptures cannot take the place of the Old Testament for Christians. After all, the Old Testament as a corpus of Hebrew literature, especially in the awkward LXX translation, must have been just as alien to the cultivated Greeks and Romans of the first Christian centuries as ever it is to modern Christians. But they never demanded that Homer or Aeschylus or Virgil should be substituted for it. The point is that there is a historical, literary and theological bond between the Old Testament and the New Testament which simply does not exist in the case of the scriptures of any other religion. There is an obligation today on Indian Christians, for instance, to take account of the Hindu scriptures. But this is not effected by the method of treating them as a substitute for the Old Testament.

We cannot understand the New Testament unless we read the Old Testament. Christianity arose out of Judaism. Jesus' claims, person and teaching would be largely unintelligible without a knowledge of the Old Testament. There must be an element of continuity as well as discontinuity between the Old Testament and the New Testament. Though Christians need not, indeed must not, claim that everything in the Old Testament finds its true fulfilment in the New Testament, some very important Old Testament elements do.

Two minor questions naturally encounter us here, which we should perhaps dispose of:

(a) What about those elements in the Old Testament which are not fulfilled in the New Testament? Are they mistaken, misleading, positively wrong and evil, or merely otiose? The greatest example of such elements is of course the command to obey the Torah in all its detail; this important question we treat below. Are some elements in the Old Testament mistaken or misleading? Yes, certainly, if isolated and not viewed in the full perspective of the Old Testament itself: 'Thou shalt not suffer a witch to live' (Exod. 22:18). What terrible acts of injustice have been committed because Christians took this as a divine command literally binding on them! We could easily find passages in the earlier part of the Old Testament which portray God as desiring the destruction of whole communities. Honesty compels us to reject the various devices by which Christians who believed in the verbal infallibility of scripture have tried to reconcile this sort of thing with the nobler concept of God found in the prophets, not to mention the revelation of God in Jesus Christ. There are also perhaps some elements in the Old Testament that, without being positively harmful when viewed apart from the New Testament, seem to Christians to be otiose or irrelevant. May we propose the dogmatic opposition to idol worship as one? Admittedly the iconoclastic passages in the Old Testament were glady used by early Christians in the face of the pagan use of images in their day; by the Iconoclast party in the eighth century and after against the Iconodules in the Eastern Church; by the Reformers of the sixteenth and seventeenth centuries against the excessive attention given to saints and images by the late medieval Western Church; and by semi-literate Christian leaders against the animism of village Hinduism in South India today. But most of the arguments against idolatry (even those of Second Isaiah) are very easily answered. Wholly aniconic worship seems strangely inappropriate for a religion which believes in the incarnation.

(b) The New Testament, we have claimed, can only be understood in the light of the Old Testament. Is the reverse true? This is really the great question of the relation between the Testaments in another guise. It comes into sharp focus if ever one has had the experience, as I have had, of taking part in a joint Jewish–Christian bible study group. Of course we had to choose a part of the bible which both religions accept as scripture. In fact we studied Isaiah 40–46. We found we could do it profitably, as long as the Christians did not make any cross-references to the New Testament. But again and again the opportunity presented itself for doing so, and often I felt that what the prophet of the exile was saying would have been admirably illustrated by a New Testament reference. I conclude therefore that, in the widest sense, the Old Testament, though not unintelligible without the New Testament, is seen in its truest and deepest significance when read with the New Testament as foil. This is a Christian judgement, but not, I believe, a tendentious one.

How, then, do we as Christians orientate ourselves towards the Old Testament? We have already said (p. 203 above) that we do not recognize one overall schema or theological theme running through the Old Testament that gives it integral unity. We have also laid it down that Christians should not try to find everything in the Old Testament fulfilled in the New Testament. The New Testament is not the only possible conclusion to the whole Old Testament. Perhaps we might use the simile of the quarry. The Old Testament is the indispensable quarry from which are taken the materials that go to make up the New Testament. New Testament writers used a very great deal of material from this quarry, but they did not use it all. There are, as we have seen, some important materials in the quarry which the New Testament writers left untouched because they had no use for them. Perhaps if we want another simile to illuminate the relationship which we are rejecting, we might take that of the space module. At various points during their space voyages the astronauts have been obliged to 'dock' the space module in which they are travelling with another space capsule. The process of 'docking' is difficult and requires much skill because it must be done with great exactness. This is a good model for the way in which most of the fathers of the Christian church believed that the Old Testament was engineered to fit with the New Testament. Everything had to be fitted in, even if in the process a good deal of violence had to be used on the text of the Old Testament. This we must repudiate. So we accept the image of the Old Testament as a quarry, not the Old Testament as a space module.

It follows that considerable areas of the Old Testament are not directly related to the New Testament and sometimes point in a different direction. Christians, for example, are not interested *as Christians* in the ritual, ceremonial or sacrificial prescriptions of the Torah. The genealogies of the patriarchs, even if they were historical (which they are not) have no particular relevance to the New Testament. The Book of Job is of great significance for us, but not for the reasons for which traditional exegesis (or, for that matter, Thomas Aquinas) valued it. It does not prophesy the resurrection of the body. But it does discuss the God–man relationship in the very profoundest terms. It can therefore be very properly related to parts of Romans. The point of connection is justification by faith. Job constantly asserts his own righteousness before God. By the end of the book he knows better. For a detailed comparison see *The Book of Job* by Anthony and Miriam Hanson, pp. 24–9. There are entire books, such as Esther and the Song of Solomon, which could be omitted from the canon as far as their relevance to the New Testament is concerned. The Books of Chronicles are more valuable for the flickering light which they throw on the condition of Israel in the post-exilic period than for the historical information concerning the period they profess to chronicle.

We value the Old Testament primarily for its account of salvation history. That is, we value it because it records the saving acts of God for his people. We can put this another way by saying that in the Old Testament, if we read it with faith, we can apprehend the revelation of God's character in history. It has often been pointed out that the bible as a whole does not attempt to give a philosophical account of God. It does not offer proofs for his existence or a systematic account of his attributes. It allows his character to become apparent by means of his acts, and in the Old Testament these acts are all, from the time of Abraham onward, concerned with his people Israel. As Kuss concludes at the end of his section on the use of scripture in Hebrews which comes in the introduction to his commentary on the Epistle (p. 66), God has revealed himself in salvation history and that revelation finds its culmination in Jesus Christ. God known in Jesus Christ is therefore the criterion which we apply to the Old Testament. The fathers of the church approached the quarry with allegory as their tool for hewing out material suitable for inclusion in the New Testament but we approach it with the tool of God's continuing revelation culminating in Jesus Christ. It is by this criterion that we can judge the earliest concepts of God in the Old Testament as being very imperfect, by this criterion that we put aside the detailed prescriptions of the Torah as irrelevant.

Those parts of the Old Testament that are most congenial to us, those parts which we can speak of as being 'fulfilled' in the New Testament, are therefore those passages where we encounter the living, saving God, where faith in God because of what he has done is emphasized as the core of religion, where there is a sense of expectation, an awareness that God has yet more light to show, has still a world destiny for Israel, has still a reckoning to make with Israel and with the world. In effect, this means that for us the vital elements in the Old Testament are the prophets and the writings in which an eschatological strain comes to the fore. We find affinity also, as Paul does, with those passages where the call of Abraham is described and discussed, since this is exactly where faith in response to God's calling is made the basis of Israel's religion. This is not an arbitrary or tendentious way of approaching the Old Testament because in fact the works of the great prophets were not composed with the Torah, as later Judaism knew it, in mind and were not originally preserved and handed on because they witnessed to the Torah. They were composed by the prophets themselves because they believed that God had spoken to them directly; and they were preserved and transmitted by those who believed that God had spoken directly to their authors, not primarily because the authors had any relation to the Torah. The habit of reading the prophets in the light of the Torah only dates from the post-exilic period. Could one not say that Jesus, far from reading the prophets in the light of the Torah, read the Torah in the light of the prophets? That certainly is what we find the earliest Christians doing as soon as we have any evidence of their existence.

We have claimed the prophets, the eschatological element (running through various types of literature), and the descriptions of the men and women of faith as being those parts of the Old Testament which we value most as Christians. What about the rest? We have already reminded ourselves that it is God's character which we find revealed, so anything that seems to throw genuine light on that is of interest of us. That is why we claim the first three chapters of Genesis as our heritage: God is known as creator, one who addresses man on a personal plane, one who hates sin but grants man the perilous gift of freedom. We have said, moreover, that God's acts in the Old Testament from Abraham onward are concerned with his people Israel. Hence nothing that has to do with the history of Israel can be without interest for us. Even the mythological period of the patriarchs and the legendary period of the exodus and the wilderness sojourn must interest us, not because it can tell us very much about the pre-history of Israel, but because it does inform us how the Israel which has emerged into the light of history by the beginning of the first millennium BC thought of itself and its origin. The historical books, therefore, which the Jews very profoundly call 'the former prophets', are of interest to us.

What of the writings, the third section of the Jewish bible, which we Christians, following the Alexandrian arrangement, have distributed among the historical books, or inserted between the former and the latter prophets? Psalms is for us of primary importance, not because it records dialogues between the Father and the Son as the New Testament writers believed, but because it contains some of the most intimate and personal approaches to God, clothed in beautiful poetry. That God is a personal God and that he is a living God is something which no one who uses the psalms in prayer and worship can ever forget. Job we have dealt with above. Proverbs I suppose we value most for that element in it which some of the New Testament writers also most prized, its contribution to the wisdom tradition. This tradition was later to prove invaluable to the earliest Christian theologians in their task of constructing a Christology that would express the full stature of the Christ event and also begin to meet the demands of philosophy. We shall have a little more to say of that below. Qoheleth is difficult to fit in anywhere, but perhaps its very difficulty may prove its value: we cannot help admiring a religious tradition that produced its own critic and voiced its own doubts. The author of Ecclesiastes is perhaps the Søren Kierkegaard of the Old Testament. The Book of Daniel we value not because of its historical witness: its stories of Jewish heroism in the face of persecution are pure legend. Nor do we appreciate it for its prophetic power: it is nearly all prophecy *post eventum*, and when the author ventures into genuine prophecy he gets it wrong. No: in as far as we value it at all, we value it as a witness to the growing mood of apocalyptic, we value it for the bizarre but unforgettable symbols of brute force and military might with which it provided the author of Revelation, and no doubt also for the author's serene trust in the overruling providence of God even in the most disastrous circumstances.

Nor must we fail to mention the Book of Jonah. This book, which New Testament writers seem to have valued chiefly for its supposed witness to Christ's resurrection, has been greatly illuminated by the advent of the critical approach to the Old Testament. We now know that it is not an historical narrative at all, but a brilliant parable in which Jonah represents exclusive Judaism, and the great fish perhaps the experience of the exile. The author wishes to teach his people that God's concern extends beyond the limits of Judaism to the Gentile world, and that far from condemning all non-Jews as inveterate sinners, he desires them also to know of his mercy. Viewed thus, Jonah is one of the most Christlike books in the Old Testament and a striking witness to the concept of God which was later fully disclosed in Jesus Christ.

We have said that our criterion for the Old Testament is Jesus Christ. It would be more accurate to say that it is God revealed in Jesus Christ. We are concerned with the full significance of Jesus Christ in his life, ministry, teaching, death and resurrection. In this we see the supreme action of God, now not merely for the temporal salvation of his people Israel, but for the salvation of the whole world. We will therefore expect to see fulfilled in his entire career not a series of exact fulfilments of prophetical intimations uttered centuries before, but the whole purpose, design and *character* of God. This will preserve us from an atomistic or 'magical' interpretation of messianic texts such as we find for example in Justin's *Dialogue with Trypho*, and such as occasionally we find in the New Testament, notably perhaps in Matthew's Gospel. It also means that we completely eschew the attempt to find Jesus in the Old Testament apart from God – that is, to dissociate him too much from the saving action of God in Israel's history, or even to suggest that it was not God but Jesus who appeared in the theophanies of the Old Testament. This is a tendency of which some of the New Testament writers are not wholly guiltless. I suspect that when John emphasizes that no one has ever seen God (John 1:18; 5:37), he means that anyone in the Old Testament who is described as having seen God has really seen the pre-existent Word, not God the Father. John guards himself from representing the Father as a wholly transcendent and 'absent' figure by his constant emphasis on the fact that the Son really does reveal the Father. The Father is made known in the Son. But later theologians were not so careful. The habit of tracing the activity of the pre-existent Christ in the Old Testament became very general right up to the middle of the fourth century. It was the rise of Arianism that finally persuaded what proved to be the orthodox party to abandon the practice. The Arians were only too glad to find the Logos and not the Father in the Old Testament, because they believed in a Father who was too transcendent to be embroiled in a merely phenomenal world, and in a Logos who was so much of a cosmic mediator that he could not be God in the ultimate sense.

One other point must be made before we define our concept of revelation in the Old Testament more exactly: we have said that God is known by means of his acts in history as recorded in the Old Testament. But some of the greatest of these acts, those often on which both Old Testament and New Testament writers put most emphasis, come from a period in Israel's career which we must describe as legendary, if not mythological. We cannot in all honesty describe anything recorded of Abraham as historical at all. The comparison with King Arthur is not exaggerated. He may have been an historical character; but he may be simply the representative of the first ancestor, a necessary symbol of the beginning of the people. Even when we come to the time of Moses, we are still moving in the sphere of legend. Some of Israel's ancestors came up from Egypt. About the exact details of how this took place, we cannot be at all sure. Moses must have been an historical character; there must have been some cult event connected with Sinai–Horeb. But we can have no certainty as to whether Moses is the originator of any of the Torah. Only when Israel arrives in Canaan does she emerge from the mists of legend into the light of history.

Several scholars, as we have seen, are fully aware of the fact that we are so often dependent on Israel's faith for our knowledge of God's acts (see von Rad (1) p. 45; Knight p. 152). We are, for the opening acts of God's revelation of himself, wholly dependent on Israel's faith. God is known to us in the Old Testament as far as those incidents are concerned not by what actually happened, but by Israel's interpretation of what actually happened. To be absolutely exact, it is the interpretation of what actually happened given by those who wrote the Old Testament, committing to writing Israel's tradition about itself. I do not think that we should be upset by this. It is not as if the entire Old Testament is concerned with legendary events: legend passes into history, and the interpretation is essentially the same. The picture of faithful legendary Abraham is borne out completely by the picture of the entirely historical Jeremiah. God, whom Israel believed to have carried them on eagles' wings through the legendary period of the desert, carried them in just the same way through the historical period of the Babylonian exile. It is in any case a matter of 'from faith to faith', because the account, for instance, which Jeremiah gives of his call by God, his wrestlings with God's declared destiny for him, and his inability to abandon his vocation, would be quite meaningless without Jeremiah's faith in God and our faith in his veracity. It is quite open to the Freudian psychologist to explain away Jeremiah's sense of vocation as the vagaries of his super-ego; and for the Marxist to account for his behaviour in terms of the state of the fig market in Judah in the year 600 BC.

This does not mean that our claim to see God revealed in his acts through Israel's history is all makebelieve or subjective fancy. There is something there to be explained: the existence of Israel, the career of Jeremiah, the phenomenon of the great prophets, the fact of Judaism, the person of Jesus of Nazareth, the origin of Christianity, etc. But the link between the Old Testament and the New Testament is for Christians a matter of faith – not of blind faith; it is a faith well based on facts; it can give an excellent account of itself. But it is still a matter of faith, as is any attempt to explain the true significance of the Old Testament. Christians have no reason at all to be alarmed at this. It is a principle which lies at the very heart of the New Testament witness: God as Saviour can only be known by faith – whatever we or the New Testament writers might be disposed to say about God as creator. Jesus can only be recognized as Christ by faith – it is a matter of revelation, as Matthew's account of the Caesarea Philippi incident brings out (Matt. 16:17). And Christians can only construct a Christology which does justice to the New Testament witness if they are willing to make the act of faith. So, in saying that the earliest witness to God's acts in the Old Testament is based as far as we are concerned on Israel's faith concerning what happened, we are not committing ourselves to a realm of uncontrolled fancy or imagination. We are in fact relying on the truth of God, what the Old Testament calls his 'emet, his consistence with himself. What he has revealed himself to be in history which we can to some extent check, such we can safely believe him to have been during the period when we are dependent on the account of their experience given by faithful Israelites.

Our account of the Old Testament has assumed that the concept of God, and of many other things also, to be found in it is not fixed and monochrome. At the same time we have claimed that the Old Testament is the record of the revelation of God to Israel. From this it must follow that the revelation was a developing or progressive one: the earlier ideas about God which Israel held were cruder, but under the influence of developing revelation they became more refined and therefore more just and true. This used to be called the concept of 'progressive revelation'. Recently, however, no doubt under the influence of the Barthian reaction against the 'liberal' theology of the nineteenth century, there has been a tendency to repudiate the phrase 'progressive revelation' on the grounds that it is a concept which owes too much to nineteenth-century ideas of evolutionism. Thus D. L. Baker rejects the phrase (p. 74), saying that the concept is now 'outmoded along with the progressive evolutionary idea of history which is presupposed'. Von Rad, rather more to the point, takes a concrete instance of someone who supported this concept, Julius Wellhausen, the great biblical scholar of the last century. 'Wellhausen', he writes (see (1) p. 113) 'was in the last analysis strongly influenced by Hegel; he looked on Israel's history as a history of ideas and presented it above all from the standpoint of a spiritual evolution.'

This criticism of Wellhausen is no doubt justified, but I do not see how we can afford to dispense with the concept of at least a developing revelation. God is not revealed with equal truth and clarity in all parts of the Old Testament. What emerges of God's character in the Jahwistic tradition is not as high or as close to the New Testament tradition as what emerges from the utterances of the great prophet of the exile. It is true of course that the developing revelation did not develop steadily. It is not the case that the later books of the Old Testament to be written contain *ipso facto* a higher concept of God than those written some time before them. The highest reaches of revelation were perhaps achieved in the prophecies of Second Isaiah. What comes after may well be described as an anticlimax (though we must except the Book of Jonah). But we must accept degrees of revelation, and if we do that we must be able to say at least roughly which part of the Old Testament records the clearer and which the less adequate revelation. And on the whole, the earlier parts of the Old Testament reflect the earlier understanding of God, even if the latest parts do not necessarily reflect the highest and clearest apprehension.

Perhaps an example may be the best way of explaining what we mean by developing revelation. It is one offered by B. Anderson (pp. 25–32) and is worked out by him at some length. His example is Genesis 22, the story of the sacrifice of Isaac. Anderson points out that behind the narrative as we have it in Genesis lies a very considerable development already: the earliest form was a cult legend designed to explain why the Israelites commute the offering of the firstborn with an animal sacrifice. Then it got attached to the cycle of stories connected with Abraham. This then became joined up with the stories about the other patriarchs, and it begins to take its place in salvation history with the promise of a glorious future for the race given as a reward of Abraham's faith. The whole becomes part of the E tradition, a document composed about 850 BC with an eye to encountering some of the challenges with which contemporary Israel was faced, one of which was certainly ritual child sacrifice. Last of all it is included in the Pentateuch (centuries later) and became part of scripture. Within the course of this history we can see the concept of God being moralized, refined and clarified. But this is one of the earlier parts of the Old Testament! We must therefore always be ready to recognize in the Old Testament varying degrees of knowledge of God, which means in effect varying degrees of revelation.

Vriezen has an interesting comment which is relevant to this topic. He does not like the use of the word 'process' in connection with God's revelation (p. 152, n.); but 'a Christian need not shrink back from the idea of a true development which is implicit in the idea of history – for a Christian believes that God has a plan, and he may try to trace this plan, if only he realizes that this plan is fully known only to God'. We find here the same fear of any Hegelian suggestion of process; but in fact he makes a bolder claim than any we have been making above. We have been content to say that God's character is revealed through the record of the Old Testament. Vriezen suggests that we can actually have some sort of access to God's mind or intention. I believe that in fact that claim may and should be made by Christians: we discuss this in greater detail below under the rubric of the fulfilment of prophecy. But Vriezen is using 'development' here to apply to a phenomenon different from that which we have been discussing. He is thinking of a process of events developing throughout a period of history. We mean a developing understanding of God's character. We need both sorts of development if we are rightly to relate the Old Testament to the New Testament. We need the concept of salvation history (a development of events) and of a developing revelation (developing understanding).

Clements has still another point to make about revelation which we should not ignore. He says (Laurin p. 135) that the Old Testament itself shows us a changing pattern of revelation, from revelation through prophets to revelation through law. He means no doubt that the period of the great prophets was succeeded by a period in which the Pentateuch having been finally put together, law observance became the centre of Israel's religion. I am not sure that I think 'revelation through law' is a satisfactory way of expressing it; but we shall be discussing law more fully below. Clements has well reminded us at any rate that the revelation in the Old Testament, besides varying in degree, is mediated by a wide variety of vehicles. Prophecy and law are by no means the only vehicles; even if we were to confine ourselves to the *kᵉtūbīm*, which were for the most part written after the exile, we encounter a striking variety of media of revelation: there is sacred hymn or poetic meditation (the psalms); the extended parable (Ruth and

Jonah); the lament (Lamentations); the exhortation, almost a diatribe in the original sense of the word (Qoheleth); the theological poem (Job); the liturgical history (Chronicles); the book of legends and prophecy by hindsight (Daniel). Of course the degree of revelation here varies as much from one book to another as does the literary form; but all can be, and all are in *some* degree, the vehicle of revelation.

The reader may be surprised not to have encountered in this discussion the question of inspiration. Are we not in these last three chapters actually asking questions about the inspiration of the Old Testament? In fact I have used the adjective 'inspired' already on p. 211 above, but only in order to reject it. I do not think that the concept of inspiration is a useful one in connection with our topic of the relation between the Testaments. To describe any book of the entire bible as inspired is to attribute to it a quality which would seem to set it apart from all other literature. But when we ask what it is that sets the bible apart from all other literature, we can only reply that it has the quality of being the record of God's revelation; and that brings us back to assessing the various books of the bible in terms of revelation again. We can easily allow a greater or lesser degree of revelation, but a greater or lesser degree of inspiration, if it means anything different, would seem to bring us into a dangerous area. We should be making claims for an inspired book that it is more reliable, less inadequate just because it is inspired, and not because of its contents or circumstances of writing. It is this perilous notion of inspiration that placed Mr Selwyn Hughes in a situation where he felt himself bound to interpret what is the product of a very early fertility rite as if it was the most profound utterance of the great prophets; and that persuaded him into using the most unconvincing arguments to defend the internal harmony of everything in the bible. It is this notion of 'inspiration', or lack of it, that moved the Reformers to reject and often denigrate the Apocrypha, and Tridentine Catholics to treat it as being on the same level as the noblest parts of the Old Testament. I therefore conclude that if we leave the notion of the inspiration of the Old Testament altogether on one side, we will not be the losers.

The Fulfilment of Prophecy

We must next explain what we mean by the fulfilment of Old Testament prophecy in the New Testament. We have already used the category of eschatology to describe large parts of the Old Testament. In such places we meet a sense of expectation: God has yet to manifest himself fully, and so on. In this sense the history of Israel recorded in the Old Testament may rightly be said to be moving towards an end. Beyse well points out that Stephen's speech in Acts 7 is an excellent example of this; Stephen does not repudiate the history of his people, but he sees it as having a goal (12–13). Several Old Testament scholars show themselves as anxious to emphasize that not too much stress must be put on the literal fulfilment of particular prophecies. Knight (p. 295) goes so far as to claim that 'it is the Old Testament as a whole that is messianic . . . and not merely a few elements in its composition'. This seems to be an exaggeration: one could point to many parts of the Old Testament that are not messianic at all, large parts of the Torah, for example, or the Book of Esther. Eichrodt (p. 502) specifically rejects the idea that 'a complete picture of Christ is foreshadowed in the messianic prophecies'. Von Rad very relevantly maintains that there are plenty of examples of unfulfilled prophecy within the Old Testament itself. He writes of the historical Isaiah: 'Not one of all the great sayings about Zion came true. The nation showed no faith, and Jahweh did not protect his city.' He goes on to say that this did not puzzle Isaiah (2, p. 167). Proksch believes that one very prominent element in messianic expectation, the Davidic kingship, was quite irrelevant to the Second Isaiah: 'In Second Isaiah Yahweh, and not David, is king, and the prophet stands at the point of time where the new kingdom is breaking into history' (Proksch, quoted by J. N. Schofield in Laurin p. 105).

We must therefore regard the relation of Old Testament prophecy to the era of the New Testament in terms of revelation rather than in terms of prediction and fulfilment. We cannot accept the traditional belief that inspired prophets in Old Testament times knew about events which were to take place hundreds of years later. This is partly because such a notion is too close to the attribution of magical knowledge to the prophets, but there are deeper reasons. If detailed knowledge of the remote future was available even to only occasional figures in Old Testament history, it raises difficult problems about predestination and human freedom. To take an example within the Old Testament itself: in 1 Kings 13:2 we have a story in which a man of God prophesies against King Jeroboam: 'A son shall be born to the house of David, Josiah by name, and he shall sacrifice upon you [the altar where Jeroboam was offering incense] the priests of the high places', etc. If this had really been an event that took place in the time of Jeroboam, how are we to think of the freedom of action of Josiah's parents 300 years later when they were naming their son? Were they divinely inspired to choose the name 'Josiah' so that the prophecy should come true? A far more probable solution is that we have in 1 Kings 13 an interpolation in the narrative belonging to the time of Josiah. In other words, we do not need the dubious assumption of supernaturally endowed foresight about specific events.

We must, rather, think of the greatest of the prophets as having understood something of the mind of God. In the particular circumstances in which they lived they attempted to declare the mind and will of God, always with respect to the events of their own day. In as far as they did understand God's will, the same mind or design will appear in the life and ministry of Jesus Christ, if he is, as Christians believe, the clearest revelation of God's character. For example, in the figure of the suffering servant of the Second Isaiah we have the picture of one who obeys God's will through suffering and perhaps death, and the suggestion is made that the suffering of God's obedient servants is God's way of dealing with sin and bringing about reconciliation. When the perfectly obedient servant, Jesus Christ, appears, essentially the same pattern of divine activity becomes manifest. Jesus is the fulfilment of the highest expectations of the Old Testament because the way God brings about his purposes becomes partially clear in the work of the Old Testament prophets, and wholly clear in the work of Jesus Christ. The fulfilment of prophecy means the partial insights which the prophets had to God's character and designs becoming fully clear in the career of Jesus Christ. It is not a question of miraculous prediction and fulfilment, but of partial understanding naturally pointing forward to full understanding.

When we today read the Old Testament christocentrically we do not mean exactly the same thing as did our forefathers when they spoke about the fulfilment of the messianic prophecies. In fact the most obviously messianic prophecies such as Isaiah 9:1f. and 11:1f. are relatively unimportant as far as fulfilment is concerned. This fits in well with what we can hope to know of Jesus' consciousness of his own mission. I believe indeed that he could not have avoided the challenge of Messiahship. But his messianic expectation does not fit in with any *messianic* expectation in the Old Testament though it fits in with other expectations, as for example those we find in the servant figure of the Second Isaiah and of the psalms.

Professor Hans Hübner is therefore justified in saying that Jesus is not the Jewish Messiah (see his article 'Der "Messias Israels" und der Christus des Neuen Testaments'). Jesus is the greatest and final prophet of the Jews, and their saviour in the sense in which he is the saviour of all men. The concept of a Messiah arose during the intertestamental period, based on some elements in the Old Testament, but also informed by the historical circumstances of the centuries immediately before the birth of Jesus. When Jesus arose to manifest the ultimate revelation of God, he had to encounter, and to some extent make use of, the concept of Messiahship. But his full significance greatly transcended the idea of Messiahship; his relation to the Kingdom, his filial consciousness with regard to the Father, his authoritative teaching about God's mercy and man's righteousness are just as important in assessing his status as is Messiahship in itself – indeed, much more important. We call him Jesus *Christ* primarily because the advent of the Messiah was to mark the dawning of the end time, and in this Jesus certainly did fulfil the concept. The Messiah is an eschatological figure; but when the end came it was so very different from what any picture of the Messiah in the Old Testament or beyond it ever envisaged, that the Messiahship is simply transcended and left behind. It was inevitable that the first Christians should describe the risen Jesus in terms of Messiahship because they were Jews. But, just as Paul believed Jesus to be Messiah while attributing a much more exalted status to him, so we can use the title Christ for him while seeing in him someone much greater than the Messiah of the Jews. The Jews will not in fact be sent any other Messiah, but Jesus did not exactly fulfil the role of Messiah. If he had, he could never have been what he has become to Christians.

One point more must be made about the fulfilment of Old Testament prophecy: the prophecies of the Old Testament are either fulfilled in the New Testament or they are not fulfilled at all. This point has been excellently made by Simon Barrington-Ward, General Secretary of the Church Missionary Society, in a recent newsletter. He writes: 'The temptation to see in contemporary events the fulfilment of certain Old Testament prophecies must be for Christians, as for Zionist Jews, one of the subtlest and most insidious forms of a drift into idolatry and the secularization of the Bible. The danger of over-simple and rapid identification of biblical persons and events with what seem to be their modern counterparts is always with us. For some, the beasts and demonic forms of the Apocalypse all too easily become, say, the multinationals, and the saints are seen as liberation movements of which the Exodus becomes the archetype. For others, to the right, it seems to be flying in the face of biblical evidence not to see in the re-establishment of the nation of Israel, after 2000 years, a palpable disclosure of God's plan. The forces of light have been variously perceived as the British Empire, the United States or the revival of Israel itself. The forces of destruction translate more naturally and obviously into Russia and "Red" China closing in with all their hosts on a restored Jerusalem. . . For Christians, surely the true message of the whole Bible must be precisely the opposite. The Old Testament finds its entire fulfilment, its true exegesis, in Jesus Christ.'

This is an admirably expressed protest against what is basically a superstitious method of treating the bible. This method views the bible as a sort of Old Moore's Almanac. We cannot of course agree with Barrington-Ward's much too sweeping claim that the Old Testament finds its entire fulfilment in Jesus Christ: the true exegesis of only parts of it, though very important and central parts, is a Christian exegesis. But he has made a point that needs to be remembered particularly today when world insecurity has produced a renewal of biblical 'Fundamentalism'.

Christians and the Torah

We owe it to Judaism to take the Torah seriously. The prevailing liberal Protestant approach of the last century that the Torah represented a legalistic and inferior form of Judaism, an unspiritual piling-up of merits by correct observances, will not pass today. The Jews rightly point out that a very large part of the Old Testament is concerned with the necessity of observing the law of Moses. And they often add that as far as the evidence is available it seems that Jesus did not oppose the Torah but observed it himself. We must admit that genuine devotion and humility is entirely compatible with Torah observance. A poem such as Psalm 119, with its passionate commitment to obeying the Torah, is very far from meriting the epithet unspiritual.

The traditional Christian view is that the Torah was intended by God as a disciplinary and restricting régime for the Jews until the Messiah should come and abrogate it, and it was often added that the Jews were an exceptionally stiff-necked and hard-hearted race (by the admission of their own prophets) who needed a detailed prescription of observances in order to keep them under control. This is totally unfair and unhistorical. The Jews, in fact, by the witness of their own prophets, have shown themselves to possess a genius for self-criticism and self-understanding which Christians might well envy. But we now know that we may not think of Israel as having been given a detailed rule of life hundreds of years before the time of the great prophets. We do not need therefore to ask why God gave the law of Moses to the Jews. They only acquired a detailed Torah relatively late in the period of Old Testament history. Concentration on detailed Torah observance was a reaction to exile and the conditions of the return. It was not a divinely given ordinance.

Knight expresses an extraordinarily favourable view of the Torah; he writes: 'It reveals itself in its final, post-exilic form not as a set of legislations which Israel will later necessarily outgrow, but as one harmonious whole of revelation such as is necessary for the understanding of the *hesed* which God showed to Israel in the first place, and which Israel is to show to God in return'

(p. 240). It is quite true that the Torah is viewed as God's gift, and obedience to it is an act of gratitude. But the 'one harmonious whole' of which Knight writes is only achieved by ignoring the conclusions of the critical approach to the Old Testament; and the writers of the New Testament, to a man, would surely have protested against the implication here that *all* the prescriptions of the Torah are binding on all believers.

We can appreciate some admirable features of the Torah, as Paul could. The picture of the man after God's heart which it portrays is an attractive one. The element of liturgical and festal observance which it commands is essential for any living religion. The constant emphasis on moral principle (however unfashionable today) is good and necessary for Christianity. But in the long run a religion centred on the Torah has two deadly deficiencies:

1   It tends towards legalism and self-righteousness, however humble, however self-critical individual devotees may be. I remember a few years ago attending a talk by a Jewish rabbi on the Jewish way of life. Among other things he explained how the *tephillim* or phylacteries were made, small leather cases containing vellum strips inscribed with passages from the Old Testament. He said that these strips had to be written by someone who was a pious Jew. When he was asked how one identified a pious Jew, he described him as one who scrupulously observed all the prescriptions of the Torah, including those concerning ritual purity. Piety is defined in terms of observance.

2   The second deficiency is closely connected with the first: the Torah consists of prescriptions many of which are purely ritual or ceremonial. Among them is a strong element of merely ritual purity. Purity means not incurring ritual contamination. This can lead to most embarrassing situations: I have known a case where a ministrant belonging to the synagogue refused to shake hands with a woman in case she might be (menstrually) impure and thus disqualify him from carrying out his ritual duties concerning the preparation of food. The concept of merely ritual impurity is an anachronism and a scandal in modern orthodox Judaism. But it is inextricably connected with full Torah observance.

In his Introduction to his novel *Quentin Durward*, Walter Scott imagines a conversation between an upper-class Scotsman and a French marquis of the old régime taking place not long after Waterloo in the ruins of the old marquis's country mansion. The marquis invites the Scotsman (who is of course a Presbyterian) to lunch but apologizes for the austere diet, because it is a fast-day. Scott writes (*Quentin Durward*, Waverley edn (Edinburgh 1829), p. xlix): 'I hastened to assure him that, though they might differ from those of my own, I had every possible respect for the religious rules of every Christian community, sensible that we addressed the same Deity, on the same grand principle of salvation, though with different forms; which variety of worship had it pleased the Almighty not to permit, our observances would have been as distinctly prescribed to us as they are laid down under the Mosaic law.' An admirable piece of early ecumenism! We note that Scott, who evidently had never heard of the critical approach to the Old Testament, agrees with Selwyn Hughes 150 years later, that God had prescribed a set of specific observances for the Jews. But he realizes that God has not done so for Christians and this is precisely the point. We do not have a Torah to teach us what not to eat or how precisely to worship. We do not need one, and critical scholarship now tells us that the detailed observances of Judaism cannot claim the sanctity of Mosaic authorship and therefore lose a great deal of their authority.

The concept of revelation necessarily implies minds to apprehend the revelation. But here we run into an apparent difficulty. The Old Testament, it seems, does not operate in conceptual terms. Vriezen (pp. 154–6) insists that knowing God implies communion and faith – such knowledge is 'not ontological but existential' (p. 155), and he concludes that 'completely alien to the Old Testament, therefore, is the making of an image in the mind' (p. 156). All speculation about the being of God is thus avoided. Knight likewise claims that one cannot demythologize the Old Testament because word and thing are so closely connected (p. 271).

All this is true as far as it goes, but it does not dispense with the need to give an intelligible account of the Old Testament revelation. The reason why rational concepts are not used is simply that only at the very end of the Old Testament period did Israel encounter Greek philosophy and Greek rationalists who demanded an intellectually intelligible account of God. When they did encounter this, acute and devout minds in Israel produced the wisdom tradition, which was, as we have seen (see pp. 201–2 above), the beginning of a philosophy of religion. It is true that in the Old Testament to know God is to acknowledge him and right behaviour is an essential element in knowledge of God. But the rejection of concepts is not the same thing as the apophatic way so enthusiastically embraced by the mystical theologians of the Eastern Orthodox Church. God is not presented as essentially unknowable. It must be said also that the Old Testament is very far from eschewing images of God. On the contrary, it is extraordinarily fertile in them: he is creator, father, husband, judge – not to mention even more far-fetched images such as pregnant woman (Isa. 42:14), barber (Isa. 7:20), vinedresser (Isa. 5:1–7) or blood-stained warrior (Isa. 63:1–6). If these are not images in the mind, what are they?

As for the impossibility of demythologizing the Old Testament, here too we must be careful not to make claims which will involve us in difficulties when they are universally applied. We have already (see pp. 205–6 above) observed the danger of accepting as an adequate picture of God everything that is presented to us in the Old Testament. We do not want to find ourselves compelled to admit that God is a demon who demands blood if he is not propitiated by the offering of a foreskin, as he is delineated in Exodus 4:24–6. If we may not demythologize this passage, what are we to do with it? Reject it, no doubt, because it gives a totally inadequate and misleading picture of God. But, in saying this, we have already in a sense demythologized it. We have transposed it into the category of 'passage expressing something of God's character', then we have implicitly compared it with God's character as revealed in Jesus Christ; and by that criterion it has been found wanting. Those who attempt to evade the application of rational concepts to the revelation of God in the Old Testament by declaring that the Old Testament only operates on 'existential' or 'non-conceptual' lines have not, it seems to me, really thought out their position. The Old Testament, if you like, mostly operates at the pre-speculative, the poetic or iconic level. It cannot be transferred bodily into the categories of modern existentialism without grave misrepresentation.

Our Relation to the New Testament Interpretation of Scripture

We have now reached the point where we can give in summary form our answer to the question with which these last three chapters have been concerned, and which indeed can hardly have been far from our minds throughout the book: how far can we today agree with the New Testament interpretation of the Old Testament? The main lines of the answer will of course have become clear by now, but we should end the work by stating unambiguously our answer to this question.

At the most fundamental level we are in agreement with the writers of the New Testament. We all agree that the story of the Old Testament is the story of salvation history, of how God called a people, made himself known to them in a special way, and finally in Jesus Christ gave them the highest and ultimate revelation which was to be proclaimed not only to the Jews but also to the whole world. We all agree that, as far as Christians are concerned, Christ is the centre and meaning of the bible; in him the revelation which was begun in Old Testament times reached its point of greatest clarity. We all agree that God had a design in history and that it finds its fulfilment in Jesus Christ. We all agree that this final revelation came at the end of the days, and that with the coming of Jesus Christ a new era has begun which is the inauguration of the Kingdom of God. Thus we all agree that God uttered many invaluable words during the period covered by the Old Testament, but that Jesus Christ is his last Word. These are very important beliefs and principles, and the fact that we are one with the writers of the New Testament in accepting and believing them shows that we are very far from being in the unhappy position of having nothing in common with their interpretation of the Old Testament. On the contrary, we are in agreement about the most basic and important matters.

We can also agree sometimes at a more specific level. For example, we have said that God had a design in history which we can to some extent trace through the Old Testament and find fulfilled in the life of Christ. This means that when we hear the Gospel writers saying that Christ had to suffer (e.g. Luke 24:26), we can agree with them. The necessity was a moral, not a physical or natural, one. Christ had to suffer if he was to be true to his calling, i.e. if God's purpose was to be carried out. He could have refused his calling, as Jeremiah could have refused his (despite Jer. 20:9!), but he did not do so. No doubt all the writers of the New Testament would have agreed that it was a moral necessity. In this respect we can at least sympathize with the New Testament writers when they use typology; if God has a design and if he works in certain ways, it is not at all unreasonable to expect that one set of events in the Old Testament in which his design can be traced will have a certain correspondence with the set of events in Christ's life by means of which the design is fully revealed. As we have seen (see pp. 186f. above), our disagreement over typology concerns the historicity of the Old Testament events, not the principle of typology itself.

Another specific point where we can agree with the New Testament writers' interpretation of the Old Testament is in their recognition of the figure of the servant. We have seen how frequently this occurs when New Testament writers are expounding the Old Testament, and we ought to be able to agree that, by and large, they are right in saying that Jesus fulfilled the servant role which we can trace in the Old Testament. He probably himself saw it as his own role; it makes the best sense of his work.

A third specific point might be found in what could be called the unexpectedness of God's mode of salvation in Jesus Christ. New Testament writers are fond of quoting texts from the Old Testament to confirm this: 'The very stone which the builders rejected has become the head of the corner' (Ps. 118:22, cf. Luke 20:17; 1 Peter 2:7); 'I will destroy the wisdom of the wise, and the cleverness of the clever I will thwart' (Isa. 29:14, quoted in 1 Cor. 1:19); 'I do a deed in your days, a deed you will never believe, if one declares it to you' (Hab. 1:5, quoted in Acts 13:41). This divine quality of unexpectedness finds its climax in the crucifixion of Jesus Christ but it is also to be traced in the actions of the living, sovereign God recorded in the Old Testament.

But there are important beliefs about which we cannot agree with the New Testament writers in their interpretation of the Old Testament. In the first place, as we have made sufficiently clear already, we cannot agree that the whole of the Old Testament is fulfilled in Jesus Christ. This is a belief certainly held by the writers of the New Testament, though perhaps it is never actually put into writing. But a passage such as Luke 24:27 certainly carries this implication; and so no doubt does John 5:46.

Perhaps this might not make so very much difference; but we must go on to say that we cannot agree with the view which the New Testament writers, together with all Jewish scholars, held about the nature of the prophets' inspiration – and we must remember that Moses and David counted as prophets in their estimation. The prophets, we must maintain, were not given miraculous knowledge of future events that were to take place in the messianic era. They spoke as men of faith, not of sight. What they said came from their knowledge and experience of God gained in just the same way that we can gain it. Their insight was, of course, the work of God's Spirit in them, and it came by grace. It was, therefore, supernatural (for grace by definition transcends nature), but not superhuman. There is a sense in which the greatest theologians of the New Testament might agree here. Paul and John, I believe, would have said that one can only know God as Saviour by faith. But this does not alter the fact that they believe, as did all Jews, in the miraculous inspiration of the prophets.

Consequently, entire categories of New Testament exegesis cannot be admitted as valid by us. That dialogue between God and the pre-existent Son which is a feature of Paul, Hebrews and John is not something we can possibly admit as a reasonable way of interpreting the Old Testament; for examples see Romans 15:3, 9; 2 Corinthians 4:13, 6:2; Hebrews 1:5–13; John 10:35 (all these have been expounded in the relevant chapters above). Nor can we be content to trace the activities of the pre-existent Christ in Old Testament history, as is done by so many New Testament writers. The utmost we can concede here is that such a bizarre interpretation at least witnesses to a profound truth: the God whom we know in Jesus Christ has always been such as we now know him. Hence, if anyone in Old Testament times really encountered him (which we cannot possibly doubt), the God whom he encountered was the same God as we know. Most Christians would add that he is the Trinity, God as Three in One.

But this is not the same thing as Paul's statement: 'The Rock was Christ', in 1 Corinthians 10:4.

A fourth point where we differ is where New Testament writers use allegory to interpret the Old Testament. As we have seen, this is rare. It is mostly a case of typology becoming too elaborate and merging into allegory. This is not, therefore, a very important difference, but it becomes very important when we pass to the traditional interpretation of the Old Testament by the fathers of the church and their successors. Allegory became the accepted method of interpreting any part of the Old Testament that could not be immediately and obviously related to the New Testament. The Reformers made a protest against the excessive use of allegory, but the fact that Selwyn Hughes still employs it so extensively shows that it still appeals to those who take a 'literalist' approach to scripture. The advent of critical study has of course put it completely out of court.

There is also a species of New Testament exegesis which seems to occupy a middle position as far as we are concerned today. There are images or titles taken from the Old Testament by New Testament writers and applied to Christ of which we can say that, though this is not plausible exegesis, these images do provide appropriate figures for understanding Christ. Such is Paul's great image of Christ as the second Adam. No doubt Paul believed that Genesis 2:7 applied to Christ in some sense (see 1 Cor. 15:45), but as far as we are concerned, it is the figure of Adam that supplies the significance, not the fulfilment of scripture. The same thing might be said about the author of Hebrews' sustained argument about Christ as the true and eternal high priest. Priesthood as expounded in Hebrews is a suitable category to apply to the work of Christ. Another such appropriate figure is the wisdom of God which plays such an important part in New Testament Christology. We must not claim that the author of Proverbs 8:22–31 had Jesus Christ or the eternal Son in mind as he composed that poem; but certainly the wisdom of God is an appropriate figure for describing the relation of Christ to the Father. Other such figures are Messiah, with which we have already dealt, and Son of Man, which hardly qualifies as an Old Testament category at all – or at least owes as much to intertestamental literature as to the canonical Old Testament. John the Divine uses this technique of applying Old Testament images to Christ throughout his work; but he does not challenge comparison with the other Old Testament writers since he never claims to expound the fulfilment of scripture.

In conclusion, the writers of the New Testament and modern Christian students of the Old Testament are engaged in the same task, the understanding of the Old Testament in the light of Christ.

They share the same fundamental convictions, as we have seen. But the techniques of the two groups are different. The New Testament writers used typology, *pesher* fulfilment, etc., indeed the whole paraphernalia of Jewish exegesis, the only tools they had for the task. Our tools are the techniques of modern biblical criticism and the concept of developing revelation. We cannot accept the assumptions about the nature of scripture which lie behind their technique, just as it would never have occurred to them to consider the assumptions which lie behind our approach to the Old Testament. But because we are, like them, believers in God-in-Christ, we have enough in common to profit from their exegesis, to admire it when it makes sense in our terms, and to understand it and sympathize with it when it does not.

BOOKS AND ARTICLES REFERRED TO IN THE TEXT

Abbott, T. K. *A Critical and Exegetical Commentary on the Epistles to the Ephesians and to the Colossians* (Edinburgh 1909)

Aletti, J-N. *Colossiens 1:15–20, Genre et Exégèse du texte* (Rome 1981)

Anderson, B. W. *The Living World of the Bible* (London 1979)

Anderson, H. art. 'The Old Testament in Mark's Gospel' in Efird, J. M. (q.v.)

Baker, D. L. *Two Testaments, One Bible* (Leicester 1976)

Barrington-Ward, S. *CMS Newsletter* 449 (London Oct. 1982)

Beare, F. W. *The First Epistle of Peter* (Oxford 1947)

Beasley-Murray, G. R. *The Book of Revelation* (London 1974)

Bernard, J. H. *A Critical and Exegetical Commentary on the Gospel according to St John*, 2 vols. (Edinburgh 1928)

Best, E. *Following Jesus* (Sheffield 1981) *1 Peter* (London 1971)

Betz, O. art. 'Der Gebrauch von (TG) Jesaja 52:13—53:12 in Römerbrief' (unpublished, 1981)

Beyse, W. *Das Alttestament in der Apostelgeschichte* (Munich 1939)

Billerbeck, P. see Strack, H. L.

Borgen, P. *Bread from Heaven* (Leiden 1969)

Bottini, G. C. *La Preghiera di Elia in Giacomo 5:17–18* (Jerusalem 1981)

Bousset, W. *Die Offenbarung Johannes* (6th edn Göttingen 1906)

Bovon, F. *Luc le Théologien* (Neuchâtel–Paris 1978)

Braude, W. G. ed. *Midrash on the Psalms* (New Haven 1959), ed. *Pesikta Rabbati* (New Haven and Yale 1968), ed. with Kapstein, A. *Pesikta de Rab Kahana* (London 1975)

Brown, R. E. *The Community of the Beloved Disciple* (London 1979)

Bruce, F. F. *Commentary on the Epistle to the Hebrews* (London and Edinburgh 1964)

Bultmann, R. *Das Evangelium des Johannes* (10th edn Göttingen 1962)

Burney, C. F. art. 'Christ as the ARCHE of creation (Prov. 8:22, Col. 1:15–18, Rev. 3:14)' in *JTS* 27 (OS) (1926), pp. 160–77

Cadbury, H. J. see Lake, K.

Charles, R. H. ed. *Apocrypha and Pseudepigrapha of the Old Testament*, 2 vols. (London 1913); *A Critical and Exegetical Commentary on the Revelation of St John*, 2 vols. (Edinburgh 1920)

Chilton, B. *God in Strength* (Freistadt 1979)

Cohn, L. and Wendland, P. ed. *Philonis Alexandri Opera Quae Supersunt* (Berlin 1896)

Conzelmann, H. *Die Apostelgeschichte* (2nd edn Tübingen 1972)

Court, J. M. *Myth and History in the Book of Revelation* (London 1979)

Delcor, M. *Les Hymnes de Qumran* (Paris 1962)

Derrett, J. D. M. *Law in the New Testament* (London 1970)

Dibelius, M. *An die Kolosser, Epheser, an Philemon*, ed. H. Greeven (3rd edn Tübingen 1953); *Der Jakobusbrief* ed. H. Greeven (Göttingen 1964)

Dunn, J. D. G. *Christology in the Making* (London 1980)

Edgar, S. L. art. 'New Testament and Rabbinic Interpretation' in *NTS* 5 (1958–9), pp. 47–54

Efird, J. M. ed. *The Use of the Old Testament in the New, and Other Essays* (Duke Univ. Durham NC 1972)

Eichrodt, W. *Theology of the Old Testament* (6th edn Eng. trans. London 1961 of German edn Stuttgart 1959)

Ellis, E. E. *Paul's Use of the Old Testament* (Edinburgh and London 1957)

Etheridge, J. W. E. *The Targums of Onkelos and Jonathan ben Uzziel on the Pentateuch* (new edn New York 1968)

Farrar, F. W. *History of Interpretation* (London 1886)

Fiorenza, E. art. 'Apokalypsis and Propheteia' in Lambrecht, J. (q.v.)

Fornberg, T. *An Early Church in a Pluralistic Society* (Gleerup 1977)

France, R. T. *Jesus and the Old Testament* (London 1971)

Freed, E. D. *Old Testament Quotations in the Gospel of John* (Leiden 1965)

Gerhardsson, B. *The Testing of God's Son* (Gleerup 1966)

Gnilka, J. *Der Kolosserbrief* (Freiburg–Basel–Vienna 1980)

Goppelt, L. *Der Erste Petrusbrief* (Göttingen 1978)

Greeven, H. see Dibelius, O.

Grigsby, B. H. art. 'The Cross as an Expiatory Sacrifice in the Fourth Gospel' in *JSNT* 15 (July 1982), pp. 51–80

Gundry, R. H. *The Use of the Old Testament in Matthew's Gospel* (Leiden 1967)

Haenchen, E. von art. 'Schriftzitate und Textüberlieferung in der Apostelgeschichte' in *ZTK* (1954), pp. 51, 153–67

Hanson, A. T. art. 'Philo's Etymologies' in *JTS* 18 (NS) (1967); *Jesus Christ in the Old Testament* (London 1965); *Studies in Paul's Technique and Theology* (London 1974); *The New Testament Interpretation of Scripture* (London 1980); *Studies in the Pastoral Epistles* (London 1968); *The Image of the Invisible God* (London 1982); with Hanson, E. M. *The Book of Job* (London 1953); *The Pastoral Epistles* (London 1982); art. 'The use of Scripture in the Pastoral Epistles' in *Irish Biblical Studies*, autumn 1981; art. 'The Midrash on 2 Corinthians 3: a Reconsideration' in *JSNT* 9 (Oct. 1980); art. 'Vessels of Wrath or Instruments of Wrath? Romans ix, 22–3' in *JTS* 22/2 (NS) (1981); art. 'John's Citation of Psalm lxxxii' in *NTS* 11 (1965), pp. 158–62; art. 'John's Citation of Psalm lxxxii Reconsidered' *NTS* 13 (1966), pp. 363–7; art. 'The Old Testament Background to the Raising of Lazarus' in *Studia Evangelica* (Berlin 1973), pp. 252–5; art. 'Rahab the Harlot in Early Christian Tradition' in *JSNT* 1 (1978), pp. 53–60

Hanson, E. M. see Hanson, A. T.

Hanson, R. P. C. *Allegory and Event* (London 1959)

Harris J. T. *Testimonies* Part i (Cambridge 1916) Part ii (Cambridge 1920)

Holtz, T. von *Untersuchungen über die Alttestamentlichen Zitaten bei Lukas* (Berlin 1968)

Hooker, M. D. and Wilson, S. G. eds. *Paul and Paulinism* (London 1982)

Horgan, M. P. *Pesharim: Qumran Interpretation of Biblical Books* (Washington 1979)

Houlden, J. H. *Paul's Letters from Prison* (London 1970)

Howard, G. art. 'Hebrews and the Old Testament Quotations' in *NT* 10 (1968), pp. 208–16

Hübner, H. *Das Gesetz bei Paulus* (Göttingen 1978); art. 'Der "Messias Israels" und der Christus des Neuen Testament' in *Kerygma und Dogma* 27 (July–Sept 1981), pp. 216–39

Hughes, S. *Every Day with Jesus* (Walton on Thames 1982)

Jackson, F. J. F. ed. *The Beginnings of Christianity,* 5 vols. (London 1920–33)

Jellicoe, S. *The Septuagint and Modern Study* (Oxford 1968)

Jenkins, F. *The Old Testament in the Book of Revelation* (Grand Rapids 1972)

Kapstein, A. see Braude, W. G.

Kelly, J. N. D. *A Commentary on the Epistles of Peter and of Jude* (London 1969)

Kilpatrick, G. D. art. 'Some Quotations in Acts' in Kremer, J. (q.v.)

Knight, G. A. F. *A Christian Theology of the Old Testament* (London 1959)

Kremer, J. ed. *Les Actes des Apôtres; traditions, rédaction, théologie* (Paris and Leuven 1979)

Kuhn, K. G. *Der Tannaitische Midrash Sifre zu Numeri* (Stuttgart 1959)

Kuss, O. *Der Brief an die Hebräer* (Regensburg 1966)

Lake, K. and Cadbury, H. J. *The Beginnings of Christianity*, vol. 4 (London 1933), and see Jackson, F. J. F.

Lambrecht, J. see Vanni, U.

Laurin, R. B. ed. *Contemporary Old Testament Theologians* (London 1970)

Le Déaut, R. and Robert, J. *Targum des Chroniques,* 2 vols. (Rome 1971) *Targum du Pentateuque* (Paris 1978); *The Message of the New Testament and the Aramaic Bible* (Eng. trans. Rome 1982)

Lightfoot, J. B. *The Epistle to the Colossians* (new edn London 1979)

Lindars, B. *New Testament Apologetic* (London 1961)

Lock, W. *A Critical and Exegetical Commentary on the Pastoral Epistles* (Edinburgh 1924)

Lohmeyer, E. *Die Briefe an die Philipper, an die Kolosser, und an Philemon* (9th edn Göttingen 1961); *Die Offenbarung des Johannes* (3rd edn Tübingen 1970)

Lohse, E. *Die Briefe an die Kolosser und an Philemon* (Göttingen 1968)

Longenecker, R. *Biblical Exegesis in the Apostolic Period* (Grand Rapids 1975)

McConnell, R. S. *Law and Prophecy in Matthew's Gospel* (Basel 1969)

McKelvey, R. J. *The New Temple* (Oxford 1969)

McNamara, M. *Targum and Testament* (Shannon 1972)

Manson T. W. art. 'The Old Testament in the Teaching of Jesus' in *John Rylands Library Bulletin* 34 (1951–2)

Mansoor, M. *The Thanksgiving Hymns* (Leiden 1961)

Marcus, R. ed. *Philo: Questions on Genesis*, 2 vols. (London and Cambridge, Mass. 1953) ed. *Questions on Exodus*, 2 vols.

Masuda, S. art. 'The Good News of the Miracle of the Bread' in *NTS* 28/2 (Apr. 1982)

Michel, O. *Der Brief an die Hebräer* (4th edn Göttingen 1960)

Milligan, G. see Moulton, J. H.

Moffatt, J. *A Critical and Exegetical Commentary on the Epistle to the Hebrews* (Edinburgh 1924)

Moule, C. F. D. *The Epistle to the Colossians and to Philemon* (Cambridge 1958)

Moulton, J. H. and Milligan, G. *The Vocabulary of the Greek New Testament*, 1 vol. (ed. London 1954)

Philo see Cohn, L.

Rese, M. art. 'Die Funktion der alttestamentliche Zitate und Ausspielungen in den Reden der Apostelgeschichte' in J. Kremer (q.v.)

Robert, J. see Le Déaut, R.

Robinson, J. A. *St Paul's Epistle to the Ephesians* (London 1909)

Schlatter, A. art. 'Das Alttestament in der Johannischen Apokalypse' in *Beit. z Ford. christl. Theol 1616* (Gütersloh 1912), pp. 1–108

Schneider, G. *Die Apostelgeschichte* (Freiburg–Basel–Vienna 1980)

Schweizer, E. art. 'Paul's Christology and Gnosticism' in Hooker, M. D. and Wilson, S. G. (q.v.)

Scott, R. B. Y. art. 'Wisdom in Creation: the *'āmōn* of Proverbs viii, 30' in *VT* 10 (1960), pp. 213–23

Scott, Sir Walter *Quentin Durward* (Edinburgh 1829)

Selwyn, E. G. *The First Epistle of Peter* (2nd edn London 1947)

Smith, D. Moody art. 'The Use of the Old Testament in the New' in Efird, J. M. (q.v.)

Sowers, S. G. *The Hermeneutics of Philo and Hebrews* (Zürich 1915)

Spicq. C. *L'Épître aux Hébreux* (3rd edn Paris 1952) *Les Épîtres Pastorales,* 2 vols. (4th edn Paris 1969)

Stanton, G. N. *Jesus of Nazareth in New Testament Preaching* (Cambridge 1974)

Stendahl, K. *The School of St Matthew* (2nd edn Lund 1967)

Stenning, J. E. *The Targum on Isaiah* (Oxford 1953)

Strack, H. L. and Billerbeck, P. *Kommentar zum Neuen Testament aus Talmud und Midrasch*, 3 vols. (3rd edn Munich 1961)

Suhl, A. *Die Funktion der Alttestamentlichen Zitate und Ausspielungen im Markusevangelium* (Gütersloh 1965)

Sweet, J. *Revelation* (London 1979)

Swete, H. B. *The Gospel according to St Mark* (3rd edn London 1920) *The Apocalypse of St John* (2nd edn London 1967)

Taylor, V. *The Gospel according to St Mark* (London–New York 1959)

Thomas, K. J. art. 'The Old Testament Citations in Hebrews' in *NTS* 11 (July 1965), pp. 303–25

Trudinger, L. P. art. 'Some Observations concerning the Text of the Old Testament in the Book of Revelation' in *JTS* 17 (NS) (1966), pp. 82–8

Vanni, U. art. 'L'Apocalypse johannique, État de la question' in Lambrecht, J. ed. *L'Apocalypse johannique et l'Apocalyptique dans le Nouveau Testament* (Leuven–Gembloux 1980)

Vermes, G. *The Dead Sea Scrolls in English* (London 1962)

Von Rad, G. *Old Testament Theology*, 2 vols. (Eng. trans. vol. 1 London 1965 from German edn of Munich 1957; vol. 2 London 1975 from German edn of Munich 1960)

Von Soden, H. *Die Briefe an die Kolosser, Epheser, Philemon, die Pastoralbriefe*, vol. 3 (Freiburg 1891)

Vriezen, T. C. *An Outline of Old Testament Theology* (Eng. trans. Oxford 1970 from 3rd Dutch edn 1966)

Waard, J. de *A Comparative Study of the Old Testament Text in the Dead Sea Scrolls and in the New Testament* (Leiden 1966)

Weingreen, J. *From Bible to Mishna* (Manchester 1976)

Wendland, P. see Cohn, L.

Wernberg-Møller, P. *The Manual of Discipline* (London 1957)

Westcott, B. F. *The Epistle to the Hebrews* (2nd edn London 1892)

Wilcox, M. *The Semitisms of Acts* (Oxford 1965)

Williamson, R. *Philo and the Epistle to the Hebrews* (London 1970)
Wilson, S. G. see Hooker, M. D.
Zarb, P. S. M. *De Historia Canonis Utriusque Testamenti* (2nd edn Rome 1934)
Zunz, G. G. *The Text of the Epistles* (London 1953)

INDEX OF NAMES

INDEX OF SCRIPTURAL REFERENCES

(Covers the Bible, Qumran, Greek and Latin Authors and Rabbinic Literature)